Taking

NATURE

By the Hand

Harold A. Tichenor

Published by Harold A. Tichenor, Rural Route #4, Box 1016,
Napton, MO 65340-9226

www.HaroldTichenor.com

Library of Congress Control Number: 2002093459

ISBN 0-615-12152-7

Manufactured in the United States of America
by Thomson-Shore, Inc., Dexter, Michigan.

O Zeus, if there be a Zeus,
For I know of him only by report.
Euripides

I have frankly taken nature by the hand, accepting
in my farthest speculations, the animal faith I live
by from day to day.
George Santayana

CONTENTS

CONTENTS

INTRODUCTION

This book began as an explanation to my children. While they are not unaware that my position in philosophy is at odds with the religions of the community in which I live, there are details I wish them to have. I also have wished, thinking of later generations, to make it readable by young readers. Although, I may have failed in this, there are traces of my efforts in some parenthetical definitions, the detailed index and the many references which direct the reader to pages on which the subject at hand is mentioned, and in some cases discussed more fully. This is a feature I have wished for myself, when reading some books. As the work progressed, I became interested in making a credible case for naturalism in philosophy and began to dream about publication.

My education in philosophy, such as it is, is self taught, and if that is not handicap enough, my sources are limited to mostly my own library which was somewhat haphazardly acquired. Buying books is like other sins: one leads to another.

Often I express myself in the words of others to show that most of what I have to say has been said by others and because, perhaps, it is a little more persuasive than if I said the same thing in my own words. This practice lends moral support, but I have no illusions about the quotations being "proof." Proof in philosophy is elusive and that is a principal theme in this book, but that fact does not make a case for skepticism. That is another theme in the book.

One does not make the case for naturalism without stepping on the toes of those who take philosophy in another direction. My psychologist, if I had one, would likely say that there is a note of retaliation in some of my remarks. It is true that there is reason for suspicion of such action, for I have heard myself indirectly described, as an unbeliever, as worthy of eternal damnation more times that I like to remember. This wisdom has occurred, but not on every occasion, in the eulogy of a departed neighbor. I really should not add that in a few cases I was not able to recognize the deceased from the speaker's eulogy, but I want the reader to know that in such cases I took Mark Twain's advice on etiquette at a funeral, and did not elbow the person next to me when it happened.

I plead innocent of any recrimination. Indeed, if I were a praying man, I would say "Father forgive them, for they know not what they do." It is a point I make in this book that such "uncommon" sense has a natural origin as does common sense, and I have no heart to buck the inevitable. In my view, ideas, including religious ones, are natural events, and nature is what this book is about. My quarrel is with metaphysics[t] (which will be explained) not churches and my neighbor's practice in attending them. Nor do I want to change anyone's mind about their theology, I simply want to be understood. Indeed, I have a passion to be understood.

We learn from the philosophers themselves that there is a good deal of nonsense in philosophy. The nonsense is always in the work of someone else than the one we are reading. I will indulge this time-honored practice in this book with no holds barred. That I do not admit that anything I say is nonsense will not surprise the reader. I would not be saying it if I thought it was nonsense. However, I claim only certainty[1] (which will be explained) for my ideas. This, the elusiveness of proof, is the reason why the classical writings of philosophers, nonsense and all, gets repeatedly republished and are treated with a degree of reverence, giving them the near status of the books of a philosophical bible. I ask the reader to accept my criticism as benign irreverence.

In my effort to make a very detailed index--for there are few words that lack philosophical import--it has turned out to be too much of a good thing, I fear. It is faulty in two respects: some words are so numerous as to make them worthless to index; and the scope of the indexing is so wide as to include words of little value in the index. To ameliorate the former, I have diluted the effect in many cases by making sub entries under them which directs the reader to different uses of the words. For the latter, I have happened on the happy philosophical principle that "it can't hurt." Further, rather than face the frustrations of trying to correct these errors, I propose to apologize to the reader. Reader, I apologize for the index.

Hoping that this will get me off to a good start with my readers, I ask them, even if they can do it only imaginatively, to take nature by the hand with me, as we progress through these pages.

CHILDHOOD THOUGHTS

I had philosophical questions on my mind at about the age of thirteen. They were epistemological, although I had no idea what the word meant at the time. My memories of those troubling thoughts are as vivid as if they had happened only yesterday. I can remember just exactly where I was, walking home from school, when, as I experienced it, I "realized" that there is no such thing as knowing; we only believe.

Church and Sunday school attendance at the Baptist church in Napton was fixed in my family comparable to the sunrise. Missing was never considered unless one was sick or snow drifts or floods made it impossible to get there. I had reached the age when most children were joining the church and was pondering how one could know which religion was true. I had just emerged from my first innocent phase of religious convictions. I believed that the Baptists had the true religion; the Methodists, who had a church in sight of my home, were not too bad but didn't have the whole truth; the Presbyterians, whose church was farther away, were further in the dark; and the Catholics, about whose church I heard some uncomplimentary remarks, were little better than superstitious.

But on that day I remember so well, I awoke, if I may borrow from Kant, from my dogmatic slumbers. I ceased to see a difference in kind among religious denominations. There were among my neighbors members of all these churches. I felt that I could not in fairness accuse them of not being as sincere and as certain as the Baptist, nor did it seem fair to think that the devil made them do it or that God had led the Baptists in the right way but had not the others; as a matter of fact; I believed that the members of the other denominations were as sincere and certain as the Baptist, and I did not believe the devil made them do it. But, besides the local denominations there were many religions in the world whose adherents were equally sincere and certain. The conclusion was unavoidable: certainty does not guarantee truth. My thoughts from "How do you determine which religion is true?" changed to "How can you know if any religion is true?" Then, having put all denominations on the same level as beliefs, with the conviction that there should be good reasons for selecting one over the other, I found no *reasonable* way to do so. There were--there had to be--causes for beliefs, but they were not reasons. The contrast between reason and cause was stark.

Perhaps there is no precept urged on us in our youth more persistently than to be fair with our fellows. I took it seriously, and the question arose, if one is going to be charitable and fair, how do you do it without giving others credit for being as likely to be correct in controversial matters--matters where honest men disagree--as you are yourself?

I then pondered just what "knowing" could be. We must have been studying the Civil War in school at the time, as Lincoln's statement to the effect that the South had no oath registered in heaven to do what they were doing, filled my mind. "Oath registered in Heaven?"! It pointed up the dilemma of certifying anything to be true. How can any opinion be certified true? If only there were some place, some person, some thing where one could get it certified. Heaven seemed to be the ultimate, but those who claimed to get their certification from heaven were, as a group, notoriously untrustworthy because of their disagreement. If not heaven, then what? There seemed no place or person. I was left standing alone with my questions and opinions. Perhaps certainty came from the philosopher's pen. In time I would look into that.

If I experienced something like Cartesian doubt (see page 54), it was short lived. I was soon aware that I did not doubt the existence of all those people who made up the various religious sects, nor that they believed what they did. I did not doubt that the road would bear me up as I walked home, that the house would be there when I got home, nor that it would get dark later and the sun would come up the next morning. I did not doubt the existence of what I would someday find philosophers called "the external world." Instead of further doubts, I began thinking in terms of cultural determinism although I did not use those words. Most children adopted the religion of their parents, for example. Their nature being such and the influence and pressures being such that they were "caused" to accept their parents' religion.

In time I became aware, or so I thought, that there are two certainties. Just as seeing is believing, believing is being certain. This is one certainty--the feeling, the experience, the function--that is part of us. The other certainty is belief and that belief being certified somehow as true.

The first certainty, which I will call certainty^1, is the one we live by; a fact of life. The second certainty, which I will call certainty^2, is the desired, the ideal, seemingly just out of reach at times, the philosopher's dream and/or illusion. Certainty^1 is belief. Certainty^2 is, or would be if we had it, knowledge as sought by philosophers. I had met epistemology and dismissed it as impossible.

In saying this, I do not dismiss the word "knowledge" from my vocabulary. My position on knowledge, which came some years after my introduction to philosophy, and involved the pondering of a "critique of reason," appears on pages 188-190. The following paragraph will serve as a preview.

 "How do we reason our way to knowledge (certainty^2)?" is not an answerable question. The answerable question is asked in a specific situation, for example, when eating an apple, "Is it reasonable to doubt that I know that I am eating an apple?" When we answer, "It is not," we are expressing "knowledge" of common usage, common naturalistic usage, and I use it just that way.

If this is only certainty^1, we have the consolation that, when correct, it does everything that certainty^2 would do. (Plato, to give credit where credit is due, made the same point, but his terms were "right [correct] opinion" and "knowledge."[FD, 86]) The certainty^1 that goes into making a wheel, serves us just as well as if it came with a certificate from heaven. I do not believe there is a paradox here. I would prefer the word predicament.

I called myself an agnostic for several years before admitting to myself that I believed only in nature and nature's laws. That experience was *emancipation*. I was free at last of what seemed a compulsion to treat an unpalatable theology as believable. Gone were all the problems it entailed. Among other things I no longer worried about people spending eternity in hell because of their beliefs. It may be unsophisticated and unphilosophical to state that your philosophy is naturalism, however, I did just that.

NOTE TO THE READER

It is my goal in writing this book to make the case for naturalism in philosophy. I include a history of naturalism which does a great deal to that end. However, it takes up the greater part of the book, and those who are not students of philosophy may find it tedious. In the interest of holding on to my readers, I suggest that those who do find it tedious skip some or all of the history and resume reading on page 171. In offering the reader this option, I am gambling that my theories will generate interest in the history and the reader will return to it. I warn you that if you do skip the history permanently you will miss some of the highlights of philosophy and some of my arguments and criticism.

NATURALISM DEFINED

I suggest that the most elemental term in philosophy and in discourse in general, for that matter, is "thing." Let us look at a few sentences, all taken from philosophical writings. Disregard the points made by these remarks. They are of no interest in this case, and without the context in which some of them were used, their meaning can not be ascertained anyway. What I want to call attention to is the word, *thing,* used as the elemental term of what the people are writing about.

In classic Latin Essence was the idea or law of a thing.[DOP, 112]

But it is of the essence of material things to be material.[DOP, 112]

But only individual things are generated and exist.[DOP, 321]

Note that according to Aristotle, the substance of a thing is always intelligible.[DOP, 321]

Let things be what they are; move like water; be tranquil like a mirror; respond like an echo[DOP, 329]

The only things which shall be debatable among philosophers shall be things definable in terms drawn from experience. . . .[DOP, 105]

God's existence follows from the fact that things exist.[DOP, 84]

But the name nature taken in this sense is seen to signify the essence of a thing.[AOB, 167]

For it is evident that matter alone is not the essence of the thing.[AOB, 167]

There is no unitary, unvaried or simple thing in a multiplicity of singular things.[AOB, 208]

Our enjoyment must be more than "casual" before we can assign value to the things we like.[AOA, 177]

The understanding, like the eye, whilst it makes us see and perceive all other things, takes no notice of itself.[AOE, 34]

In the nineteenth century, philosophy continued to be in part, a repository of hitherto unsolved problems concerning the nature of things.[AOI, 22]

Such an unbridled "speculative" use of reason is characteristic of the previous uncritical and dogmatic assertions of the rationalists concerning the ultimate nature and cause of things.[AOI, 35]

This order, the same for all things, no one of gods or men has made; but it always was, and is, and shall be.[SOP, 52]

All things arise and pass away.[SOP, 52]

What is the formula of the growth and decay of all things.[SOP, 276]

> To be useful, reasoning must be about things, and must keep in touch with them at every step.[SOP, 360]

By the usage in these quotations, then, philosophy is *about* things. Discourse about nothing (*no things*) is not philosophy at all. To this, the reader may agree and even think it a trite remark, which it is, but philosophers, perhaps most of them, believe otherwise. One tells us that it is "naive," to believe we are dealing with things. "Philosophy is a little more sophisticated, and realizes that the whole material of science consists of sensations, perceptions and conceptions, rather than of things."[SOP, 207] It is interesting that the author of this remark (which was part of his definition of idealism) is also the author of the quotation immediately above this paragraph, and that both remarks appear in the same book. Further discussion of "things" must await our discussion of Immanuel Kant.

What the reader may not assent to is that things are natural things; that there are no *meta*-things. It is obvious from what follows that this is my position. Although it has several meanings, "we must recognize at least two principal meanings in the word Nature. In one sense, it means all the powers existing in either the outer or the inner world and everything which takes place by means of those powers. In another sense, it means, not everything which happens, but only what takes place without the agency, or without the voluntary and intentional agency, of man."[ON, 9] It is the first of these meanings that is naturalism in philosophy. For further elaboration I take excerpts from the definition given in a dictionary of philosophy:

> Naturalism . . . holds that the universe requires no supernatural cause and government, but is self-existent, self-explanatory, self-operating, and self-directing; that the world-process is not teleological and anthropocentric, but purposeless, deterministic. . . , and only incidentally productive of man; that human life, physical, mental, moral and spiritual, is an ordinary natural event attributable in all respects to the ordinary operations of nature.[DOP, 221]

Also in somewhat different words,

> [Naturalism is] the general philosophical position which has as its fundamental tenet the proposition that the natural world is the whole of reality. . . naturalism means to assert that there is but one system or level of reality; that this system is the totality of objects and events in space and time; and that the behavior of this system is determined only by its own character and is reducible to a set of causal laws. Nature is thus conceived as self-contained and self-dependent, and

from this view spring certain negations that define to a great extent the influence of naturalism. First, it is denied that nature is derived from or dependent upon any transcendent, supernatural entities. From this follows the denial that the order of natural events can be intruded upon. And this in turn entails the denial of freedom, purpose, and transcendent destiny.[DOP, 221]

This writer goes on to say,

The beneficent task that naturalism recurrently performs is that of recalling attention from a blind absorption in theory to a fresh consideration of the facts and values exhibited in nature and life.[DOP, 205]

To this I add a "principle" from Leucippus, "that all qualitative differences in nature may be reduced to quantitative ones."[DOP, 183] This is a point I will make when discussing the empiricists. Also, Kepler said somewhere "when the mind leaves the realm of quantity it wanders in darkness and doubt."

I suggest that (the concept of) nature is as important for the theist as the atheist. The concept of miracles makes no sense at all without nature, for it is nature that is interrupted and overruled when the gods work a wonder. Nature is basic in our concepts, as the supernatural can be denoted, referred to, made explicit, said, only with reference to the natural. For if nature is not conceived when expressing supernature the word (supernatural) is superfluous. It can denote only what allegedly is. Nature (natural things) is basic, ground zero, to our concepts.

I omitted the references to ethics and "tychistic" (chance) events given in these definitions. From naturalistic premises, it follows that nothing happens by chance, interpreted as meaning events occurring without causes; therefore chance does not belong in the definition of naturalism. The problem is, where we speak of chance, the reality is probability. Probability pertains to, and only to, prediction; and prediction, like all human acts, has its cause. Take for example the weatherman's prediction of the weather. Among those things we would ascribe causes of his doing so are that he is getting paid for it and that he believes in meteorologic causation.

In the case in which the weatherman's prediction is of a 25% "chance" of rain, there is no chance regarding rain. It will either rain or it will not according to the natural conditions that exist. This means that a prediction of rain, based on past observations, has a one chance (probability) in four of being correct. In no way does the calculation of probability pertain to the basic assumptions of the meteorologist's science, natural causation and induction. If Hume (discussed later) gave us anything of lasting value, it is his pointing this out (discussed on page 114). In his words, "probability is founded on the presumption of a resemblance betwixt those objects of which we have had experience, and those which we have had none; and, therefore, it is impossible that this presumption can arise from probability."[AOE, 189, 190] In the words of one commentator, "Probability rests on the unbolsterable principle of induction, and cannot itself be used to bolster it up."[AOE, 190] Those epistemologists who deprecate science as knowledge because it is probabilistic have missed this point. Probability cannot be used to bring science into question. One is up to his pate in science when using probability. It is a function within science. One cannot discard science and keep probability.

NATURALISM FROM THALES TO DESCARTES

It is my plan to make a brief, therefore necessarily incomplete, survey of naturalism in western philosophy with some comments along the way, which will make clear the importance of naturalism in the struggle for knowledge. It will, I believe, expose the relative unimportance of metaphysics. I will leave the definition of metaphysics in limbo for the time being. As a term it came into use as a classification to distinguish much of Aristotle's philosophy from his physics. For centuries in the middle ages metaphysics was virtually synonymous with philosophy.

As far as we know "pre-Hellenic [before the immediate successors of Aristotle] peoples explained every obscure operation in nature by some supernatural agency; everywhere there were gods,"[SOP, 51] but naturalism characterized most of early Greek philosophy to the time of Socrates. I will use Will Durant's "dizzy and superficial summary."

> Apparently it was the Ionian Greeks who first dared to give natural explanations of cosmic complexities and mysterious incidents: they sought in physics the natural causes of particular events, and in philosophy a natural theory of the whole. Thales (640-550 B.C.), "the Father of Philosophy," was primarily an astronomer, who astonished the natives of Miletus by informing them that the sun and stars (which they were wont to worship as gods) were merely balls of fire. His pupil Anaximander (610-540) B.C.), the first Greek to make astronomical and geographical charts, believed that the universe had begun as an undifferentiated mass, from which all things had arisen by the separation of opposites; that the astronomic history periodically repeated itself in the evolution and dissolution of an infinite number of worlds; that the earth was at rest in space by a balance of internal impulsions. . . ; that all our planets had once been fluid, but had been evaporated by the sun; that life had first been formed in the sea, but had been driven upon the land by the subsidence of the water; that of these stranded animals some had developed the capacity to breathe air, and had so become the progenitors of all later land life; that man could not from the beginning have been what he is now, for if man, on his first appearance, had been so helpless at birth, and had required so long adolescence, as in these later days, he could not possibly have survived. Anaximenes, another Milesian (fl. 450 B.C.) described the primeval condition of things as a very rarefied mass, gradually condensing into wind, cloud, water, earth, and stone; the three forms of matter--gas, liquid and solid--were progressive stages of condensation; heat

and cold were merely rarefaction and condensation; earthquakes were due to the solidification of an originally fluid earth; life and soul were one, an animating and expansive force present in everything everywhere. Anaxagoras (500--428 B.C.), teacher of Pericles, seems to have given a correct explanation of solar and lunar eclipses: he discovered the process of respiration in plants and fishes; and he explained man's intelligence by the power of manipulation that came when the fore-limbs were freed from the tasks of locomotion. Slowly in these men, knowledge grew into science.

   Heraclitus (530-470 B.C.). . . turned science from astronomy to earthier concerns. All things forever flow and change, he said; even in the stillest matter there is unseen flux and movement. Cosmic history runs in repetitious cycles, each beginning and ending in fire. . . . "Through strife" says Heraclitus, "all things arise and pass away. . . . War is the father and king of all: some he has made gods, and some men; some slaves, and some free." Where there is no strife there is decay: "the mixture which is not shaken decomposes." In this flux of change and struggle and selection, only one thing is constant, and that is law. "This order, the same for all things, no one of the gods or man has made; but it always was, and is and shall be." Empedocles (fl. 445 B.C. in Sicily) developed a further stage the idea of evolution. Organs arise not by design but by selection. Nature makes many trials and experiments with organisms, combining organs variously; where the combination meets environmental needs the organism survives and perpetuates its like: where the combination fails, the organism is weeded out; as time goes on, organisms are more and more intricately and successfully adapted to their surroundings. Finally, in Leucippus (fl. 445 B. C.) and Democritus (460--360) B. C.), . . . we get the last stage of pre-Aristotelian science--materialistic, deterministic atomism. "Everything," said Leucippus, "is driven by necessity [natural law; universal causation]."   "In reality," said Democritus, "there are only atoms and the void." Perception is due to the expulsion of atoms from the object upon the sense organ. There is or have been or will be an infinite number of worlds; at every moment planets are colliding and dying, and new worlds are rising out of chaos by the selective aggregation of atoms of similar size and shape. There is no design; the universe is a machine.[SOP, 51, 52]

We must give more room to Democritus who has been called the greatest of ancient philosophers. He is credited with publications in several fields of science as well as music and art. He held that there is no such thing as chance. Matter is not created and none is ever destroyed. The only change is in the combinations of atoms. His atom theory included the mind, of course,

Although trusting the senses for practical purposes, he deprecated them. Citing color, temperature, sound, etc., as examples of instances of the senses deceiving us, he claimed these "secondary qualities" are in us not in things, a mistaken idea that prevailed until the time of John Locke, who gave it great exposure. For all the clout Democritus's philosophy had as science, he was a rationalist; genuine knowledge coming only by investigation and thought. The senses, he thought, give us only obscure knowledge, or opinion. Presumably "investigation," for him, did not include the use of the senses.

We will pass over the Sophists lightly in the interest of brevity. Worthy of mention is their invention of grammar, the natural rules of language. Protagoras, [481-411 B.C.] the most renowned of them, is given credit for that. Their criticism of tradition and morals may have contributed to the deterioration of morals in Greece during their time. Some of them argued that regardless of law, what nature permitted was good. I will make the point that this is not a part of naturalism in my discussion of ethics on page 209.

We also pass over Socrates (469-399 B. C.) who asked many questions and answered few. He gave us such wisdom as the wise man is he who knows that he knows nothing, and the unexamined life is not worth living. Nevertheless, he proclaimed that knowledge is virtue[EGP, 253] and "dismissed natural philosophy as 'sheer folly'"[EGP, 22] which shows that he thought he knew a few things. Of more interest to the history of naturalism are some of his followers, the Cynics.

The founder of the Cynic school was Antisthenes of Cyrene (440-365 B. C.). He opened his own school but after hearing Socrates's discourse, took his pupils to learn from him. The essence of the Cynic philosophy is to live on bare necessities in order that the soul may be as free as possible. Antisthenes lived by his philosophy. His motto was "I do not posses, in order not to be possessed." He resumed his teaching after Socrates's death at the Gymnasium Cynosarges (Dogfish) a place maintained for people of a low station in life. It was this place rather than the creed that gave the name Cynic to the philosophy.

Diogenes (412?-323), a pupil of Antisthenes, was happy to learn that the simple life was part of virtue and wisdom and exceeded his teacher in its practice making it famous in Greece by living it in the extreme. He imitated the life of animals in so far as he could, sleeping on the ground, eating wherever he could, begging at times. He answered the call of nature including sex in public, advocating free love.   He advocated freedom of speech and made great use of it, punctuating it with humor and wit.   He refused to recognize laws, but harmed no one.   This is just a sample of his peculiar ideas.

This seems to us more a life style than a philosophy but for the cynics it was an ethic, because for them the aim of life is happiness found through living the simple life.   Wealth destroys peace and promotes envy.   Religion except in the practice of virtue, which had to be its own reward, was a superstition.   They gave metaphysics no more respect than they gave religion.

After Diogenes the Cynics became more of a religious order than a philosophy, making poverty a rule of life, living on alms but maintaining schools of philosophy, teaching in the streets where they slept for they had no homes.   Through Diogenes' disciples Stilpo and Crates, the Cynic philosophy survived into the Hellenistic age and influenced Stoicism.

I pause here for a definition of idealism, a term that will show up from time to time as we proceed.   There are so many subspecies of the term that the definition in a dictionary of philosophy[DOP] runs to three pages.   It is usually considered the opposite of materialism and realism, but I think of it as the opposite of naturalism.   Idealism is "in metaphysics, the doctrine that ideas, or thought, are the fundamental reality."[SOP, 400]   Or, a variation of this: the ontological (having to do with existence) view that everything is spiritual or mental.   This view is usually associated in Western philosophy with Berkeley (discussed on page 86) and Hegel (barely mentioned page 158).

The father of idealism was perhaps Parmenides (6th century B. C.) who held that reality is the One, whatever that could mean.   Idealists mistrusted the senses.   Motion, change, and development of any kind were illusions of superficial sense.   Beneath this reality was a motionless unity which was Being, Truth, and God, a position known as monism (the universe is comprised of one kind of stuff).   There is more, but I will stop with this much of a philosophy that is not a part of the history of naturalism.   Plato was the culmination of a development that began with Parmenides and was the most famous philosopher of idealism of all time or until after Immanuel Kant, but we turn first to Zeno of Elea, a follower of Parmenides.

Zeno of Elea, (fl.475 B.C.) attempted to show that the ideas of plurality [the universe is comprised of more than one kind of stuff] and motion were as impossible as a motionless one.   He published a book of paradoxes, nine of which have survived. Every school boy and girl, almost, knows the story of the hare and tortoise, a variant of one of Zeno's paradoxes. Zeno appeared in Athens about 450 B. C. where he spent his time reducing the theories of other philosophers to absurdities. He was perhaps the father of logic, which gives him a place in the history of naturalism. Logic, I will argue, is a part of naturalism. In his old age he referred to his paradoxes as pranks; however, he was an influence on Pyhrro and Carneades.

Pyhrro (365-275 B.C.), whose name is a synonym for skepticism, wrote no books, but a pupil spread the word. He held that everything is opinion. Nothing is certain. His alleged culprit was the senses, that mainstay of anti-naturalism, but he berated reason as well. He counseled suspending judgement on philosophical questions; accepting the current myths is as good as anything else, nothing is quite true. Carneades, (213-129) who came to Athens about 193 B.C., echoed Pyhrro and taught his students to be satisfied with probability and the customs of their time. This skepticism does not, on the surface, seem to have much to do with naturalism, but I have included these two philosophers in order to point out the naturalism in the use of "probability." No one seemed to notice until David Hume, whom we will meet later, the fact mentioned above that probability rests on induction--on laws of nature--on naturalism--on the fact that some opinions must be valid in order to reach a position that is probable. I will mention, also, that "everything is opinion" is something like my "certainty[1]," but that "nothing is quite true" does not follow.

Plato (428/7--348/7 B.C.), founded the Academy, named for the local god Academus in 386 B C. This university became the intellectual center of Greece for centuries to come. Socrates was an influence that caused him to drop his interest in politics and poetry and become a philosopher at the age of 20. Philosophy and mathematics were the principal studies at the Academy. A plaque over the portal read, "Let no one without geometry enter here." Men who studied there made most of the advances in mathematics in the fourth century B.C.

But for all Plato's stature as an educator and philosopher there is much to criticize in his naturalism, which includes a very naive psychology in *The Republic*. In the "Myth of the Cave" he has us imagine men bound in a cave since childhood in such a way that they can not turn their heads, therefore, can see nothing behind then. There is light from fire behind and above them. Between the lights and the prisoners is a road on which men are passing carrying various objects. There is a wall in front of them. All the prisoners can see is shadows, their own and those of the men and objects behind them. Voices of the men behind them echo from the wall and the men mistake them and the shadows for reality.

The men, having been so deprived "all their lives," would not be able walk and talk. Nevertheless, Plato has us imagine further that one prisoner is released and made to walk toward the fire. Looking at the light would be painful; he would too confused to see properly the objects that had been making the shadows which was reality for him. If he were told that what he was seeing is reality and what he was used to was illusion he would not be unable to understand. If he were then dragged out in to the sunlight he would be overwhelmed by the sunlight and could not see real objects. Gradually he would recognize the objects he sees as reality and lastly see the sun (which is thought to be Plato's allegory of enlightenment).

If the prisoner, after this enlightenment, would return to the cave and explain to the prisoners that their beliefs were illusions they would not believe him; and if released would turn on him and kill him for disturbing their illusions. This is thought to be an allusion to Socrates who was made to drink the hemlock because he disturbed people's beliefs.

We might reasonably suspect that Plato's mission was to demonstrate the importance of experience in education, but such is not the case. His direction is 180 degrees from the empirical (relying on or derived from observation or experience). Plato's theory of knowledge is that knowledge is recollection. We have knowledge within us. Education is bringing it out. With an argument, the logic of which escapes me, he concludes that we must reject the conception that knowledge can be put into the mind. It would be like putting sight into a blind eye. He thinks that he has shown that "this capacity" is innate. He also uses the term "faculty" in his explanation. With these terms he makes a syntactical jump, his terminology changing from "knowledge is within" us to terms more conducive to explaining that the mind takes in knowledge. For all I know, however, something may have been lost in the translation.

The utopia Plato proposes in the *Republic* is a naturalistic theory for the most part, but a poor one in which he flunks political science, psychology, and economics (my assessment).

The theme of the *Republic* is, at least nominally, justice, what justice is, how it is obtained, etc. The book literally reeks with comments on and implications concerning human nature, which range from the commonplace fact that people vary in aptitude to the less credible idea that people can be made altruistic by education. Plato names four kinds of government, timarchy (something like what Sparta had at the time), oligarchy, democracy, and tyranny, and finds them all unjust. He had no vision of representative government, the kind that in our time has proven to serve mankind the best. Only philosophers could produce a just government according to Plato, and he proceeds to explain how this utopia, this justice, could be created.

There will be no families, the children will be brought up by the state, all will have the same education, and class (in society) will not be hereditary. Girls will have an equal chance with boys, and there will be no slaves. This is not done in the interest of civil rights; all considerations are for what is best for the state. What is best for the state will be justice. Plato has no concept of civil rights. The best of one sex will be united with the best of the other, but the inferior are to be mated as little as possible, and "the children of the inferior Guardians, and any defective offspring of the others, will be quietly got rid of."[TR, 216]

Education will include censorship, and with training and tests at various stages each person will be placed in the occupation that he/she can perform the best. The results will be three classes. At the bottom are the businessmen, workingmen, and farmers who can have private property; next are soldiers who can have no private property but will live in military communism. Those who pass the final training and test will be guardians, which will be a small minority. The effects of education will be cumulative. "By maintaining a sound system of education you produce citizens of good character, and citizens of sound character, with the advantage of a good education, produce in turn children better than themselves and better able to produce still better children in their turn, as can be seen with animals."[TR, 169]

This is not a sound analogy; animals are improved by selection for hereditary traits not by education. His emphasis on education reminds me of what a prominent US Senator said a generation ago, that if you educate a fool you just have an educated fool. If Plato had been a good historian, he would have known that criminals come from all educational levels.

There is to be no legislation in Plato's utopia; the well-educated guardians will know what to do. The guardians will own no property, have no money and no families lest these thing corrupt them. They are to see that in the other classes there is no poverty and no excessive wealth (which would corrupt). Plato had no conception of the value of incentive in economics and would no doubt have been appalled by Adam Smith. He lived too early to learn from Lord Acton *(Essays on Freedom and Power)* that power of any kind corrupts.

For all the power the guardians have they must share it with the Oracle at Delphi who will see to "the founding of the temples and the institutions of sacrifices, and other services to the gods and spirits and heroes, besides the arrangements for the burial of the dead and the rites we must pay to the powers of the other world to secure their goodwill."[TR, 175]

Having thought that Plato was serious about his utopia, I was surprised to find that he claims that it is only "Ideal" and that it can never happen until-- but I will let him explain (talking to a friend):

> The society we have described can never grow into reality or see light of day, and there will be no end to the troubles of states, or indeed, my dear Glaucon, of humanity itself, till philosophers become kings in this world this world or till those we now call kings and rulers really and truly become philosophers.[TR, 233]

Presumably everyone else except the Hitlers of the world would know better than to try to institute Plato's utopia. The lesson in all this is that naturalism is no exception to the fact that there can be nonsense in philosophy.

So much for Plato's naturalism. In metaphysics he reaches reality in something he calls "Forms" or "Ideas" which are the source of all reality. To one like myself for whom they make no sense, they may perhaps be described as a mystical something, reminiscent of universals, which is the reality that exists before things and brings them into being. Mere things get their reality by participating in the forms or ideas. Your dog, for example, has reality by imitating or participating in the form dog or dogness. As a mere thing he is inferior to and an imitation of the form dog. The same for all material things.

Matter is merely possibility. It requires soul or God, a self-moving force, to give it form and being. In Plato's dialogue called the *Phaedo* he puts his own words in the mouth of Socrates who has a sidekick called Simmias, who contributes little to the dialogue except to rubber stamp what Socrates says. After several paragraphs in which he considers the body and soul as separate entities, he belittles the body as a hinderance to philosophy and the senses as untrustworthy, he insists that the philosopher frees the soul from association with the body as much as possible. He then declares that there are such things as the Just, the Beautiful, and the Good, which is the position that universals (defined on page 38) are real. The direction he takes philosophy is away from Science.

> Have you ever grasped them [the Just, the Beautiful, and the Good] with any of your bodily senses? I am speaking of all things such as Size, Health, Strength and, in a word, the reality of all other things, that which each of them essentially is. Is what is most true in them contemplated through the body, or is this the position: whoever of us prepares himself best and most accurately to grasp that thing itself which he is investigating will come closest to the knowledge of it?
> Obviously [replies Simmias]
> Then he will do the most perfectly who approaches the object with thought alone, without associating any sight with his thought, or dragging in any sense perception with his reasoning, but who, using pure thought alone, tries to track down each reality pure and by itself, freeing himself as far as possible from eyes and ears, and in a word, from the whole body, because the body confuses the soul and does not allow it to acquire truth and wisdom whenever it is associated with it. Will that man reach reality, Simmias, if anyone does?
> What you say, said Simmias, is indeed true.[FD, 102]

Plato so separated the soul from the body that the soul could and did exist before we are born. With a dialogue which will be followed no further, for it has no saving thread of logic in it, Plato uses this to support his claim that knowledge is recollection; we recall what has been learned in a previous life when the soul was in another body.[FD, 114, 115] Epistemology must be added to the list of subjects at which Plato failed.

The followers of Plato transformed his rejection of sense knowledge into a skepticism as complete as Pyhrro's, but he (Plato) would be resurrected by Christianity as the purveyor of truth, as would Aristotle.

Aristotle (384-322 B.C.) modified Plato's theory of Forms but did not entirely dispose of them. He made a distinction between Form and Matter, a distinction that can be made only in thought, not in fact. Forms are embedded in particular things. They are not separate entities.

We get back the reality of particular things, which concept is congenial to naturalism, but it is nothing to write home about. I cannot envision a metaphysical entity (form) imbedded in a physical one (particular thing). Nevertheless, Aristotle took a step backward toward his predecessors, the materialists, and his work was prodigious. "The extant works of Aristotle cover almost all the sciences known in his time."[DOP, 35] "A very large part of our technical vocabulary, both in science and in philosophy, is but the translation into modern tongues of the terms used by Aristotle."[DOP, 38]

But in his naturalistic explanations of things, he drifts into metaphysics. "Against the earlier nature-philosophies that found their explanatory principles in matter, to the neglect of form, Aristotle affirms that matter must be conceived as a locus of determinate potentialities that become actualized only through the activity of forms. . . . Aristotle recognizes what he calls 'necessity' in nature; but the products of the latter, since they are aberrations from form, cannot be made the object of scientific knowl-edge."[DOP, 36] I must confess that an exposition on (or about or of) "form" is the cloudiest of metaphysics for me. In fact I find it unintelligible.

For Aristotle "Science in the strict sense of the word, is demonstrated knowledge of the cause of things. Such demonstrated knowledge is obtained by syllogistic deduction from premises in themselves certain." The center of his logic, known to him as "analytic," was the "syllogism, or that form of reasoning whereby, given two propositions, a third follows necessarily from them."[DOP, 36] According to him "the causes which it is the aim of scientific inquiry to discover are four sorts: the material cause (that of which a thing is made), the efficient cause (that by which it comes into being), the formal cause (its essence or nature, i.e. what it is) and the final cause (its end, or that for which it exists)."[DOP, 36] And all this has a beginning. All causes regress to the First Cause Uncaused, and this source is God. Despite this aberration in logic, his logical treatises, the *Organon*, as it was named after his death, reigned as the text book of logic until recent times. He observed that his predecessors drew their theories out of their heads instead of from investigation but was not free of that fault himself.

He seems to confuse definition with science. Definition itself is for Aristotle the classification of an object or idea by naming the genus or class to which it belongs and defining sub classes by their difference within the genus, an activity not altogether useless. As to what is universal for all things, he arranged the mode or aspects by which all things can be considered into ten categories: substance, quantity, quality, relation, place, time, position, possession, activity, passivity.

His greatest achievement, but not without many mistakes, was in biology in which he consolidated previous discoveries and collected data on the fauna and flora of the Aegean countries. It was said that Alexander gave orders to his hunters, fishermen, etc., to help in the project. It was the first scientific collection of animals and plants. Aristotle was weakest in mathematics and physic and missed the big one, the heliocentric theory of the solar system, something he shared with those who followed him.

We find no scientific revolution stemming directly from Aristotle's "science." Except for his logic, his philosophy was unknown to early Christian philosophers but eventually had a revival after being translated in the ninth century. The influence of Aristotle's philosophy was greatly increased by the work of St. Thomas in the thirteenth century, but his science developed in a completely sterile form. In the seventeenth century Galileo, Francis Bacon, and others reacted against it. Bacon criticized the doctrine of "final causes," the doctrine that the cause of an event is explained or found in some end or purpose. He argued that the Aristotelian logic provided no method for discovering new facts. Being deductive in nature, it gave only the logical consequences of what is already known. The resulting science therefore had a purely classificatory character, dividing the known contents of the world into "species" and "genera". It provided no understanding of the causality of the characteristics by which objects could be so classified.

Hellenistic Philosophy

We will touch lightly on the Greek philosophers of the "Hellenic period" (after Aristotle), principally the Stoics and Epicureans, ending with Plotinus (204-270), a neo-Platonist. Epicurus founded a school in Athens in 306 B.C. His philosophy is principally ethics and wholly naturalistic. His ethics, briefly and over simplified, is that pleasure is good and pain is bad. Virtue and knowledge are not good in themselves but good because they lead to pleasure. He thought that the aim of philosophy was to free men from fear, above all the fear of the gods. He opposed religion because, he thought, it promotes and thrives on ignorance and darkens life with the terror of celestial spies. Thus, religion causes pain not pleasure. He did not deny the existence of the gods but gave them no place in the design and guidance of the world.

Epicurus had no more use for metaphysics in general than he had for religion. Two thousands years before the debate between the rationalists and empiricists, whom we will discuss in order, he was on the side of the empiricists. The final test of truth is experience. Reason alone cannot give us truth for it gets its data from experience. We know nothing of a supersensible world. Except for the gods way up there somewhere doing nothing, all reality is composed of the Void and Atoms. Even the mind is material. Lucretius (94-55 B.C.), in a poem, *On the Nature of Things,* is an important source of Epicureanism. I will quote him on the mind.

> Now this I say, that mind and soul are held in union and together form a single nature, but the guiding power, which I call mind or understanding, is the chief, and lords it, so to speak throughout the body. . . . But, when the mind is moved by some intense fear, we see that all the soul has fellow-feeling 'mid the limbs, that sweats and pallor thus break out o'er all the body, that the speech is broken and the voice miscarries, that the eyes are misty, that there is a ringing in the ears, and that the legs give way: in fine we often notice men collapse from terror of the mind; whence anyone can learn with ease that soul is closely joined with mind, and when the force of mind has struck it, it forthwith propels and strikes the body.
>
> This doctrine also shows that mind and soul have a material nature. For, when you see them move the limbs, catch up the frame from sleep, transform the look, and guide and turn about the total man--none of which things we know can happen without touch, nor touch in its turn without substance--must you not admit that they consist of a material nature?[HP, 23]

Lucretius believed the mind is "formed of particles exceedingly minute."[HP, 23] As we have seen, Greek philosophy before Socrates was naturalistic, or materialistic, as it is usually called, and became overshadowed by Plato's Forms or Ideas. The Epicureans and their contemporaries, the Stoics, were not willing to abandon materialism without a more determined attempt to base truth on sensation, therefore; their arguments "may be considered as a reaction against the Ideas and Forms."[HP, 54] There were parallels in their philosophy. Both believed that nothing is real, for example, which does not occupy space, but the Stoics believed that in the atoms "there is a force which permeates all that exists so that each thing is a spontaneous being."[HP, 56] "They strained their conception of body until it approached the notion of spirit."[HP, 58] It would be tedious to separate their naturalism from their metaphysics.

There was a great difference between the ethics of the Stoics and Epicureans. The withdrawal from the obligations of family and state by the

Epicureans[HP, 53] contrasted with the Stoics, who (if they lived up to their philosophy) contented themselves with little and accepted without complaint the difficulties and disappointments of life. Despite belief in determinism, the Stoic held himself and others morally responsible for every action. He suppressed all feelings that would obstruct the course or question the wisdom of Nature, which he studied in order to live by. Will Durant says somewhere that a civilization is born Stoic and dies Epicurean.

Hellenistic Science

We have seen naturalistic tendencies in Hellenistic philosophy, but there are some philosophers of the era whom we can call scientists as we use the term today. While philosophers palavered, these men made a impressive addition to knowledge.

In about the year 300 B.C., Euclid collected the known works of others in geometry into his *Elements*. As every one who has studied the subject knows, it is confined to such figures and proofs as can be made with only a ruler and compass. It would be the textbook in geometry in the western world until the twentieth century. He also summarized the works of others on the geometry of the cone in his *Conics* which has not survived.

Apollonius of Perga (3rd century B. C.), who studied in Euclid's school, took this treatise as the starting point of his own *Conics*, in which he studied the properties of the four curves generated by the intersection of a right circular cone with a plane. One is the circle. He gave the names, parabola, ellipse, and hyperbola to the other three, names they have to this day. His work made possible the theory of projectiles and advanced astronomy, mechanics, and navigation.

Archimedes (287?-212 B. C.), was interested in pure science as we use the word today and was the greatest of ancient scientists. Ten of his works survive. Some of the subjects covered in them are: parabola, ellipse, spirals, sphere, cylinder, conic section, the center of gravity of bodies, and alternative hypotheses in plane geometry. He discovered that the surface of any liquid body at rest and in equilibrium is spherical, and has the same center as the earth. He founded hydrostatics and calculated the value of pi, the ratio of the circumference to the diameter of a circle, as between 3 1/7 and 3 10/71. He squared the circle by proving that the area of a circle is equal to a right triangle whose long leg is equal to the circumference and whose short leg is equal to the radius of the circle. His work on the laws of the lever and balance was not improved on for many centuries.

Archimedes discovered a method for measuring specific gravity when given the task of determining if the king's crown was pure gold. King Hieron had the crown made, supplying the gold. When delivered it weighed as much as the gold but the suspicion arose that part of the crown was silver. Archimedes discovered that equal weights of gold and silver displaced different volumes of water. The crown did not displace exactly the volume of water expected of pure gold. Further measurements determined that part of the crown was silver. On his discovery of this method, according to one story he dashed out naked into the street crying *"Eureka! eureka!"*-- I have found it! I have found it! Of equal fame as this statement, perhaps paraphrased, is "Give me a lever long enough and a place to stand and I will move the earth." It is a forgivable mistake, considering that the laws of gravity were not known at the time. With a lever long enough to move the earth, (neglecting the gravitational pull of other bodies in the solar system), Archimedes would have been nearly weightless and the pull would be virtually parallel to the lever.

Aristarchus of Samos (280-264 B. C.) was an astronomer. Although there is no hint of heliocentricism in his works, he is credited by Archimedes with the a hypothesis to that effect but seems to have abandoned it on the grounds that it did not agree with the prevailing belief that the orbits were perfect circles, a dogma that held until the time of Kepler. We will find even Galileo holding this view.

Hipparchus of Nicaea (in Bithynia) (160?-125 B C.), was a scientist and was an important astronomer despite one colossal mistake. The Ptolemaic astronomy, named for Claudius Ptolemy, that had all heavenly bodies revolving around the earth, was based on Hipparchus' research and calculations. To his credit he calculated the solar year at 365 1/4 days minus 4 minutes and 48 seconds, a mean lunar month at 29 days, 12 hours, 44 minutes, and 2 1/2 seconds, both close to currant calculations. With less accuracy but close, he calculated the distance of the moon from the earth as 250,000 miles. His measurements of the angle between the plane of the earth's orbit with that of the earth's equator (obliquity of the ecliptic), the moon's orbit, and the interval between two successive conjunctions of the planets with the sun (synodic periods) are impressive compared to present measurements. He mapped in terms of celestial latitude and longitude the positions of 1080 fixed stars completing it about 129 B. C.. He compared this work with a chart Timochares made 166 years earlier. From this he was able to calculate that the stars had shifted their positions some two degrees during that time. Growing out of this was his discovery that the equinoxes occurred earlier each year. His calculation of this (precession of the equinoxes) was thirty-six seconds per year. Today's calculation is fifty. He created trigonometry by formulating a table of sines. As an inventor, he improved the astrolabe and quadrant.

The reputation of Eratosthenes of Cyrene (276?-195?) for varied knowledge made him head of the Alexandrian Library at age forty. As a geographer he brought together the reports of Alexander's surveyors, travelers, and explorers in his *Geographica*. His descriptions were, of course, limited to the part of the earth known to Greece, but he mentioned India and China. He attempted to give a scientific explanation of the features of various regions of the earth by citing such natural causes as volcanic eruptions, earthquakes and water erosion, thinking that would in time grow into the science of geology.

He saw the narrow mindedness of the Greeks in their division of mankind into Hellenes and barbarians--better people and lesser people--and called attention to the refinement of people in other nations. He was accomplished in mathematics and measured the earth's circumference as 24,662 miles and the obliquity of the ecliptic at $23°51'$. The latter was very close to accurate, and science measures the earth's circumference today as 24,847 miles.
He gets our attention by writing that India could be reached by sea from Iberia (Spain) by keeping to the same parallel, were the Atlantic Ocean not an obstacle.

Theophrastus (372-287 B.C.) was Aristotle's successor in biology. He was a naturalist not only in biology but also in philosophy, rejecting the supernatural explanations of the time. His methods were an improvement over Aristotle's in studying hundreds of species. He attributed sexual reproduction only to a few species such as the date palm or fig tree. He described the fertilization of the latter where flower clusters of the caprifig are hung from the branches of the edible fig allowing wasps to carry the pollen of the former to the latter, a practice probably acquired from the Babylonians. Beyond this he showed no knowledge of sexual reproduction listing the methods of generation as from seeds, twigs, branches, roots, small pieces of wood, or from the trunk, all of which had evidence to support them, but also listed spontaneous reproduction. He classified plants into trees, bushes, shrubs, and herbs. He named the parts of the plant as root, stem, branch, twig, leaf, flower, and fruit. These classifications prevailed for centuries. He discussed the industrial uses of plants and the climatic conditions most favorable for their growth and noted their geographical distribution.

Advances were made in medicine in this era, boosted by the study of Egyptian medicine. The dissection of cadavers was permitted, promoting human anatomy to a science. Herophilus of Chalcedon (fl. 300 B. C.) possibly the greatest anatomist of antiquity, working at Alexandria about 285 B.C., dissected and described the eye, the brain, ovaries, the uterus, the seminal vesicles, and the prostrate gland and examined the liver and the pancreas. He understood the function of the nerves and named the brain as the seat of thought. He divided the nerves into sensory and motor. In his work on the brain, he left his name in the *torcular Herophili*. He understood the differences in the arteries and veins, discovered that the arteries carried the blood from the heart throughout the body, and seemed close to discovering the circulation of the blood. He valued taking the pulse in diagnosis, but was not the first to do so. He gave the duodenum the name used today. His careful science reduced the mistakes inherited from Aristotle.

Erasistratus a 3rd century B. C. physiologist, probably the most notable of the era, expected all functions of the body to be explained by natural causes, rejecting any non-natural ones. He practiced medicine in Alexandria about 258 B. C., advocating preventive medicine through hygiene diet and exercise, opposing frequent use of drugs and bloodletting. He declared that every organ is connected with the rest of the body by artery, vein, and nerve. He studied the brain by making experiments on living subjects and did original study of the heart.

While these scientists were not free from mistakes, their knowledge was an oasis in a broad plateau of metaphysics.

I apologize to the shades of all the Greek and Roman philosophers I have omitted or slighted in this history and pass on to a Roman Plato.

Philosophy of the Age of Faith

Plotinus (205-270) was an idealist and the last of the notable pagan philosophers. His philosophy was congenial to Christianity and lasted until the fifth century. From Plotinus' time for a thousand years reason would be in thrall to theology. In order to know what naturalism is up against, we will take a sampling of Plotinus' idealism (interpreted):

> All reality consists of a series of emanations, from the One, the eternal source of all being. The first, necessary emanation is that of Nous (mind or intelligence), the second that of Psyche (soul). At the periphery of the universe is found matter. Man belongs partly in the realm of spirit and partly in the sphere of matter. . . .
>
> The object of sensation are of a lower order of being than the perceiving organism. The inferior cannot act upon the superior. Hence sensation is an activity of the sensory agent upon its objects. Sensation provides a direct, realistic perception of material things, but, since they are ever-changing, such knowledge is not valuable. In internal sense perception, the imagination also functions actively, memory is attributed to the imaginative power and it serves not only in the recall of sensory images but also in the retention of the verbal formulae in which intellectual concepts are expressed. The human soul can look either upward or downward; up to the sphere of pure spirit, or down to the evil regions of matter. Rational knowledge is a cognition of intelligible realities, or Ideas in the realm of Mind which is often referred to as Divine. The climax of knowledge consists in an intuitive and mystical union with the One; this is experienced by few.[DOP, 256]

As I am one of the many, I will stop with this much of Plotinus' philosophy. Naturalism now takes a back seat as it will for centuries to come. Until the 17th century, "there was no generally recognized, clear line of distinction between philosophy and the natural sciences; 'natural philosophy' was the common term which could embrace both what we would call metaphysics and what we would call physics."[AOR, 14] This is not to say that there were not naturalistic beliefs and assumptions in most philosophers' writings.

This brings us to the Christian Era and what is called patristic philosophy, which overlaps Plotinus in time. In eventually developing their theology, the Christians were presented with the problem of reconciling the new beliefs with pagan positions. The Fathers of the first 200 years,

> most of them converts from paganism, proclaimed the Christian religion as "the

true philosophy." Their works were mostly apologetic [defensive] in nature, directed either against pagan prejudices and misconceptions or the religious speculations of Gnosticism. . . In general, patristic philosophy is differentiated from medieval and modern philosophies in that it failed to distinguish adequately between the conclusions of reason and the [alleged] facts of revelation."[DOP, 242]

The period from the year 200 to 450 ended with the works of Augustine. In this period: "With the catechetic school of Alexandria and in particular with Clement and Origin, the work of reconciliation between Hellenistic philosophy and the Christian religion formally begins."[DOP, 242]

As one would expect, this was not exactly a hotbed of naturalism, but Clement (about 150-210) on one occasion used a naturalistic argument to discredit the "Heathen Gods:"

> Those whom you worship were once men, and in process of time died; but myths and time have crowned them with honour. People readily come to despise the present because they live in it; whilst the past, which cannot be directly examined and is hidden in the darkness of the ages, is invested with honor by imagination and fiction. We are suspicious of the present, full of admiration for the past. In this way the dead men of antiquity, being reverenced through the long prevalence of error, are thought to be gods by their successors.[TFWT, 138, 139]

This argument of natural causes of religious belief could as well be made today as in Clement's time. Origin (185-254), who is credited with being one of the first theologians,[DOP, 237] and "was the first great Christian teacher who was born of a Christian family,"[TFWT, 147] explained difficulties in the Bible as allegories, which show that he had a naturalistic bent:

> "Will any man of sense," he writes, "suppose that a first, a second and a third day, morning and evening, existed without sun and moon and stars? . . . And who is so silly as to imagine that God, like a husbandman, planted a garden in Eden and put in it a tree of life, which could be seen and felt so that anyone who tasted the fruit with his bodily teeth received the gift of life? . . . Why, even the Gospels are filled with narratives of the same kind. We read of the Devil leading Jesus up on to a high mountain to show him the kingdoms of the world and their glory. Who but a careless reader of these things would not condemn the supposition that with the bodily eye . . . Jesus beheld the kingdoms of Persia, Scythia, India and Parthia and the glory of their rulers among men?"[TFWT, 150]

We find that one taking such a common-sense approach could also believe in magic.

> "Magic is not, as the Epicureans and Aristotelians suppose, utterly incoherent, but, as the experts prove, a consistent system which has principles known to very few." One of the fundamental principles of magic is, as is well known, the use of the correct names of spiritual beings. "Our Jesus," says Origin, "keeps to the same philosophy of names; for His name has been clearly proved to drive our countless demons from souls and bodies, powerfully working on those from whom they were expelled."[TFWT, 151]

And, of course, today the faithful pray "in Jesus' name."

The period of patristic philosophy from 450 to the 8th century is "generally characterized by the *elaboration* and *systematization* of truths [beliefs] already formularized. Platonic and Neo-Platonic influences predominate, though Aristotle's *logic* holds an honored place through this pre-Scholastic era."[DOP, 243]

Although in this era, as in the Scholastic one to follow, theology and philosophy were so intertwined as to make it hard to speak of one without including the other, the existence of God being assumed in all speculations, there were matters that we may classify as problems of dogma. Gnosticism, which, as we saw, Clement opposed and which meant for Christian Gnostics "an esoteric knowledge of higher religious and philosophic truths to be acquired by an elite group of intellectually developed believers,"[DOP, 132] was one such problem. Another, and perhaps the greatest one, was Arianism, the view of Arius, (256-336) who held

> that Jesus and God were not of the same substance (the orthodox position). He maintained that although the Son was subordinate to the Father he was of a similar nature. The controversy on the relation of Jesus to God involved the question of the divine status of Jesus. If he were not divine, how could the church justify him as an object of worship, of trust, and adoration? If he is divine, how could such a belief square with the doctrine of one God (monotheism)? Arianism tended toward the doctrine of the subordination of Jesus to God, involving the extreme Arians who held Jesus to be unlike God and the moderate Arians who held that Jesus was of similar essence with God although not of the same substance. Some eighteen councils were convened to consider this burning question, parties in power condemning and placing each other under the ban. The Council of Nicea in 325 repudiated Arian tendencies

but the issue was fought with uncertain outcome until the Council of Constantinople in 381 reaffirmed the orthodox view.[DOP, 34] [The view of those who won the battle became the orthodox view.]

While the fathers of the church were fighting it out over points of dogma, the pagan religions were overcome by Christianity. The last Christian arguments against the pagans were made by Augustine. However, in the process Christianity became to a significant degree paganized Judaism. The church changed the worship of the pagan gods with worship of the saints. God as the Father, the Son, and the Holy Ghost gave additional multiplicity that was congenial to paganism. A man that was a god was easily accepted by pagan converts. Thus polytheism was not entirely taken away from them. Ancient pagan rites were transformed and remained in Christianity. Pagan celebrations were replaced with Christian ones including the Saturnalia with Christmas. Pagan altars were made Christian and pagan statues were renamed Mary and Jesus, undermining the old beliefs.

But to return to what is called philosophy, there were two kinds of Christian philosophers: "those who believed that 'since God has spoken to us it is no longer necessary to think,' and the others who believed that 'the divine law required man to seek God by the rational methods of philosophy' because it is man's first duty to use his God-given reason.' "[AOB, xii]

Tertullian (169-220) a Christian philosopher (or anti-philosopher) of the former kind was famous for his saying "The Son of God died; it must be believed because it is absurd."[TFWT, 175] Martin Luther (1583-1546) who made Christianity "not only irrational but anti-rational," did much the same thirteen centuries later. In *The Bondage of the Will*, a reply to Erasmus's (1466-1536) pamphlet on *Free Will*, he wrote,

> This is the highest degree of faith--to believe He is merciful, who saves so few and damns so many; to believe Him just, who according to His own will makes us necessarily damnable, that He may seem, as Erasmus says, "to delight in the torments of the miserable, and to be an object of hatred rather than love." If, therefore, I could by any means comprehend how that same God can be merciful and just who carries the appearance of so much wrath and iniquity, there would be no need of faith. But now, since that cannot be comprehended, there is room for exercising faith.[AOAv, 149]

Luther would have had room for even greater faith had he proof that God did not exist. Was it Mark Twain who said that faith was believing in something you know is not so?

Augustine (354-430) was the first Christian philosopher of repute. Despite his insistence that faith must precede understanding, he was the type of philosopher who thought it was his duty to use his God-given reason. These philosophers produced the most of the literature. Augustine was influenced by Plotinus and other neo-Platonists and their conception of "immaterial reality." It is said that he Christianized Plato, that is, interpreted him to fit his (Augustine's) theology. I find Augustine's Platonism no more comprehensible than Plato's, but he was a reasoner and "reason" I will venture, always has one foot, or at least a finger or two, in naturalism.

Augustine contemplates time in his *Confessions*, his best known writings, with some intriguing remarks and concludes that it is all in the mind. We measure time, Augustine writes, but there are three times, the past, now, and the future. The past is not (no longer exists) and the future is not yet (has not occurred). We cannot measure something that is not. The present has no space. We can measure time only as it passes. We measure that which is not, through the present which has no space to measure it in. Do we measure time and know not what we measure? Could I measure the length of a body and how long the space in which it moves from one place to another without measuring the time in which it moved? We measure the spaces of stanzas by the spaces of verses and the spaces of verses by the spaces of the feet, etc., but we get no certain measure of time because one verse pronounced may take longer than another. At this point Augustine thinks that time is nothing but protraction but of what, he does not know. Perhaps it is the mind. The impressions that things make in the mind as they pass in time remains after the events pass. It is this that I measure not what passes by to make the impression.

How, he asks, is the future diminished when it does not exist and how is the past increased when it is now no longer unless three things occur. The mind expects, considers, and remembers. That which is expected passes through what is considered into what is remembered. It is not the future and the past that is long but rather we have a long memory of the past and a long expectation of the future.[TC]

It seems to me that it is the natural properties of time that Augustine is trying to fathom. We will encounter other comments on time and will try to make some sense of it after doing so.

Elsewhere Augustine discusses learning and concludes with a little illogic.

Do we learn by signs? Signs are anything that presents something to the mind, as far as I can determine. There is nothing that can be learned by signs, Augustine tells us, for if a sign is presented me and I know not what it is, it teaches me nothing. If, when it is presented, I know what it is, what does it teach?

Augustine develops an argument which he feels proves the existence of God *(The Confessions)*. Whatever faith tells him, he still wants a philosophical proof and his weapon is "reason." He will acknowledge to be God that one than whom it is proved nothing is superior. He feels that if he proves (with the use of reason) that there is something above and superior to reason, it will prove that God exists. He does not offer a proof of this, but treats it a axiomatic.

He begins by pointing out that each person's senses are his own, else one could not see what another does not see. Everyone has his own reason as is evident by the fact that one person can know something that another does not know. (Intellect would have been a better word than reason, for in his next step he shows reason makes many things common to everyone.) Numbers (mathematics) does not belong to the senses but is unchangeable, a thing seen by all who use reason. We will find that later philosophers call this "knowing a priori," But unlike them he includes physical objects in these "truths." The objects we sense by the eyes and ears as colors and sounds do not belong to the nature of our senses, but are physical qualities to be identified by us. Many other things, he says, are present in common, in a manner public. They are seen by every individual who uses reason and these "objectives" are inviolate and changeless. These "objective truths" which we each see by our individual minds are the same to everyone, but they do not belong to us individually.

Having enumerated several "immutable truths," Augustine proceeds to treat them as one "truth." There is an immutable truth which contains all things immutably true which presents itself as a universal light to all who can fathom that which is immutably true. As this truth is neither inferior nor on the same plane, it follows that it is superior and more excellent (than our minds). He considers that he has shown that there is something that is higher than our minds and our reason and that it is truth itself.[TC]

Augustine had said at the beginning of the demonstration that if he proved that there is something superior to our reason, it would prove the existence of God, therefore this is his proof of the existence of God (This "truth" *was*

God?). If the reader cannot see this, he/she is not alone. Augustine had reasoned his way to God. It is this tendency to "reason" that makes men philosophers. The faithful do not live by faith alone. Reason would be the mainstay of philosophy until and when it reached its apex in the seventeenth century, after which it would be deflated by philosophers of observation and experience--in a word, empiricism.

It is interesting that in the bit about physical objects, Augustine was making the case for the naturalistic common-sense position that they do exist, although this was not his objective. It may seem to the reader that support for this position is unnecessary but we will be finding philosophers who hold that physical objects exist only in the mind or only when they are perceived.

The Scholastics

"Those who taught the seven liberal arts or theology in the cloister and cathedral schools," [DOP, 297] were known as Schoolmen or Scholastics. The term Skolastikos originated with the Greeks and from "Roman antiquity the expression was handed down to the ninth century, when *doctores scholastici* came into general usage"[DOP, 297] Anselm (1033-1109) and Thomas Aquinas (1225-1274), among them and saints of the church, constructed proofs of God's existence using, presumably, their God-given but natural reason. The latter dismissed the proof of the former only to have Kant (18th century) dismiss them both. Anselm, taking Augustine's advice, said "I do not seek to understand that I may believe, but I believe in order to understand. For this also I believe, that unless I believe, I should not understand,"[AOB, 88] but was not above using what he thought was reason to prove God's existence which he managed by the magic of equating or identifying a concept of a being with the being itself (my own criticism) that being that "than which nothing greater can be conceived."[AOB, 88] To put what is virtually my criticism into philosophical jargon, "Anselm has been reproached, . . . for unduly passing from the field of logical to the field of ontological or existential reasoning. This criticism has been repeated by many authors, among them Aquinas."[DOP, 235] Here is an interpretation of Anselm's proof:

> I have an idea of a Being than which nothing greater can be conceived; this
> idea is that of the most perfect, complete, infinite Being, the greatest

conceivable; now an idea which exists in reality . . . is greater than one which exists only in conception; . . . hence, if my idea is the greatest it must exists in reality. Accordingly, God, the Perfect Idea, Being, exists.[DOP, 28]

This interpreter adds that "Anselm's argument rests upon the basis of the realistic metaphysics of Plato." By this he is not saying that Plato's metaphysics is realistic, although presumably he believed that it was, but that Anselm's argument was based on Plato's philosophy that the real is Idea. Anselm's own argument runs to several pages, and I do not know if this is the best interpretation. The "proof," as stated, is an illogical attempt to prove the existence of God by logic. Some, perhaps most, philosophers rejected it, but Kant was "responsible for the final demolition of the 'ontological proof'"[AOR, 67] as he and later philosophers called it.[DOP, 235] Kant's refutation:

> This argument is fallacious precisely because it requires us to regard "existence" as a predicate which names an attribute on all fours with the other attributes, such as omniscience, that are traditionally assigned to God. But "existence" is not a predicate, and does not name an attribute or characteristic of the things to which it is ascribed. "To illustrate his point, Kant gives the example of the difference between a hundred real dollars and a hundred possible dollars. The only difference lies in the fact that the former exists, and the latter do not. The concept of a hundred dollars is precisely the same in both cases."[AOI, 36]

We seem to have gotten rather far afield from the history of naturalism, but Anselm was using (or trying to use) what our next philosopher, St. Thomas Aquinas (1225-1274), called our own natural powers of reason. It will be worthwhile to read a sketch about medieval Europe--St. Thomas's Europe:

> The historical background was melting into newer scenes. There is a remarkable passage in Lucretius which describes the decay of agriculture of the Roman state, and attributes it to the exhaustion of the soil. Whatever the cause, the wealth of Rome passed into poverty, the organization into disintegration, the power and pride into decadence and apathy. Cities faded back into the undistinguished hinterland; the roads fell into disrepair and no longer hummed with trade; the small families of the educated Romans were out bred by the vigorous and untutored German stocks that crept, year after year, across the frontier; pagan culture yielded to Oriental cults; and almost imperceptibly the Empire passed into the Papacy.

The Church, supported in its earlier centuries by the emperors whose powers it gradually absorbed, grew rapidly in numbers, wealth, and range of influence. By the thirteenth century it owned one-third of the soil of Europe, and its coffers bulged with donations of rich and poor. For a thousand years it united, with the magic of an unvarying creed, most of the peoples of a continent; never before or since was organization so widespread or so pacific. But this unity demanded, as the Church thought, a common faith exalted by supernatural sanctions beyond the changes and corrosion of time, therefore dogma, definite and defined, was cast like a shell over the adolescent mind of medieval Europe. It was within this shell that Scholastic philosophy moved narrowly from faith to reason and back again, in a baffling circuit of uncriticized assumptions and pre-ordained conclusions. In the thirteenth century all Christendom was startled and stimulated by Arabic and Jewish translations of Aristotle; but the power of the Church was still adequate to secure, through Thomas Aquinas and others, the transmogrification of Aristotle into a medieval theologian. The result was subtlety, but not wisdom. . . . Sooner or later the intellect of Europe would burst out of this shell. [SOP, 79, 82]

For St. Thomas natural knowledge, what we would call scientific knowledge, comes from the senses and natural reason. This knowledge is of the sensory world--natural things. It is limited but within these limits it trustworthy. We can have indirect knowledge that God exists by sense experience because we experience His effects (the stars and rolling thunder, perhaps) but of the supernatural world, God, the Trinity, His essence, we can have knowledge only by divine revelation. If our knowledge were complete we would see no contradiction between revelation and science. Therefore, St. Thomas does not discount science but, as we would expect of a theologian, he sees much more than nature to have knowledge about.

And just what are these things about which we can have knowledge? All things are either substance or accident: Substances are things like balls and bats, separate entities, physical objects. Accidents exist only as qualities in a substance. Examples are colors, sounds, tastes, density. Other philosophers call these "secondary qualities" and call substances "primary qualities." We will find this concept and terminology still in use in the 17th century when the empiricists argued that all knowledge is from experience. Aquinas's philosophy varied considerably from Augustine's and changed the philosophy of the church.

Plato's metaphysics reigned until Aquinas Christianized Aristotle as

Augustine had done with Plato. While the philosophers made a big thing of the differences and there was much disputation, it was mostly suffocating metaphysics with scarcely a breath of fresh air for a naturalist. Aristotle's works had mostly been lost in the Dark Ages and were rediscovered in the later part of the 12th century. They

> came to be for European philosophy what the Bible was for theology--an almost infallible text, with solutions for every problem. In 1215 the Papal legate in Paris forbade teachers to lecture on his works; in 1231 Gregory I appointed a commission to expurgate him; by 1260 he was *de rigueur* in every Christian School and ecclesiastical assemblies penalized deviations from his views.'[SOP, 73]

For Aquinas the philosopher uses reason and theology uses revelation. But he also reasoned in theology as far as it would take him without contradicting faith. He gave the church the best of both worlds, reason and faith, nature and God. Although not declared free from error, his philosophy is today the philosophy of the Catholic Church.

Aquinas had the wisdom to see the importance of science (what he called natural philosophy) and held it to be the reasonable method of dealing with the real natural world and, of course, took the position that it was compatible with his faith. Having accepted them both as truth, he had the difficult job of reconciling them. Anyone who holds to these two kinds of "truth" has to take something like the position Aquinas took. It is the price one pays for the two "truths." No one has done better at squaring faith and science to the satisfaction of the believer.

Aquinas sorts out science and faith: All objects of science are self evident, in a manner, "seen" (experienced). Objects of faith are not. Therefore, it is not possible that one thing can be believed and be seen by the same person. However, what is an object of science for one person can be an object of belief for another (one who has not "seen" it) and he quotes I Cor. xiii. 12: "We see now through a glass in a dark manner; but then face to face." He uses the trinity as an example. It is faith now (seeing it through a dark glass) but in time it will be seen. He concludes that faith and science cannot be about the same thing.

However, Aquinas is not identifying faith and belief (opinion) as it may appear. As he continues we learn that opinion is deemed possible to be otherwise (than true) while faith is certain (which is a revelation to me). The object of opinion is deemed possible to be otherwise, while the object of science should be deemed impossible to be otherwise than it is. Also, the objects of faith because of their certainty are deemed impossible to be otherwise. Faith and science cannot be about the same object, the reason being that an object of faith is unseen and the object of science is seen.

I confess that I am seeing this through a glass darkly, but the happy result of this is that science and faith both being true and about different objects cannot contradict. I have heard individuals of the faith hold this view, perhaps having studied St. Thomas. From this position it follows that if science says that the sun is the center of the solar system and faith says that the earth is the center, there is no contradiction. But, this is not Aquinas' position, for he adds that if there is a contradiction, science in that instance is simply not true (or not science). This was the position of the church in its shameful treatment of Galileo. In that case science and faith were historically about the same things, contrary to St. Thomas's dictum.

St. Thomas uses a terminology inherited or acquired from Aristotle, making great use of such terms as act, potency, actuation, quiddity, essence, being, quality, accident, form, and substance in explaining nature and supernature alike. He, also, like Aristotle, uses definition as if it were a science. A few paragraphs will suffice to show his use of some of these terms. From a piece on "Potency and Act in Various Compositions:"

> Now, the composition of matter and form is not to be explained in the same way as that of substance and the act of being, even though both be compositions of potency and act.
>
> First of all, this is so because matter is not substance itself, for then it would follow that all forms are accidents, as the ancient natural philosophers thought. Rather, matter is a part of substance.
>
> Secondly, it is so because the very act of being [ipsom esse] is not the proper act of matter but of the whole substance. That, of which we can say that it is, is the item whose act is to be. Now, we do not predicate *to be* of matter but of the whole. Hence, matter cannot be called that which is; instead, substance itself is that which is.
>
> It is clear, then, that the composition of act and potency has greater extension than the composition of form and matter. Consequently, matter and form are divisions of material substance, while potency and act are divisions of common being. For this reason, whatever concomitants potency and act have, as such, are common to both material and immaterial created substances; for instance, to receive and to be received to perfect and to be perfected. However, whatever

characteristics are proper to matter and form as such, as, for instance, to be generated and corrupted, and the like, these are peculiar to material substances and in no way appropriate to immaterial created substances. [TPA, 169]

From a piece on "How Various Acts Are Distinguished:"

> Neither is an angel, nor in any creature, is a perfected power or an operative potency the same as its essence. This is clear from the following. Since potency gets its meaning from act, the diversification of potencies must depend on the diversity of acts. This is why it is said that the appropriate act corresponds to the appropriate potency. Now in every created thing, essence differs from its act of being and is related to it as potency to act, as is clear from what has been said.
>
> The act to which operative potency corresponds is operation. Now, the acts of understanding and of being are not the same in an angel; nor is any other operation, either in the angel or in any other kind of creature, identical with its act of being. Consequently, an angel's essence is not its intellectual potency, nor is the essence of any created being its operative potency. [TPA, 171]

Presumably here St. Thomas was using his "natural powers of reason." Despite this, this is a good example of why scholastic philosophy did little for the advancement of knowledge. I have mentioned (page 19) that Aristotelianism at the hands of Aquinas and others developed in a completely sterile form. This is not to say that Aquinas did not make sense at times.

One commentator tells us that Aquinas's philosophy "can be understood as a systematic critique and elimination of Platonism in metaphysics, psychology and epistemology." [DOP, 32] (I give him my blessing). What he

> appears to have insisted on most in using Aristotle as a pillar of his own thought was the rehabilitation of man and the universe as stable realities and genuine causes. This insistence had been called by some his *naturalism*. Against the tendency of thirteenth century Augustinians to disparage the native ability of the human reason to know truth, St. Thomas insisted on the capacity of the reason to act as a genuine and sufficient cause of true knowledge within the natural order. [DOP,32]

With faith being certain, it seems that Aquinas did not need a separate proof of God's existence; however, as mentioned, he rejected Anselm's proof of God and did himself prove God's existence five ways, some of which had been used by a previous philosopher. One holds about as much water as another so I will mention only one. With his "natural theology," he begins with an appeal to observation (a posteriori). In what he calls the world of sense (the empirically knowable), efficient causes follow one another in order. There is the first cause followed by an intermediate cause which may be one or several. The ultimate cause follows the intermediate cause. If there is no cause there is no effect, therefore if there is no first cause there is no intermediate cause and no ultimate cause. If causes could go on to infinity there could be no first efficient cause and no ultimate effect. This is all obviously false; therefore there is a first efficient cause which is God.

If this were a sound logical argument, it seems to me that it would be a case of science (of objects seen) and faith (of objects unseen) being about the same thing, namely causation, contrary to St. Thomas' declaration above.

Despite his opposition to Augustine's Platonism, his position on eternity is similar to Augustine's. He contrasts the natural properties of time with his conception of eternity which is outside of time. In the natural world, there is movement, succession, before and after, and time is nothing but this movement. Further, there is a beginning and end in that which moves. Experiencing all this makes us apprehend time. In a like manner, the apprehension of uniformity, that is, where there is no movement, no succession, gives us the idea of eternity. Eternity is known from two sources. We know it because that which is eternal has no beginning nor end and it has no succession, being whatever it is simultaneously.

Will Durant, who omitted scholastic philosophy from his *The Story of Philosophy*, admitted in the second edition that to do so was an "outrage, forgivable only in one who had suffered much from it in college and seminary, and resented it thereafter as rather a disguised theology than an honest philosophy."[SOP, viii] Aquinas's philosophy as the philosophy of the Catholic Church (as has been noted) is still a source of student suffering. "Students in ecclesiastical seminaries are to become familiar with the thought and method (ratio) of Aquinas, [but] not to the exclusion of other important writers or of the findings of science."[TPA, xix] His published writings fill 10,000 double-column folio pages. Thus the volume itself is, shall we say, insufferable. In my view little is learned except some history of ideas by reading Aquinas.

Although philosophers have classified the seventeenth century as "the age of reason," for reasons (by evidence) we shall see, the centuries from Augustine through the Middle Ages (from the 5th century to about the 14th or 15th), which is called the age of faith, was also an age of reason, that is, their principle weapon, although mostly specious, was reason. They used "reason as a handmaiden in the service of faith."[AOAv, 27] The faithful do not live by faith alone. Natural theology was, for the scholastics, that obtained by the natural (reasoning) powers of the mind.

Perhaps the subject of the hottest disputes was universals. I was shocked and disgusted to learn that belief in the reality of universals was called realism, something that was unreal to me. I found it hard to believe that grown, sober men could believe in such a thing. I pause here for a definition:

> The problem of Universals is: does whiteness, or fatness, or roundness, or anything that can be predicated of a number of things, really exist separately, apart from white things or fat things or round things? Or are the whiteness, the fatness, the roundness only in the things that are white and fat and round? Or are they only in our mind? Is whiteness merely a mental idea given us by all the white things we have ever known, and fatness the sum of all the fat things, and roundness the glomerate impression of all the round things we have ever perceived? If your reply is that whiteness exists quite separately and substantially, then philosophically you are a realist; if you believe whiteness is only the mind's idea of the sum of things that are white, then in philosophy you are called a nominalist. [AOB, 20]

The disputes over universals have been called "a tempestuous controversy that is not yet, and perhaps by its nature cannot be, resolved,"[AOB, 20] but the same person in the same book quotes approvingly another's view that William of Ockham undermined realism fatally.[AOB, 210] I do not know if realism received a fatal blow, but as many people have an attraction for metaphysics, I doubt it.

One writer observes,

> Whatever happens in history is temporal, and must follow the same sequence of birth, through growth, to death. This is as true of philosophical systems as it is of individuals, and the particular expression of each idea has its decline as it had its heyday or its incipience.[AOB, 201]

I break in here to observe that this remark is a piece of natural philosophy and that natural philosophy began a rise after the era we are discussing and has not only gone through a long period of growth, it is in acceleration. The writer continues,

The beginning of the end came for scholastic philosophy around 1320, when many theologians began to fear for the future of religion itself amidst the complications of the conflicting systems. . . . The various fourteenth century thinkers each propounded their own varieties of attack on the given scholastic positions, but it is William of Ockham who stands, if any single man can claim such a position, at the end of the Middle Ages as the great iconoclast, clearing the encumbered ground and preparing a beach-head for the philosophers of the Renaissance, for such men as Francis Bacon and Thomas Hobbes.[AOB, 201]

In Ockham (ca 1280-ca 1349), as he is called, I finally found a philosopher of the middle ages who made sense. He is best known for his "famous principle, that entities are not to be multiplied without necessity [having a basis in logic or experience]," which is known as Ockham's razor.[AOB, 202] His followers were known, naturally enough, as Ockhamists. Here is his position, known as nominalism, outlined.

Among Ockham's early works, composed at Oxford was an *Exposition* on Aristotle's *Physics*, in which several of Ockham's most original and famous ideas appear. In this *Exposition* Ockham explains that some authors have said things possess a common nature, and that the idea of such a common nature plus some new concept *individualizes* in creatures, and this makes them universals, or rather *universalizes* them in the intellect. Intelligences cannot perceive this common quality or nature; indeed intelligence cannot know an individual directly, as an object, but only by reflection, by a reflex action, at second bounce, as it were. This, Ockham said, is nonsense: by no twist of the intellect can a man be a goat, or Socrates at home when he is walking on the street. No more can the intellect make the mobile immobile; the perishable, the eternal; or the singular, universal. *Only* individuals are real, singly; there is no such thing as an individual universalized. The object of scientific enquiry or research is always the individual, never the universal, and the object perceived exists before the act of perceiving it. Nothing, Ockham says, exists before knowledge of an object except the object that is known; and the object of the senses and of the intelligence must be the same.

Matter, Ockham continues, and form, cannot be known by us in themselves. We can only know them in the relations and opposition they have with each other. We are unable ever to form simple concepts, *propter sibi*, as such, but only composite concepts. And if this is so with regard to sensible objects, to things whose reality we can ascertain from their properties, and whose nature we can infer, how much more so with regard to God, none of whose attributes we can experience, none of whose attributes can be the object of our experiment? God, it will be argued, is in relation to the world as a cause to its effect, and by knowing the effect, we can know the cause. This is an error. For actions are caused by individual agents. All causes are individualized realities, and differ each from the other, as knowledge of Plato from that of Socrates, and we can never arrive at a knowledge of the cause by an analysis of the effect, unless we have grasped the cause by a previous intuition. Divine nature is thus unintelligible to us. Indeed, we cannot know certainly that God is, and all the customary proofs are only arguments as to the probability of His existence, and nothing more.[AOB, 203, 204]

Ockham held "that all our conceptions are mental signs which signify the external things, and that 'a sign is anything, that, as apprehended, presents something else to cognition,' [and in doing so] he disassociated logic and metaphysics, philosophy and theology."[AOB, 211] One writer

regards Ockham's "natural philosophy" as a forerunner of the mathematico-mechanical world-view of Descartes and Newton. Of Ockham's theory of motion he says "the affirmation that the continuation of the local motion does not need any moving cause is the law of inertia itself, formulated by Descartes and at the time of Ockham too new to be admitted."[AOB, 207]

We find natural "determinism" as opposed to supernatural in one Ockhamist, John Buridan (d. shortly after 1358). He held that "every good set before us by the intellect, exercises on the will, which is undetermined of itself, a natural attraction, and we necessarily choose what appears to be the better."[AOB, 212] In connection with this we hear the so-called story of Buridan's ass: An ass placed between two equally attractive bales of hay placed equal distances from him died of hunger because he could not decide between them. We are told that the story is not found in Buridan's writings.[DOP, 58] The mystery is why anyone would look for it there. The story is obviously told to support free will and to counter, and to attempt to make ridiculous, Buridan's stand on determinism. As I am a determinist I will add to the story by saying that when the ass swung his head to shoo flies the bales of hay were no longer equidistant from him. Buridan argued that the motion of the planets and stars, including the daily rotation of the earth are governed by the same natural laws as operate here on earth. He discounted the angelic intelligences which Aristotle and Aquinas had assigned that task.

The scholastics gradually made themselves absurd by arguing more etiolated problems--of which a favorite (though fictitious) example is how many angels could stand on the point of a needle. . . . Philosophy proper . . . marked time between William of Ockham and René Descartes, while the old structure of scholasticism was being torn down by the reformation.[AOB, 212, 213]

Skepticism Again

As was the case with the ancient Greeks, much disputation by the scholastics led to skepticism of the possibility of knowledge. For an example we will skip to the 16th century and the *Essais* [Essays] of Michel de Montaigne (1533-1592). In his case the disputes of the scholastics may not have been a great influence. He valued travel and history as the best education and may have gotten most of his thoughts from the observation of life. I would classify the *Essais*, a best seller which grew to three volumes, as literature rather than philosophy.

Stoicism for a time was Montaigne's ideal but later he rebelled against it for preaching the following of 'Nature' and at the same time suppressing nature in man. He interpreted Nature through his own nature, and decided to follow his natural desires whenever they did no perceivable harm. He mixed considerable natural philosophy with his skepticism.

Long before Locke, Montaigne affirms that "all knowledge is addressed to us by the senses," and that reason depends upon the senses; but the senses are deceptive in their reports and severely limited in their range; therefore reason is unreliable. "Both the inward and the outward parts of man are full of weakness and falsehood." (Here, at the very outset of the Age of Reason, a generation before Bacon and Descartes, Montaigne asks the question that they would not stop to ask, that Pascal would ask eighty years later, that the philosophers would not face till Hume and Kant: Why should we trust reason?) Even instinct is safer guide than reason. See how well the animals get along by instinct--sometimes more wisely than men. "There is greater difference between many a man and many another man than between many a man and many an animal." Man is no more the center of life than the earth is the center of the universe. It is presumptuous of man to think that God resembles him, or that human affairs are the center of God's interest, or that the world exists to serve man. And it is ridiculous to suppose that the mind of man can fathom the nature of God. "O senseless man, who cannot make a worm and yet will make gods by the dozen!" [Quite a lot of certainty here for a skeptic.]

Montaigne arrives at skepticism by another route--by contemplating the variety and fluctuation of beliefs in laws and morals, in science, philosophy and religion; which of these truths is truth? He prefers the Copernican to the Ptolemaic astronomy, but: "Who knows whether, a thousand years hence, a third opinion will rise, which haply may overthrow these two," and "whether it be not more likely that this huge body, which we call the World, is another manner of thing than we judge it?" "There is no science," only the proud hypotheses of immodest minds. Of all the philosophies the best is Pyhrro's--that we know nothing. "The greatest part of what we know is the least part of what we know not." "Nothing is so firmly believed as that which is least known," and "a persuasion of certainty is a manifest testimony of foolishness." "In few words, there is no constant existence, neither of our being nor of the objects. And we and our judgement, and all mortal things else, do incessantly roll, turn, and pass away. Thus nothing can be certainly established. We have no communication with being." Then, to heal all wounds, Montaigne ends by reaffirming his Christian faith and singing a pantheistic paean to the unknowable God.

Thereafter he applied his skepticism to everything, always with an obeisance to the Church. . . . "What do I know?" became his motto, engraved on his seal and inscribed on his library ceiling. Other mottos adorned the rafters "The for and against are both possible"; "It may be and it may not be"; I determine nothing. I do not comprehend things; I suspend judgement; I examine."[AORB, 407, 408]

But, his comments on human nature--ideas of which he is not skeptical-- belie his skepticism:

> He perceives that a man's religion and his moral ideas are usually determined by his environment. "The taste of good and evil greatly depends upon the opinion we have of them," The laws of conscience proceed not from God but from custom. Conscience is the discomfort we feel when violating the mores of our tribe.[AORB, 408]

At bottom, Montaigne's skepticism was based on the senses which he found deceptive. Reason depends on the senses; therefore it is unreliable. Instinct he thought a better guide and pointed out how well animals get along with instinct, forgetting, or not realizing, that trusting the senses is an indispensable instinct of animals. "So whilst all the animals trust their senses and live, philosophy would persuade man alone not to trust them and, if he was consistent, to stop living."[SAAF, 297]

Montaigne could have been a good psychologist had he not been so irresponsible with his skepticism. But, his book made good reading and was an influence not only on Bacon and Descartes, but on Pascal who became intensely disturbed trying to salvage his faith from Montaigne's questioning. He was also an influence on the psychological analysis of mind and character in French Literature. We leave him, as we have others, without doing him justice.

The Advance of Science

A funny thing happened to us on the way to Descartes. While no one was watching, no one in philosophy proper that is, natural philosophy was putting metaphysics, the "first philosophy" of the Scholastics, to shame in the advancement of knowledge.

Roger Bacon (ca, 1214-1292) thought that a universal is merely the similarity of several individuals, that only individual things are real. Although he held many orthodox theological views and contributed little to science, he was the most famous of medieval scientists. He became disgusted with the metaphysics of the schools, and would burn all the books of Aristotle as a fountain of error and a stream of ignorance. But despite this he continued to quote Aristotle.

He made the case for experience in acquiring knowledge. He insisted that there are two ways to acquire knowledge, reasoning and experience. He uses fire as an example. A person who had never seen fire could not determine by reason that it burns, but when he has had actual experience his mind is made certain. Reason alone does not suffice; every thing must be verified by experience. He spoke of science as experimental and understood the importance of mathematics. "Observation he insisted, was required for certification in mathematical physics."[AOB, 137, 138]

Bacon had a vision of modern inventions, not without a blend of popular ideas of his time. He allowed that one fifth of experimental science was concerned with the fabrication of useful machines. He mentioned flying machines, but thought they would have flapping wings. He envisioned on the ground machines moving without animals with great speed; machines which would lift great weights with little labor; and machines made to operate on the bottom of the sea. He believed that rays passed through all physical objects and all physical object radiates force.

Leonardo Da Vinci (1452-1519), as every school boy and girl knows, was a genius. He took a stand against those who discounted the senses in the pursuit of knowledge. "Philosophers in turn have repeatedly--and heatedly-- denied Leonardo, the 'man without letters,' a place in their midst."[AOAv, 67] He extolled the laws of nature: "Oh marvelous Necessity! [natural law] Thou with supreme reason constrainest all effects to be the direct result of their causes, and by a supreme and irrevocable law every natural action obeys thee by the shortest possible process."[AOAv, 83]

He had an impressive career in looking into the nature of things. He rejected alchemy and astrology. He cast doubt on the possibility of a universal flood. He pointed out that there would be no place for the water to move to after the flood. "At this point natural causes fail us, and therefore in order to resolve such a doubt we must needs either call in a miracle to our aid or else say that all this water was evaporated by the heat of the sun."[AOAv, 81]

He valued experience over authorities and was active in almost every science. A small sample: He studied and explained the operation of the eye. He described the anatomy of man in drawings and well as words. He had some but not a complete conception of the circulation of the blood and did a credible job of tracing the blood vessels, muscles and nerves of the body. He dissected many cadavers in the study of the body. He described sound as transmitted by waves of air. He believed that the earth was not the center of the universe. He wrote hundred of pages on optics, color, heat, acoustics, hydraulics, magnetism, motion, and weight, and understood the importance of mathematics in science. He concluded from the fossil shells of marine animals found at high elevations that the waters has once been at those levels. He was an inventor in many fields and the whole world knows about his drawings and paintings.

Between the time of Da Vinci and Descartes natural philosophy produced inventions and discoveries at a rate unknown before. Some of them were: 1590, the compound microscope; 1608, the telescope; 1643, the barometer; 1642, first measurement of the speed of sound (but considerably wide of the mark); 1591, formation of the primary rainbow explained; 1621, law of refraction of light formulated; 1600, discovery of the earth's magnetic poles; 1604, the first systematic treatise on scientific chemistry and the coining of the word, chemistry; 1613, gunpowder used in mine blasting; 1568, "Mercator's projection" maps; 1583, first systematic classification of plants; 1612, method of producing coke devised; 1628, demonstration of the circulation of the blood. Engineers accomplished feats in this era that even today would merit admiration. Astronomers furnished the science on which the Gregorian calendar was based in 1582.

And there was that Copernican revolution, the heliocentric theory of the solar system. Copernicus (1473-1543), summarized his conclusions in 1514 and distributed some manuscript copies as trial balloons, but the reaction was so unfavorable that he could not be persuaded to publish it until late in life, in fact, the year of his death. Kepler (1571-1630) supported, clarified, and amended the Copernican system. In 1604 he discovered that the orbit of Mars is an ellipse. In 1609 "he published the first two of 'Kepler's laws': first, each planet moves in an elliptical orbit, in which one focus is the sun; second, each planet moves more rapidly when near the sun than when farther from it, and a radius drawn from the sun to the planet covers, in its motion, equal areas in equal times."[AORB, 598] In 1619 he published his "third law: the square of the time of revolution of a planet around the sun is proportioned to the cube root of its mean distance from the sun."[AORB, 598]

I have already mentioned that Kepler declared that when the mind leaves the realm of quantity it wanders in darkness and doubt.

Galileo (1564-1642) upheld the Copernican theory and was the leading physicist of the era. He

affirmed the indestructibility of matter. He formulated the principles of the lever and the pulley, and showed that the speed of freely falling bodies increased at a uniform rate. He made many experiments with inclined planes; he argued that an object rolling down one plane would rise on a similar plane to a height equal to its fall if it were not for frictional or other resistance; and he concluded to the law of inertia (Newton's first law of motion)--that a moving body will continue indefinitely in the line and rate of motion unless interfered with by some external force. He proved that a projectile in a horizontal direction would fall to the earth in a parabolic curve compounding the forces of impetus and gravity. He reduced musical tones to wave lengths of air, and showed that the pitch of a note depends upon the number of vibrations made by the struck string in a given time. Notes, he taught, are felt as consonant and harmonious when their vibrations strike the ear with rhythmic regularity. Only those properties of matter belong to matter that can be dealt with mathematically--extension, position, motion, density: all other properties--sounds, tastes, odors, colors, and so on--"reside in consciousness; if the living creature were removed, all these qualities would be wiped away and annihilated." He hoped that in time these "secondary qualities" could be analyzed into primary physical qualities of matter and motion, mathematically measurable.

These were basic and fruitful contributions. They were hampered by inadequacy of instruments; so, for example, Galileo underestimated the factor of air resistance in the fall of objects and projectiles. But no man since Archimedes had ever done so much for physics.[AORB, 602, 603]

But Galileo is most famous as an astronomer. Giving more time to it in at the end of the 16th century, he wrote to Kepler in 1596 telling him that he was happy to have him for an ally and that he had held the Copernican view for many years. He had many proofs against the generally accepted hypotheses but was afraid to publish them because of the fate of Copernicus who was ridiculed and condemned by countless people. The telescope was invented in 1608. Galileo, on hearing of it, made his own telescopes which magnified to three diameters at Padua in 1609.

He improved his telescope until it magnified objects a thousand times. Turning it to the sky, he was amazed to discover a new world of stars, ten times as many as had yet been catalogued. Constellations were now seen to contain a great number of stars invisible to the unaided eye; so the Pleiades were seen to be thirty-six instead of seven and Orion eighty instead of thirty-seven, and the Milky Way appeared not as a nebulous mass but a forest of stars great and small. The moon was no longer a smooth surface, but a corrugation of mountains and valleys; and the vague illumination of its unsunned half could be explained as partly due to sunshine reflected from the earth. In January 1610 Galileo discovered four of the nine "moons" or satellites of Jupiter; "these new bodies," he wrote, "moved around another great star, in the same way as Mercury and Venus, and peradventure the other known planets, move around the sun." In July he discovered the ring of Saturn, which he mistook for three stars. Critics of Copernicus had argued that if Venus revolved around the sun it should, like the moon, show phases--changes in illumination and apparent shape; and they had held that there was no sign of such changes. But in December Galileo's telescope revealed such phases, and he believed that they could be explained only by the planet's revolution around the sun.

It seems unbelievable, but Galileo, in a letter to Kepler, affirmed that the professors at Padua [university where he was teaching] refused to credit his discoveries, refused even to look in the skies through his telescopes.[AORB, 604]

Natural philosophy is no match for faith in the hands of the true believer. Galileo would soon be found in conflict with faith for his proof that the sun was the center of the solar system; and faith turned out to be what the church said it was. His defense of natural philosophy was also offensive to the church. A sample of his statements:

> Inasmuch as the Bible . . . calls for an interpretation differing from the immediate sense of the words as when it speaks of God's anger, hatred, remorse, hands and feet, it seems to me that as an authority in mathematical controversy it [the Bible] has very little standing. . . . I believe that natural processes which we either perceive by careful observation or deduced by cogent demonstration cannot be refuted by passages from the Bible.[AORB, 606]

> Nature . . . is inexorable and immutable, she never transgresses the laws imposed upon her, or cares a whit whether her abstruse reasons and methods of operation are understandable to men. For that reason it appears that nothing physical which sense-experience sets before our eyes, or which necessary demonstrations prove to us, aught to be called in question (much less condemned) upon the testimony of Biblical passages which may have some different meanings beneath their words.[AORB, 607]

"'Philosophy,' said Galileo, meaning 'natural philosophy,' or science,"

> is written in this grand book of the universe, which stands continually open to our gaze. But the book cannot be understood unless we first learn to comprehend the language and read the letters in which it is composed. It is written in the language of mathematics.[AORB, 586]

Galileo was tried for heresy and recanted and professed to believe the Ptolemaic system to save his life. He remembered Bruno's burning thirty-three years before. What else was there for him to do? Bruno (1548-1600) who believed that the sun is the center of the solar system was condemned and burned alive by the Inquisition not for this but for such heresies as denying the Trinity, the Incarnation, and transubstantiation.

Cardinal Bellarmine who had a hand in the condemning of Bruno and in the examination of Galileo for heresy was a man of great faith, but in a letter to another "Reverend Father" put his faith aside and put his trust in experience: "as to the Sun and Earth, a wise man has no need to correct his judgment, for his experience tells him plainly that the Earth is standing still and that his eyes are not deceiving when they report that the Sun, Moon, and stars are in motion."[TCOG, 100] He was upholding a naturalistic view, one based on experience which he did not know, indeed, did not bother to learn, had been superseded by another naturalistic view based on even more experience.

It was not only the Catholic Church that opposed Copernicus. Luther called Copernicus an upstart astrologer and a fool and with help of Calvin got the earth safely stabilized by quoting holy scripture. Calvin quoted Psalm XCIII: 1 and belittled accepting the authority of Copernicus over the Holy Spirit.

Descartes himself, to return to the history of science, gave analytical geometry to mathematics and the law of inertia to science among other contributions. The use of the first letters in the alphabet for known quantities and the last ones for the unknown in mathematics was established by him.

Francis Bacon (1561-1626), made a famous comment on nature:

> Man, being the servant and interpreter of Nature, can do and understand so much and so much only as he has observed in fact or in thought of the course of nature. Beyond this he neither knows anything nor can do anything. . . . Human knowledge and human power meet in one; for where the cause is not known the effect cannot be produced. Nature to be commanded must be obeyed; . . . Our only hope therefore lies in. . . true induction.

Beautifully stated! These words appear in his *Novum Organum* (1620), which was his call to make a new beginning in science. The following quotations are from the same book.

First we must clear away all the misconceptions, predigest, illusions and fallacies, superstitions, false philosophy and such which Bacon called "idols" which are now in possession of the human understanding. "The formation of ideas and axioms by true induction is no doubt the proper remedy to be applied for the keeping off and clearing away of idols. To point them out, however, is of great use." He does so at length. We will take a sampling. He points out a persistent trait of human nature that interferes with learning.

> The human understanding when it has once adopted an opinion (either as being the received opinion or as being agreeable to itself) draws all things else to support and agree with it. And though there be a greater number and weight of instances to be found on the other side, yet these it either neglects and despises, or else by some distinction sets aside and rejects, in order that by this great and pernicious predetermination the authority of its former conclusions may remain inviolate. And therefore it was a good answer that was made by one who, when they showed him hanging in a temple a picture of those who had paid their vows as having escaped shipwreck, and would have him say whether he did not now acknowledge the power of the gods - "Aye," asked he again, "but where are they painted that were drowned after their vows?" And such is the way of all

superstition.[NO]

What we want to believe is also a factor,

> For what a man had rather were true he more readily believes. Therefore he rejects difficult things from impatience of research; sober things, because they narrow hope; the deeper things of nature, from superstition; the light of experience, from arrogance and pride,[NO]

"False philosophie," which hinders the advancement of science, "is of three kinds: the Sophistical, the Empirical, and the Superstitious. . . . The most conspicuous example of the first class was Aristotle, who corrupted natural philosophy by his logic."

> But the Empirical school of philosophy gives birth to dogmas more deformed and monstrous than the Sophistical or Rational school. For it has its foundations not in the light of common notions (which though it be a faint and superficial light, is yet in a manner universal, and has reference to many things), but in the narrowness and darkness of a few experiments. To those therefore who are daily busied with these experiments and have infected their imagination with them, such a philosophy seems probable and all but certain; to all men else incredible and vain. Of this there is a notable instance in the alchemists and their dogmas.
>
> But the corruption of philosophy by superstition and an admixture of theology is far more widely spread, and does the greatest harm, whether to entire systems or to their parts. . . . For the contentious and sophistical kind of philosophy ensnares the understanding; but this kind, being fanciful and tumid and half poetical, misleads it more by flattery. For there is in man an ambition of the understanding, no less than of the will, especially in high and lofty spirits. Of this kind we have among the Greeks a striking example in Pythagoras, though he united with it a coarser and more cumbrous superstition; another in Plato and his school, more dangerous and subtle. It shows itself likewise in parts of other philosophies.[NO]

He makes a strange use of the word empirical, given the fact that empirical science is what he is advocating. I take his meaning here to be random trial and error with out theory, but this is the way Edison developed the incandescent light bulb, so one wishes Bacon had used a different word. Elsewhere he returns to the subject of superstition.

> Neither is it to be forgotten that in every age natural philosophy has had a troublesome and hard to deal with adversary - namely, superstition, and the

blind and immoderate zeal of religion. For we see among the Greeks that those
who first proposed to men's then uninitiated ears the natural causes for thunder
and for storms were thereupon found guilty of impiety. Nor was much more
forbearance shown by some of the ancient fathers of the Christian church to
those who on most convincing grounds (such as no one in his senses would now
think of contradicting) maintained that the earth was round, and of consequence
asserted the existence of the antipodes.[NO]

Again he cites false philosophy. Men "distort and color" their beliefs "in
obedience to their former fancies; a thing especially to be noticed in
Aristotle, who made his natural philosophy a mere bond servant to his logic,
thereby rendering it contentious and well-nigh useless." He makes another
dig at Aristotle and Plato. "We have as yet no natural philosophy that is
pure; all is tainted and corrupted: in Aristotle's school by logic; in Plato's
by natural theology."[NO]

Bacon gives a little history of how we acquired the philosophy of Aristotle
and Plato. "To the times of Cicero and subsequent ages, the works of the
old philosophers still remained. But in the times which followed, when on
the inundation of barbarians into the Roman empire human learning had
suffered shipwreck, then the systems of Aristotle and Plato, like planks of
lighter and less solid material, floated on the waves of time and were
preserved."[NO]

The learning institutions of his own time he found wanting. "Again, in the
customs and institutions of schools, academies, colleges, and similar bodies
destined for the abode of learned men and the cultivation of learning,
everything is found adverse to the progress of science."[NO]

If "the formation of ideas and axioms by true induction" (the true method
of science) will clear away all the idols, we, as Bacon tells us, don't really
need all this advice. What then is Bacon's method?

> But the true method of experience, on the contrary, first lights the candle, and
> then by means of the candle shows the way; commencing as it does with
> experience duly ordered and digested, not bungling or erratic, and from it
> educing axioms, and from established axioms again new experiments.
>
> Not unlike this is the true business of philosophy; for it neither relies solely
> or chiefly on the powers of the mind, nor does it take the matter which it gathers
> from natural history and mechanical experiments and lay it up in the memory
> whole, as it finds it, but lays it up in the understanding altered and digested.
> Therefore from a closer and purer league between these two faculties, the

experimental and the rational (such as has never yet been made), much may be hoped.[NO]

There is disagreement as to whether Bacon describes the true methods of science. I believe he did not do badly. There is no division here between "reason" and "empiricism" as soon developed in philosophy. The very definition of rational for Bacon is reason and experience.

Three more quotations for good measure:

> Whereas a method rightly ordered leads by an unbroken route through the woods of experience to the open ground of axioms.
>
> That reason which is elicited from facts by a just and methodical process, I call Interpretation of Nature.
>
> [His method] derives axioms from the senses and particulars, rising by a gradual and unbroken ascent, so that it arrives at the most general axioms last of all. This is the true way, but as yet untried.[NO]

For all his understanding the scientific method, it did not help him understand some of the science of his day; and it was not true that it was new and untried. It was being practiced right under his eyes. His own doctor, William Harvey, discovered the circulation of the blood, but did not publish until later. Bacon rejected the Copernican astronomy and ignored the work of Galileo and Kepler.

To his credit he kept theology and science separate, but he was not an unbeliever. He gave equal glory to God and natural philosophy.

> Natural philosophy is, after the word of God, at once the surest medicine against superstition and the most approved nourishment for faith, and therefore she is rightly given to religion as her most faithful handmaid, since the one displays the will of God, the other his power.[NO]

I have quoted here men whose natural philosophy has advanced knowledge that was available by no other means. But if they were ahead of their time in looking to nature, they were also products of their time. Not all of their theories were correct. Roger Bacon "comes near to claiming for astrology, alchemy and magic a religious, even divine, sanction."[AOB, 139] Kepler believed in witchcraft and mysticism. Galileo believed "the sun to be situated motionless in the center of the revolution of the celestial orbs," and he believed that the orbits of the planets were perfect circles. I will argue later that his concept of "secondary qualities" was a mistake. Francis Bacon after espousing a method which does not allow for the activities of deity in any way whatever, declared that he couldn't believe that "this universal frame is without a mind."[AORB, 177] He is as famous for his statement (*Essay "Of Atheism"*) that "a little philosophy inclineth a man's mind to atheism; but depth in philosophy bringeth men's minds about to religion,"[TE, 65] as he is for the one that we can conquer nature only by obeying her. We have only people for scientists.

Later philosophers treated scholasticism with some contempt. Hobbes "attacked scholastic philosophy as being a meaningless play with meaningless words--'absurd speeches . . . without any significance at all.'"[AOR, 35] Descartes's assessment of scholasticism: "We could not better prove the falsity of those principles than by saying that man has made no progress in knowledge by their means during many ages."[AOAv, 33] Locke must have been thinking of scholasticism when he said, "Vague and insignificant forms of speech, and abuse of language, have so long passed for mysteries of science, and hard or misapplied words, with little or no meaning, have, by prescription, such a right to be mistaken for deep learning and height of speculation, that it will not be easy to persuade either those who speak or those who hear them that they are but the covers for ignorance, and hindrance of true knowledge."[ECHU]

It is quite obvious that scholastic philosophers had been, for the most part, treading water; and, despite the mistakes of scientists, natural philosophy made great discoveries that would lead to an explosion of knowledge. But enough of noting the success of natural philosophy, for in Descartes we are back in philosophy proper. He is generally considered the first modern philosopher.

THE RATIONALISTS

Francis Bacon's philosophy was a call to reason but it is necessary to note the contrast between him and the three "great" rationalists. Bacon's "rationalism" was to emphasize the value of evidence and experience, a call to inductive reasoning. The rationalists held that rational thought was a means of obtaining truth about the universe greatly superior to empirical methods. Rationalism was not new. We have seen it predominate from the beginning in western philosophy, but there was a difference in concept and terminology.

We are entering an era of increased naturalism in philosophy, and our problem of separating metaphysics from naturalism is giving way to separating nonsense from sense in naturalism. The success of science was contagious to the next generations of philosophers. The progress of physics and mathematics in the seventeenth century

> transformed the generally held view of the nature of the material world, and still more, of the nature of true knowledge, to such a degree, that this epoch still stands like a barrier between us and the ages which preceded it, and makes the philosophical ideas of the Middle Ages, and even the Renaissance, seem remote, fanciful and, at times, almost unintelligible. The application of mathematical techniques--and language--to the measurable properties of what the senses revealed, became the sole true method of discovery and of exposition. Descartes and Spinoza, Leibniz and Hobbes, all seek to give their reasoning a structure of a mathematical kind. What can be said must be stateable in quasi-mathematical terms, for language less precise can turn out to conceal the fallacies and obscurities, the confused mass of superstition and prejudices, which characterized the discredited theological or other forms of dogmatic doctrine about the universe, which the new science had come to sweep away and supersede. [AOE, 14, 15]

René Descartes (1596-1650)

Descartes contributed to that science, as we have seen. Having invented analytical geometry, in 1633 he sent a manuscript on physics to a publisher, but remembering the fate of Galileo, whose views were very close to his own, he retrieved it. He thought the church had made a mistake in condemning Galileo's astronomy, and as a faithful Catholic he saw trouble for the church if it continued its opposition to science, but he didn't want to risk prison to prove it. To concealed his ideas from the church authorities, he worked them into a book on philosophy. This book, *Meditations on the First Philosophy,* was published in 1641. He wrote several books, among them *Discourse on Method* which was published in 1637, and established himself as the "foremost philosopher of his age."[AOR, 59]

When I first read Descartes, I felt a degree of empathy with him because he "made the questions 'How do I know?' and 'Can I be certain?' the first questions of philosophy."[AOR, 61] These are the questions that obsessed me as a boy. Our paths soon part, however. From what seemed to me to be clearly factual (obvious from observation) that when we are certain (have no doubt) we can be wrong, I deducted that there was no way to determine which religious denomination was true, which was the subject that filled my mind at the time. There was a degree of Cartesian doubt in my thoughts: "We do not know, we only believe; there is no such thing as knowing." But this doubt was only a temporary state. I soon became aware (to repeat remarks from page 2) as I looked back to that day when I was walking home from school and had these thoughts, that I believed that the ground would hold me as I took step after step going home; that the road led home; that the house we lived in would be there, etc.; and I would eventually realize that I was certain[1] in my initial step in believing that "when we are certain we can be wrong." I then divided "certainty" into "certainty[1]" and "certainty[2]" as explained at the beginning of this discussion.

But Descartes would not have such natural philosophy, the philosophy of Francis Bacon, until it was certified by pure reason. His philosophy briefly and oversimplified is this: There is much confusion in philosophy, and he resolved he would doubt everything until he found something that could not be doubted. He would use only clear and distinct ideas. He can not rush off pell mell in Francis Bacon's natural philosophy (my words, not his) because the senses often deceive him, and besides he could be dreaming. Even mathematics could not be trusted because he could not know that there was not an evil demon who was deceiving him. Was there anything that he could not doubt?

At last he found that indubitably he was thinking. He could not doubt that he was thinking for doubting is a kind of thinking. He then discovered his own existence and gave us one of the famous lines in philosophy when he "reasoned" that "I think therefore I am," and he identified the self with the mind (no hands and feet). If he was writing down this philosophy as he thought it up he had a problem he did not solve (the existence of his writing hand). However, if he waited until he proved he had a body to write it, he had no problem. Having proved his own existence, he then discovered in his mind innate ideas that included self, identity, substance, and God.

Descartes gave extra measure in proving the existence of God. (1) God was an innate idea in the mind. (2) He reasoned (a priori) a proof of God's existence by a method similar to that of Anselm. This "proof" was later demolished by Kant (see page 32).

With God safely back in heaven, Descartes recovered mathematics, for God would not deceive him, and with the use of math he got back the external world, (world is standard philosophical jargon for universe) a mechanism obeying the laws of physics, the kind that Francis Bacon said we had to obey in order to conquer, the mind excepted. Descartes's mind was completely free and separate from this mechanism and has been described as a ghost in a machine.[DOP, 291] He tried to solve this Body/Mind problem by theorizing that the twain met in the penal gland, an idea that got no where. He left "perceivable qualities," Galileo's secondary qualities, where Galileo left them, in the mind.

Descartes's "I think, therefore I am" was initially intriguing to me, but the fascination didn't last long. I could not conceive of thinking occurring without it being done by an (existing) person. I could only understand "I" as "I, this thinking person." Translated "I think, therefore I am" for me came out "I, this thinking (existing) person, thinks, therefore I, this thinking (existing) person, exists;" therefore Descartes had not said anything. Also I saw as much certainty[1] (I must use my own terms here) as doubt in his method. Initially he was certain[1] that there was much confusion and uncertainty[2] in philosophy, that is to say, by philosophers (existing then and in the past). Further, he was certain that philosophers and others should begin with clear and distinct ideas, and this entailed believing that philosophers and other people existed. Therefore my evaluation of Descartes's method is that he climbed down into a hole of doubt on a ladder of certainties[1], then--disowning the thoughts that were the genesis of his doubting--pushed the ladder out of the hole. I do not accuse him, however, of not doubting. If, as a matter of fact (that is, it was his true mental state), he doubted the existence of anything at all, the fact that he got there illogically does not militate against the fact that he doubted. To say that he got there illogically is to say that he is there. We can, therefore, accord him honesty in doubting but we cannot credit him with reasoning well in getting there.

Descartes reasoned to his own satisfaction that he existed, but he did not prove that he knew a priori (just flat knew it without recourse to experience) that existence gave him innate ideas. He had, I suspect, a preconceived idea that they came in the package with the self, but he did not have an impeccable series of deductions from doubt to the existence of God.

The world--the reality--he found after sufficient reasoning was the world for all time (or since it was created). He did not conceive it to have just started when he reached his conclusions. It would, as the real condition of the universe, apply for year one BCC (before Cartesian certainty[2]). The same for year two BCC, year three BCC, etc. Therefore, consistent with his conclusions, he had this knowledge in his mind innately before his doubts, and it is difficult to see how he reasonably could have been doubting.

Was Descartes consistent in invoking dreams to discredit the senses? This he did before he concluded that his thinking and only his thinking proved his existence. Did he not let a little experience in the door in his efforts to prove that reasoning a priori (without experience) is the only path to knowledge? I suggest that memories (remembering past events) is always experience and is as subject to error as the experience of the event. Furthermore, his language, "When I considered that the very same thoughts which we have when awake may also come when we are asleep, while there is at that time not one of them true, I suppose that all the objects that had ever entered into my mind when awake, had in them no more truth than the illusions of my dreams,"[AOR, 68] clearly shows, with the word, "we", that he was believing at the time that there was an "external world," namely, other people. One dreamer is part of the external world of another. An "internal world" can apply only to one thinker or dreamer.

Later Descartes "goes so far as to invoke the belief in God as the only ultimate safeguard against error even in the case of propositions that are clearly and distinctly conceived to be true."[AOR, 77] God having been derived from clear and distinct ideas in the first place, his argument was circular.

In the end he considers his proofs of the external world as purely philosophical, and does not consider them "of great utility in establishing what they prove, viz, that there is in reality a world, that men are possessed of bodies, and the like, the truth of which no-one of sound mind ever seriously doubted."[AOR, 75]

After a tortuous method--lifting nature to certainty[2] on pure reason--of getting the external world back, he writes,

> As soon as I had acquired some general notions in physics, and beginning to test them in various particular difficulties, and observed how far they can carry us, and how much they differ from the principles that have been employed up to the present time, I believed that I could not keep them concealed without offending gravely against the law by which we are bound to promote, as far as in us lies, the general good of mankind. For by them I perceived it to be possible to arrive at knowledge highly useful in life; and instead of speculative philosophy usually taught in the schools, to discover a practical philosophy, by means of which, knowing the force and action of fire, water, air, the stars, the heavens, and all the other bodies that surround us, and distinctly as we know the various crafts of our artisans, we might also apply them in the same way to all the uses to which they are adapted, and thus make ourselves the lords and possessors of nature.[AOR, 74]

So we can trust Francis Bacon's advice after all and conquer nature by obeying her. Note his use of "practical."   I will contrast this with Kant's use of the word when we get to him.

Why is Descartes, whose philosophy, a large part of which is false or very doubtful, important? Because "He stands in a uniquely important position, with one foot in the scholastic past and one in the science of the future. The theory of knowledge, [epistemology] in its modern form, begins with him."[AOR, 77] The idealistic tradition in modern philosophy (which we will meet later) began with Descartes's position that thought is the only reality directly known. He was the

> father of the subjective and idealistic (as was Bacon of the objective and realistic) tradition in modern philosophy. To his French followers and English enemies [the empiricists] the central notion in Descartes was the primacy of consciousness--his apparently obvious proposition that the mind knows itself more immediately and directly than it can ever know anything else; that it knows the "external world" only through the world's impress upon the mind in sensation and perception; that all philosophy must in consequence (though it should doubt everything else) begin with individual mind and self."[SOP, 116, 117]
> [Note: "realistic" in the quote above does not refer to universals.]

Still, Descartes offered an antidote to idealism: his conception of an objective world completely mechanical and his attempt to understand organic as well as inorganic operations in mechanical terms.

Philosophy in the seventeenth century was on its way to being divided into two camps, rationalist and empiricist, as never before. When I read the philosophers of this era the first time, I was totally confused. My stumbling block was my definition of rational and reasonable as in Francis Bacon. For me, to be reasonable was to trust evidence above hearsay and authority. It was the very definition of rational to accept the evidence given in experience. I could not make the conceptional jump required to use these "philosophical" terms as philosophers used them. I really never have. For me the debate was a priorism versus rational empiricism, not reason versus experience.

Philosophy made another change the in seventeenth century. Descartes, Hobbes, Spinoza, and Locke, among others, tried to make philosophy a substitute or basis for religion.

Thomas Hobbes (1588-1679)

Hobbes tried to make it a substitute. His philosophy, a form of mechanistic materialism reminiscent of Democritus's atomism, was congenial to empiricism but not enough to call him an empiricist. Like Descartes he was disenchanted with Scholasticism. The term determinism has been coined to describe his philosophy including his psychology. He had read Descartes and did not disagree with his mechanistic, physical side, but dispensed with the separate, metaphysical self or mind unattached to the physical body. Hobbes's materialism is synonymous with naturalism. Because of his atheism--some say deism--he was not able to republish his earlier works. He "regarded matter and motion as the least common denominator of all our percepts, and bodies and their movements as the only subject matter of philosophy."[DOP, 143, 144]

His principal concern was with what is real. He was not as concerned as Descartes was with how we know. The quotations below, as noted, are from his *Leviathan*, (defined as commonwealth or state) his most important work, published in 1651.

According to Hobbes, man's "voluntary" actions are completely determined:

Every act of man's will and every desire and inclination proceedeth from some cause, and that from another cause, in a continual chain (whose first link is in the hand of God, the first of all causes), proceed from necessity. So that to him that could see the connexion of those causes, the necessity of all men's voluntary actions would appear manifest. And therefore God, that seeth and disposeth all things, seeth also that the liberty of man in doing what he will is accompanied with the necessity of doing that which God will and no more, nor less.[L]

That is the cause of the will, but what is the will?

In deliberation, the last appetite, or aversion, immediately adhering to the action, or to the omission thereof, is that we call the will; the act, not the faculty, of willing. . . . The definition of the will, given commonly by the Schools, that it is a rational appetite, is not good. For if it were, then could there be no voluntary act against reason. For a voluntary act is that which proceedeth from the will, and no other. But if instead of a rational appetite, we shall say an appetite resulting from a precedent deliberation, then the definition is the same that I have given here. Will, therefore, is the last appetite in deliberating.[L]

Hobbes explains imagination and memory and gives us the law of inertia in the process:

That when a thing lies still, unless somewhat else stir it, it will lie still for ever, is a truth that no man doubts of. But that when a thing is in motion, it will eternally be in motion, unless somewhat else stay it, though the reason be the same (namely, that nothing can change itself), is not so easily assented to. For men measure, not only other men, but all other things, by them selves. . . . When a body is once in motion, it moveth (unless something else hinder it) eternally; and whatsoever hindreth it, cannot in an instant, but in time, and by degrees, quite extinguish it: and as we see in the water, though the wind cease, the waves give not over rolling for a long time after; so also it happeneth in that motion which is made in the internal parts of a man, then, when he sees, dreams, etc. For after the object is removed, or the eye shut, we still retain an image of the thing seen, though more obscure than when we see it. And this is it the Latins call imagination, . . . But the Greeks call it fancy, which signifies appearance, and is as proper to one sense as to another. Imagination, therefore, is nothing but decaying sense; . . . This decaying sense, when we would express the thing itself (I mean fancy itself), we call imagination, as I said before. But when we would express the decay, and signify that the sense is fading, old, and past, it is called memory. So that imagination and memory are but one thing, which for diverse considerations hath diverse names. Much memory, or memory of many things, is called experience. Again, imagination being only of those things which have been formerly perceived by sense.[L]

This gives us knowledge of fact which leads to science:

And whereas sense and memory are but knowledge of fact, which is a thing past and irrevocable, science is the knowledge of consequences, and dependence of one fact upon another; by which, out of that we can presently do, we know how to do something else when we will, or the like, another time: because when we see how anything comes about, upon what causes, and by what manner; when the like causes come into our power, we see how to make it produce the like effects.[L]

Science enables us to produce the effects we want, but it is not infallible.

No discourse whatsoever can end in absolute knowledge of fact, past or to come. For, as for the knowledge of fact, it is originally sense [sensation?], and ever after memory. And for the knowledge of consequence, which I have said before is called science, it is not absolute, but conditional. No man can know by discourse that this, or that, is, has been, or will be; which is to know absolutely: but only that if this be, that is; if this has been, that has been; if this shall be, that shall be; which is to know conditionally: and that not the consequence of one thing to another, but of one name of a thing to another name of the same thing.[L]

Hobbes proceeds to explain the cause of thoughts, what I would call concepts, tracing their development from sensation to the resulting thoughts.

Concerning the thoughts of man, . . they are every one a representation or appearance of some quality, or other accident of a body without us, which is commonly called an object. Which object worketh on the eyes, ears, and other parts of man's body, and by diversity of working produceth diversity of appearances. The original of them all is that which we call sense, (for there is no conception in a man's mind which hath not at first, totally or by parts, been begotten upon the organs of sense). . . . . The cause of sense is the external body, or object, which presseth the organ proper to each sense, either immediately, as in the taste and touch; or mediately, as in seeing, hearing, and smelling: which pressure, by the mediation of nerves and other strings and membranes of the body, continued inwards to the brain and heart, . . . All which qualities [sound, odor, hardness, softness, etc.] called sensible are in the object that causeth them but so many several motions of the matter, by which it presseth our organs diversely. Neither in us that are pressed are they anything else but diverse motions (for motion produceth nothing but motion). But their appearance to us is fancy, . . . And though at some certain distance the real and very object seem invested with the fancy it begets in us; yet still the object is one thing, the image or fancy is another. So that sense in all cases is nothing else but original fancy caused (as I have said) by the pressure that is, by the motion of external things upon our eyes, ears, and other organs, thereunto ordained.[L]

Having explained the origin of thoughts (we will find the empiricists calling them ideas) as best he could, presumably in "significant speech," he contrasts it with Aristotle.

But the philosophy schools, through all the universities of Christendom, grounded upon certain texts of Aristotle, teach another doctrine; and say, for the cause of vision, that the thing seen sendeth forth on every side a visible species, (in English) a visible show, apparition, or aspect, or a being seen; the receiving whereof into the eye is seeing. And for the cause of hearing, that the thing heard sendeth forth an audible species, that is, an audible aspect, or audible being seen; which, entering at the ear, maketh hearing. Nay, for the cause of understanding also, they say the thing understood sendeth forth an intelligible species, that is, an intelligible being seen; which, coming into the understanding, makes us understand. . . . I must let you see on all occasions by the way what things would be amended in them [Aristotle, et al]; amongst which the frequency of insignificant speech is one.[L]

Although Hobbes believed that only bodies and motion were real, he did not actually deny the existence of thoughts. He called them "phantasms" and as we have seen above "representation or appearance" and again "image or fancy." He expected to learn from science, but he called for "true ratiocination" by which he meant deduction from experience and he thought that what we lack is the proper reasoning about experience, not experience itself. This reveals that despite talk about experience, Hobbes is not an empiricist although sometimes classified as one. Truth, he says consists in the right ordering of words. Geometry is his model. There are four abuses of speech:

First, when men register their thought wrong by the inconstancy of the signification of their words; by which they register for their conceptions that which they never conceived, and so deceive themselves. Secondly, when thoughts wrong they use words metaphorically; that is, in other sense than that they are

> ordained for, and thereby deceive others. Thirdly, when by words they declare that to be their will which is not. Fourthly, when they use them to grieve one another: . . . Seeing then that truth consisteth in the right ordering of names in our affirmations, a man that seeketh precise truth had need to remember what every name he uses stands for, and to place it accordingly; or else he will find himself entangled in words, as a bird in lime twigs; the more he struggles, the more belimed. And therefore in geometry (which is the only science that it hath pleased God hitherto to bestow on mankind), men begin at settling the significations of their words; which settling of significations, they call definitions.[L]

There are no absolutes in ethics for Hobbes. We can only give the origin of the terms. I will have occasion to mention this in my discussion of ethics.

> Whatsoever is the object of any man's appetite or desire, that is it which he for his part calleth good; and the object of his hate and aversion, evil; and of his contempt, vile and inconsiderable. For these words of good, evil, and contemptible are ever used with relation to the person that useth them: there being nothing simply and absolutely so; nor any common rule of good and evil to be taken from the nature of the objects themselves.[L]

Hobbes' greatest interest was in political philosophy. He held that man was originally in a "state of nature." Man's selfish nature and strong passions cause him to enter into a "social contract," an idea not original with Hobbes's. He conceived the contract to be between man and man, not between ruled and ruler as others had, and men made the contract in order to have protection from each other; and concluded that monarchy was the best form of government. He recommended a powerful secular state, whether republican or royalist, to act independently of the Church.

Baruch Spinoza (1632-1677)

The second of the three "great rationalists," Descartes, Spinoza, Leibniz, worked God into nature as contrasted with Descartes's, who let Him have a hand in getting things started. Blaise Pascal (1623-1662), who believed that the existence of God could not be proved, and that one could and should wager that He did exist, denounced Cartesianism as atheism. Descartes, he said, would liked to have disposed of God but had to allow him a snap of the fingers to get the universe created; and afterward had no use for him. Spinoza's God is hard to find in the shadow of nature.

Spinoza was influenced by Bruno whose ideas (which we have skipped over) included (paraphrased): "All reality is one in substance, one in cause, one in origin, and God and this reality are one; . . . mind and matter are one; every particle of reality is composed inseparably of the physical and the psychical."[SOP, 116]   But, above all, Spinoza was influenced by Descartes. "What attracted him was Descartes's conception of a homogeneous 'substance' underlying all forms of matter, and another homogeneous substance underlying all forms of mind. . . . [and] Descartes's desire to explain all of the world except God and the soul by mechanical and mathematical laws,--an idea going back to Leonardo and Galileo, . . ."[SOP, 117]

Notwithstanding my considerable disagreement with him, Spinoza is another philosopher with whom I felt an emotional and intellectual kinship. As a young man he began to lose his faith, finding contradictions and improbabilities in the Old Testament. After developing his philosophy he faced opposition and abuse. As a Jew he was excommunicated by the Jews and denounced by the Christians for his beliefs. One acquaintance who had recently been converted to Catholicism wrote to Spinoza in 1675,

> How do you know that your philosophy is the best among all those which have been taught in the world, or are actually taught now, or ever will be taught in the future? . . . Have you examined all those philosophies, ancient as well as modern, which are taught here and in India and everywhere throughout the world? And even if you have duly examined them, how do you know that you have chosen the best? . . .
>
> If, however, you do not believe in Christ, you are more wretched than I can say. But the remedy is easy: return from your sins, and realize the fatal arrogance of your wretched and insane reasoning. . . . Will you, you wretched little man, vile worm of the earth, . . . dare, in your unspeakable blasphemy, to put yourself above the Incarnate, Infinite Wisdom? . . .
>
> From your principles you will not explain thoroughly even one of those things which are accomplished in witchcraft . . , nor will you be able to explain any of the stupendous phenomena among those who are possessed by demons, of all of which I have myself seen various instances, and I have heard most certain evidence.[c]

Spinoza's reply in part:

>   What I could scarcely believe when it was related me by others, I at last understand from your letter; that is, that not only have you become a member of the Roman Church . . . but that you are a very keen champion of it, and have already learned to curse and rage petulantly against your opponents. . . . I will not here recount the vices of priests and popes to turn you away from them, as the opponents of the Roman Church are wont to do. For they usually publish these things from ill-feeling, and . . . in order to annoy rather than instruct. Indeed, I will admit that there are found more men of great learning, and of an upright life, in the Roman than in any other Christian Church; for since there are more . . . members of this Church, there will also be found in it more men of every condition. . . .
>
>   You asked me, how I know that my philosophy is the best among all those which have ever been taught in the world, or are taught now, or will be taught in the future. This, indeed, I can ask you with far better right. For I do not presume that I have found the best philosophy, but I know that I think [it] the true one. . . . But you who presume that you have at last found the best religion or rather the best men, to whom you have given over your credulity, how do you know that they are the best among all those who have taught other religions, or are teaching them now or will teach them in the future? Have you examined all those religions, both ancient and modern, which are taught here and in India, and everywhere throughout the world? And even if you have duly examined them, how do you know that you have chosen the best?[c]

Spinoza's friend was correct, Spinoza's philosophy did not explain those things which are accomplished in witchcraft nor did it explain any of the stupendous phenomena among those who are possessed by demons.

Substance for Spinoza seems to mean the essential reality or God underlying all things and both are identical with nature, therefore he is a pantheist. But all do not agree with this: "Spinozism is sometimes . . . identified with pantheism although this is a highly misleading characterization."[DOP, 315] If not pantheism, then do we have a trinity: God the father, Nature the mother, and Substance, the son? No commentator I have read has suggested this, but the question arises.

Whatever his position, it is unintelligible to me. His model for reasoning, as it was for Hobbes, was geometry. However, his "argument does not, and indeed could not, follow a strictly deductive pattern, in which each step can be justified by reference to the previous proposition."[AOR, 101] It seems wise to abandon his theology and turn to his natural philosophy. For all his talk of God he appears to hold that nature does as nature would, God notwithstanding.

Spinoza put his philosophy in a book which he entitled *Ethics*, but feared the consequence of publishing it. It and some other of his writings were published late in 1677 after his death in February of that year. The quotations below, as noted, are from the *Ethics*.

The authorities who opposed his philosophy provoked this comment:

> Those who wish to seek out the causes of miracles, and to understand the things of nature as philosophers, and not stare at them in astonishment like fools, are soon considered heretical and impious, and proclaimed as such by those whom the mob adore as the interpreters of nature and the gods. For these men know that once ignorance is put aside, that wonderment would be taken away which is the only means by which their authority is preserved.[E]

Although Spinoza uses the word God often in the *Ethics*, for him everything is determined by natural law.

> Nothing comes to pass in nature, which can be set down to a flaw therein; for nature is always the same, and everywhere one and the same in her efficacy and power of action; that is, nature's laws and ordinances, whereby all things come to pass and change from one form to another, are everywhere and always the same; so that there should be one and the same method of understanding the nature of all things whatsoever, namely, through nature's universal laws and rules.[E]

Human emotions are not excepted.

> Thus the passions of hatred, anger, envy, and so on, considered in themselves, follow from this same necessity and efficacy of nature; they answer to certain definite causes, through which they are understood, ... I shall consider human actions and desires in exactly the same manner, as though I were concerned with lines, planes, and solids.[E]

Needless to say there is no place for free will in Spinoza's philosophy.

> In the mind there is no absolute or free will; but the mind is determined to wish this or that by a cause, which has also been determined by another cause, and this last by another cause, and so on to infinity.[E]

Nevertheless, "Men think themselves free because they are conscious of their volitions and desires, but are ignorant of the causes by which they are led to wish and desire"

Spinoza is aware that "it may be objected, if man does not act from free will, what will happen if the incentives to action are equally balanced, as in the case of Buridan's ass? [see page 40] Will he perish of hunger and thirst?" Spinoza does not give an inch on his complete determinism. "I am quite ready to admit, that a man placed in the equilibrium described (namely, as perceiving nothing but hunger and thirst, a certain food and a certain drink, each equally distant from him) would die of hunger and thirst."
But Spinoza points out that man and even an ass perceives more than hunger and thirst. An ass, for example, might perceive flies biting and swing his head to shoo them, leaving the food no longer equidistant from him (not Spinoza's words)(see page 40 again).
Men have ideas. Ideas in the mind, Spinoza calls concepts.

> By idea, I mean the mental conception which is formed by the mind as a thinking thing. . . . I say conception rather than perception, because the word perception seems to imply that the mind is passive in respect to the object; whereas conception seems to express an activity of the mind.[E]

Ideas are adequate and inadequate. An adequate idea is "an idea which, in so far as it is considered in itself, without relation to the object, has all the properties or intrinsic marks of a true idea." So, presumably, an adequate idea is a true conception.
When are these conceptions knowledge? Spinoza classifies three "kinds" of knowledge. He disappoints me with his disparagement of the senses in the first kind and loses me completely in the third. The first kind, "our general notions," come

> (1.) From particular things represented to our intellect fragmentarily, confusedly, and without order through our senses. . . . I have settled to call such perceptions by the name of knowledge from the mere suggestions of experience. (2.) From symbols, e.g., from the fact of having read or heard certain words we remember things and form certain ideas concerning them, similar to those through which we imagine things. . . . I shall call both these ways of regarding things knowledge of the first kind, opinion, or imagination. . . . Knowledge of the first kind is the only source of falsity, knowledge of the second and third kinds is necessarily true. . . .[E]
> From the fact that we have notions common to all men, and adequate ideas of the properties of things; this I call reason and knowledge of the second kind. . . . It is in the nature of reason to regard things, not as contingent, but as

necessary.[E]

The third kind he calls "intuition." "This kind of knowledge proceeds from an adequate idea of the absolute essence of certain attributes of God to the adequate knowledge of the essence of things. . . . Knowledge of the second and third kinds, . . teaches us to distinguish the true from the false."[E] He gives examples in mathematics which "will illustrate all three kinds of knowledge by a single example."[E] I will not go into it. It does not seem wise to use the same example to illustrate what is necessarily true and what could be false.

Descartes left us with a body-mind problem, the mind being connected in no way with the body. Spinoza has them functioning in something called "psychophysical parallelism" (not his term) which is little improvement over Descartes.

> Mind and body are one and the same thing, conceived first under the attribute of thought, secondly, under the attribute of extension. Thus it follows that the order or concatenation of things is identical, whether nature be conceived under the one attribute or the other; consequently the order of states of activity and passivity in our body, is simultaneous in nature with the order of states of activity and passivity in the mind.[E]

Despite being one and the same thing, mind and body have no effect on each other, thus the parallel action.

> That, therefore, which determines the mind to thought is a mode of thought, and not a mode of extension; that is, it is not body. This was our first point. Again, the motion and rest of a body must arise from another body, which has also been determined to a state of motion or rest by a third body, and absolutely everything which takes place in a body must spring from God, in so far as he is regarded as affected by some mode of extension, and not by some mode of thought; that is, it cannot spring from the mind, which is a mode of thought. This was our second point. Therefore body cannot determine mind, &c.[E]

Mind and body are so separate that "the human mind cannot be absolutely destroyed with the body, but there remains of it something which is eternal."[E] If he told us where these remains of the mind spend eternity in a universe determined by natural law, I missed it.

In such a determined universe, can there be sin? According to Spinoza, sin can occur only in the civil state.

> We may readily understand that there is in the state of nature nothing, which by universal consent is pronounced good or bad; for in the state of nature everyone thinks solely of his own advantage, and according to his disposition, with reference only to his individual advantage, decides what is good or bad, being bound by no law to anyone besides himself. In the state of nature, therefore, sin is inconceivable; it can only exist in a state, where good and evil are pronounced on by common consent, and where everyone is bound to obey the State authority. Sin, then, is nothing else but disobedience, which is therefore punished by the right of the State only. Obedience, on the other hand, is set down as merit, inasmuch as a man is thought worthy of merit, if he takes delight in the advantages which a State provides. . . .
>
> From all these considerations it is evident, that justice and injustice, sin and merit, are extrinsic ideas, and not attributes which display the nature of the mind.[E]

There can, nevertheless, be morality or at least desirable behavior. Reason provides it. "Men who are governed by reason--that is, who seek what is useful to them in accordance with reason,--desire for themselves nothing, which they do not also desire for the rest of mankind, and, consequently, are just, faithful, and honorable in their conduct." This expects too much of reason and is naive psychology. Spinoza is more reasonable in citing the benefit of determinism. If people cannot help doing what they do (are determined by natural law) we cannot blame them for their behavior (my words, not his).

> He who rightly realizes, that all things follow from the necessity of the divine nature, and come to pass in accordance with the eternal laws and rules of nature, will not find anything worthy of hatred, derision, or contempt, nor will he bestow pity on anything, but to the utmost extent of human virtue he will endeavour to do well, as the saying is, and to rejoice.[E]

The pleasure we derive from adapting ourselves to the basic reality and order of the universe leads us toward love of that reality. Then "love toward a being eternal and infinite [Nature/God] fills the mind completely with joy."

I take exception to the rejoicing and joy. If I understand this correctly one should look on the workings of nature, including the multiplying of cancer cells with joy.

In the place of "morality" of common parlance, Spinoza gives us the genesis of moral terms. "In no case do we strive for, wish for, long for, or desire anything, because we deem it to be good, but on the other hand we deem a thing to be good, because we strive for it, wish for it, long for it, or desire it." And again: "By good I mean that which we certainly know to be useful to us."

In the determined universe, there is still a kind of freedom, and reason gives us the only freedom we have. "I call free him who is led solely by reason."

Book V of the *Ethics* is given to the task of explaining freedom. There Spinoza says, "At length I pass to the remaining portion of my *Ethics*, which is concerned with the way leading to freedom. I shall therefore treat therein of the power of the reason, showing how far the reason can control the emotions, and what is the nature of Mental Freedom. . . ."[E] I will not attempt to follow him through it. Although not lacking merit, his arguments do not show how a person completely determined by causes outside himself, which is his position, can act on his own. I fancy I have settled this problem in my chapter on "Determinism and Choice."

At this point in time philosophers did not have a good definition for reason. We have some shocks ahead from Hume who said that reason was a slave to passion and wrote one of the most disturbing books in philosophy; and from Kant who spent eleven or twelve years writing a critique of reason.

Is time real, I mean really real? Spinoza somewhere suggested that time is a mode of thinking not an objective reality.

In political philosophy, Spinoza, like Hobbes and others, began with a "state of nature." To his credit he found for democracy, unlike Hobbes. I will skip the details.

Spinoza's three kinds of knowledge made little impression on other philosophers. He thought that his geometric method insured certainty. It was an attempt to generate knowledge with logic. His method did not succeed and created more clutter than logic. He did not seem aware that his most valuable statements could only have come from observations using the senses which he distrusted. It takes a strong stomach for repetition to read every word of the *Ethics*. His most valuable propositions (declarative sentences) are of two kinds, comments on human nature and definitions. We turn now to a philosopher who classified these respectively into "Truths of fact" and "Truths of reason."

Gottfried Wilhelm Leibniz,(1646-1716)

"Germany's greatest 17th century philosopher and one of the most universal minds of all times" was Leibniz. His philosophy was a work of odd moments, and "connects Plato with Democritus, Aristotle with Descartes, the Scholastics with the moderns, theology and morals with reason."[DOP, 182]

> He wrote many hundred of treatises and fragments, touching on almost every branch of knowledge. Even now the whole of his work has not been published. He was the last man who could hope to master the whole range of modern knowledge, and to be an encyclopedia in himself.[AOR, 143]

We will take a small sampling of his accomplishments and mistakes. He invented a computing machine which did multiplication and division as well as addition and substraction, improving a previous one invented by Pascal. He discovered the differential calculus, by 1676 the infinitesimal calculus. Although Newton had discovered it first, Leibniz had done it independently, and his notation proved more satisfactory that Newton's. He rejected Newton's absolute motion and conceived matter as energy, ideas of lasting value. He rejected the objective reality of space and time, interpreting them as perceived coexistence and perceived succession, respectively.

In a treatise on geology, entitled *Protogaea*, published after his death in 1749, he theorized that the earth had once been an incandescent globe. As it cooled it formed a crust. The oceans were formed by condensing vapors, and dissolving minerals in the crust made it salty. Water erosion and explosion of gases below the surface made other changes. He thought it possible that due to great changes in the crust of the earth over centuries "even the species of animals have many times been transformed." His explanation of fossils pointed to the theory of evolution. He thought that marine animals were the earliest forms of animal life and that other animals descended from them.

Oddly for a man with all these ideas, he found gravity unbelievable. It seemed to him a perpetual miracle for it to act through empty space through such vast distances.

Leibniz's philosophy touches on virtually every philosophical problem and is designed to cover all nature and supernature. His philosophy in contrast to his naturalism and mathematics is of mixed value. The center of Leibniz's philosophy is his distinction between two kinds of "truths"[AOR, 144] using the law of non-contradiction which

> is merely the requirement that a proposition and its opposite cannot both be true, and any proposition which implies a contradiction, or contains elements that implicitly deny each other, is false, and indeed, absurd. Leibniz is able, using this principle to distinguish what he calls "truths of reason" and "truths of fact" and, correspondingly, the concepts of necessity and contingency. A Truth of reason is a proposition which is "true in virtue of the law of non-contradiction alone"; that is, its *denial* implies a contradiction. Such propositions are necessarily true. Truths of fact, on the other hand, are propositions which are indeed true, but not necessarily so, in the strong sense of "logical necessity"; their denial does not imply a contradiction, and so is possible and conceivable. The Truths of fact are only *contingently* true.[AOR, 147, 148]

"Truths of reason" are also said to be a priori, the definition of a priori being that their "truth" is known independently of observation. "Truths of reason" also include propositions which are true by definition, for example, "all bachelors are male," and, as has been mentioned, are said to be necessary. In this case the predicate is said to be logically "contained" in the subject because the definition of "bachelor" is "unmarried man." Truths of fact in contrast to truths of reason "cannot be established to be true solely by reference to the principle of non-contradiction."[AOR, 144] "Caesar crossed the Rubicon in 49 B.C." and "an apple is on the table." are examples of "truths of fact."

Kant would later call truths of reason and truths of fact, respectively, analytic and synthetic,[AOR, 148] terms used today, but radically different types of propositions were attached to either side of the division by Leibniz and Kant.

Having made a distinction that has impressed many of his successors in philosophy, Leibniz then declared that all predicates, "except that of 'existence,' were contained in their subjects; he held that predication simply consisted in stating the properties which inhere in a substance. This might seem to destroy the distinction between analytic and synthetic propositions, . . . But it is the exception, the predicate of 'existence,' that allows a place for synthetic propositions."[AOR, 148]

God was essential to Leibniz's philosophy. He needed this exception for his proof of God. Leibniz held "that there is *one* existential proposition which is not, like all the other, contingent, viz., the proposition asserting the existence of God: for Leibniz *does* want to keep an argument . . . to prove that there must be one substance whose essence includes existence, i.e., the existence of which is a necessary truth."[AOR, 149]

This brings us to "the principle of sufficient reason." It constitutes a general test of "truths of fact".

> It is established in Leibniz's system that whether a particular substance exists, having certain properties, is a matter of contingent fact; it is not self-contradictory to suppose that different ones might have existed instead. It has also been shown that, since it is a contingent fact that certain substances exist with certain properties, the laws which state a correlation between the properties of different substances must be contingent truths. We now want to know why just *these* substances exist, and just *these* laws are true: it is this question that the principle of sufficient reason is designed to answer. It states that, for every contingent truth, a reason or cause can be given, why it should be so; there is an overruling principle in accordance with which all things come about, viz, the requirements of "good order, and perfection." God had an infinity of worlds to choose from in creating. He must have chosen, on Leibniz's view, that which is the most perfect, and that which has the greatest diversity of contents arranged in the most economical manner.[AOR, 151, 152]

What were Leibniz's substances? Monads. The universe consists

> of numberless substances called *monads*. These must be (a) completely independent of each other--they "have no windows by which anything could go out or come in"; (b) they must be indestructible by natural processes, and could not come into existence except by an act of God's creation, and they have no parts; (c) they are unchanging, in the sense that their "activity" is the product entirely of their inner nature, which contains in germ all that will happen to them; (d) they are all different. Furthermore they form a system; not, in such a way, that they can affect one another, but they have been so arranged by God that the spontaneous activity of each in fact mirrors the whole of the universe, more or less clearly or confusedly, from its particular point of view.[AOR, 164]

Everything consists of such monads, which Leibniz says are the real atoms of nature but are unlike the atoms of the scientists. There is much more of this, but enough already! Since it appears to me that there is no possible way of testing the believability of this, and as it make no sense to me, I consider it of no importance in the history of Naturalism. Leibniz pulls his philosophy out of a hat. That his head is in the hat, seems to be no help.

Still, it does not seem fair to leave Leibniz without mentioning his famous "preestablished harmony." Notwithstanding my inability to comprehend it, monads somehow result in minds and bodies apparently windowless and unable to know what the other is doing. Each follows its own laws, and they work in unison by a harmony preestablished by God (who, if I mistake not, is some kind of monad himself). For example when a metaphysician is eating an apple the mind thinks the metaphysician is eating the apple and at the same time, not missing a move, the body is eating the apple with God meticulously overseeing the process. He does not, for example, let the mind think it is playing golf however much it wants to, until of course, the body is playing golf.

This need to put theological coverings over philosophical inadequacies led Leibniz to write *Theodicee* (the justice, or justification of God). In it, his only book published in his lifetime, Leibniz declared this to be the best of all possible worlds. Voltaire, as the whole world knows, ridiculed this in *Candide*. It takes great minds to produce "great" nonsense.

The rationalists were too confident of "reason" which would be deflated by the empiricists, yet Leibniz scored one in rebuttal. When Locke, whom we will visit next, declared that "there is nothing in the intellect except what was first in the senses," Leibniz replied "nothing except the intellect itself."[SOP, 206]

THE EMPIRICISTS

The three "great" empiricists are Locke, Berkeley and Hume. Locke and Hume begin their philosophy with science, which degenerates to the verge of idealism. Berkeley, oddly enough for an empiricist, is at the opposite pole; his philosophy *is* idealism. His fight was with the dratted materialism that was infecting the philosophy of the time.

As was previously mentioned, the success of physical science was contagious to the philosophers in the eighteenth century. They attempted to apply the new scientific canons of the seventeenth century.

> Consequently only the measurable aspects of reality were to be treated as real-- those susceptible to equations connecting the variations in other phenomena. The whole nature as compounded of irreducibly different qualities and unbridgeable "natural" kinds, was to be finally discarded. The aristotelian category of final cause--the explanation of phenomena in terms of the "natural" tendency of every object to fulfill its own inner end or purpose--which was also to be the answer to the question of why it existed, and what function it was attempting to fulfill--notions for which no experimental or observable evidence can in principle be discovered--was abandoned as unscientific, and, indeed, in the case of inanimate entities without wills or purposes, as literally unintelligible. Laws formulating regular concomitances of phenomena--the observed order and conjunctions of things and events--were sufficient, without introducing impalpable entities and forces, to describe all that is describable, and predict all that is predictable, in the universe. Space, time, mass force, momentum, rest-- the terms of mechanics--are to take the place of final causes, substantial forms, divine purpose, and other metaphysical notions. Indeed the apparatus of medieval ontology and theology were to be altogether abandoned in favor of a symbolism referring to those aspects of the universe which are given to the senses, or can be measured or inferred in some other way.
>
> This attitude is exceedingly clear in the works not only of Locke and Hume, who had a profound respect for natural science, but also in those of Berkeley, who was deeply concerned to deny its metaphysical presuppositions.[AOE, 17, 18]

John Locke (1632-1704)

Naturalism in philosophy hit a new high in John Locke.

If Descartes broke the spell of scholasticism by attempting to apply the methods, standards, and some of the concepts of the mathematical and natural sciences (which he had himself done so much to advance), Locke, whose scientific attainments were exceedingly modest, emancipated philosophy from even this degree of specialization. And for the eighteenth century, at least, he rendered it no longer an esoteric study, but a discipline based on normal powers of empirical observation and common-sense judgement. Descartes only recognizes as worthy of attention arguments which proceed by rigorous deduction from premises which are self-evident or known to be true a priori; Locke appeals to observation of the natural world, seeks to examine present beliefs and states of mind by tracing them to their psychological origins and giving an account of their "natural" growth therefrom. Above all, like Hobbes, he looks on man as an object in nature, not fundamentally different from other natural objects and to be described and explained by the genetic methods of the natural science of psychology--although he did not call it that. His own theories are often fanciful enough; he is guilty of many inconsistencies and obscurities and lapses into modes of thought which he is supposing himself to combat. Nevertheless, his ideas, or at least the effects of his skill in presenting them were genuinely revolutionary. His view that many cardinal errors are due to the mistaking of words for things; that minds--or their thoughts--are capable of having their natural histories written no less than plants and animals, with equally startling and fruitful results; that the findings of philosophers must not depart too widely from the beliefs of balanced common sense (Locke may almost be said to have invented the notion of common sense); that philosophical problems are as often as not due to confusion in the mind of the philosopher rather than the difficulties inherent in the subject--all this transformed the ideas of men.[AOE, 30, 31]

He begins by telling the reader (interpreted)

that he need not, to obtain true knowledge, soar in the clouds with theologians, descend dark wells with metaphysicians, but only study his own nature, which if done conscientiously, will sweep away the "sanctuary of vanity and ignorance"--the clouds of meaningless words--and so clear a path for a solid, empirical science of man.[AOE, 32]

Locke also had a political philosophy. Like Hobbes, he theorizes man originally in a "state of nature" but much unlike Hobbes's it is a state where we are all born with God-given natural rights. "Locke's version of 'the social contract' is that all citizens consent to be ruled by a government elected by a majority for just as long as that government protects the natural rights." Some of Locke's ideas found their way into our Declaration of Independence and Constitution. I will skip the details as it is not the "philosophy" I wish to discuss. He is, however, as famous for it as for his book *An Essay Concerning Human Understanding*, which is the book that concerns us. It had great influence on philosophy in the eighteenth century. Quotations from it, as noted, follow.

Before advancing his own theory of knowledge, Locke discredits the rival epistemological theory of innate ideas. He takes classical logic as an example of what he thinks most men would claim as an innate idea.

> The argument is a dilemma. Either in saying that a proposition (e.g. "Whatever is, is" or "It is impossible for the same thing to be and not to be," the so-called Law of Identity and Law of Non-Contradiction of Classical Logic) is innate, we mean literally that a knowledge of its truth is already explicitly present in the consciousness of each man as soon as he is born, or we mean something less radical, for example, that all men are born with a capacity or faculty for knowing its truth, a capacity which is exercised only when we "come to the use of reason." But the first claim, which rests on the evidence of actual experience, is false, . . . for it is a necessary (though not . . . a sufficient) condition of the truth of this claim that all men must agree to the "innate" proposition. And this is obviously not so--Locke cites the case of children and idiots. Whereas, if we take the second horn of the dilemma, then (1) the use of the term "innate" is a very improper way of speaking," but (2) worse still, the theory now fails to distinguish between the small, privileged class of supposedly innate propositions, and any other propositions (say those of mathematics) whose truth men can come gradually to know.[AOE, 38, 39]

According to Locke's theory of knowledge "all ideas come from Sensation or Reflection":

> Let us then suppose the mind to be, as we say, white paper, void of all characters, without any ideas:- How comes it to be furnished? To this I answer, in one word, from EXPERIENCE; in that [experience] all our knowledge is founded; and from that it ultimately derives itself. Our observation employed either, about external sensible objects, or about the internal operations of our minds perceived and reflected on by ourselves, is that which supplies our understandings with all the materials of thinking. These two are the fountains

of knowledge, from whence all the ideas we have, or can naturally have, do spring.^{ECHU}

There are, then, according to Locke, two sources of our ideas: The "objects of sensation" is one, and the "operations of our minds" the other:

> The perception of the operations of our own mind within us, as it is employed about the ideas it has got;- which operations, when the soul comes to reflect on and consider, do furnish the understanding with another set of ideas, which could not be had from things without. And such are perception, thinking, doubting, believing, reasoning, knowing, willing, and all the different actings of our own minds;- which we being conscious of, and observing in ourselves, do from these receive into our understandings as distinct ideas as we do from bodies affecting our senses.^{ECHU}

Ideas are simple or complex. In acquiring simple ideas the mind is merely passive.

> The mind can neither make nor destroy them. These simple ideas, the materials of all our knowledge, are suggested and furnished to the mind only by those two ways above mentioned, viz. sensation and reflection. When the understanding is once stored with these simple ideas, it has the power to repeat, compare, and unite them, even to an almost infinite variety, and so can make at pleasure new complex ideas. But it is not in the power of the most exalted wit, or enlarged understanding, by any quickness or variety of thought, to invent or frame one new simple idea in the mind, not taken in by the ways before mentioned: nor can any force of the understanding destroy those that are there.^{ECHU}

Locke calls the objects of sensation (the things which cause ideas) qualities "to comply with the common way of speaking."

> Whatsoever the mind perceives in itself, or is the immediate object of perception, thought, or understanding, that I call idea; and the power to produce any idea in our mind, I call quality of the subject wherein that power is.^{ECHU}

And he divides them into primary and secondary qualities. He calls primary those qualities

> such as are utterly inseparable from the body, . . . and such as sense constantly finds in every particle of matter which has bulk enough to be perceived; . . . These I call original or primary qualities of body, which I think we may observe to produce simple ideas in us, viz. solidity, extension, figure, motion or rest, and number.^{ECHU}

And secondary qualities are

> such qualities, which in truth are nothing in the objects themselves but powers to produce various sensations in us by their primary qualities, i.e., by the bulk, figure, texture, and motion of their insensible parts, as colours, sounds, tastes, &c., these I call "secondary" qualities.[ECHU]

Primary qualities produce their ideas "manifestly by impulse, the only way which we can conceive bodies to operate in." The external objects are not united to our mind, yet we do perceive them, therefore "it is evident that some motion must be thence continued by our nerves, or animal spirits, by some parts of our bodies, to the brain or seat of sensation, . . ." And in the case of sight, for example "it is evident some singly imperceptible bodies must come from them [the qualities of the bodies] to the eyes, and thereby convey to the brain some motion which produces these ideas which we have of them in us."

Ideas of secondary qualities are produced

> after the same manner, that the ideas of these original qualities are produced in us, . . . by the operation of insensible particles [imperceptible bodies] on our senses. . . . let us suppose at present that the different motions and figures, bulk and number [primary qualities], of such particles, affecting the several organs of our senses, produce in us those different sensations which we have from the colours and smells [secondary qualities] of bodies; . . . it being no more impossible to conceive that God should annex such ideas to such motions, with which they have no similitude, than that he should annex the idea of pain to the motion of a piece of steel dividing our flesh, with which that idea hath no resemblance. . . .
>
> The ideas of primary qualities of bodies are resemblances of them, and their patterns do really exist in the bodies themselves, but the ideas produced in us by these secondary qualities have no resemblance of them at all. There is nothing like our ideas, existing in the bodies themselves.[ECHU]

The distinction between primary and secondary qualities is as old as Democritus. A rival theory by Leucippus that qualities are a quantity of something was an idea or concept which died on the vine. As we have seen (page 45), Galileo made use of the concepts of primary and secondary qualities, calling only quantitatively measurable properties "primary" and real. It was Locke, however, who really put the concepts on the map. He made qualities, adhering in things, not the things (bodies, objects), themselves, the cause of ideas, and he held that all knowledge was in one way or another built up from ideas. So how could he insist that we have knowledge of the existence of things when ideas were only of qualities? He made use of the time-honored concept of substance:

> So that if any one will examine himself concerning his notion of pure substance in general, he will find he has no other idea of it at all, but only a supposition of he knows not what support of such qualities which are capable of producing simple ideas in us; . . . The idea then we have, to which we give the general name substance, being nothing but the supposed, but unknown, support of those qualities we find existing, which we imagine cannot subsist. . . without something to support them. [ECHU]

Next Locke defines "particular sorts of substances:"

> We come to have the ideas of particular sorts of substances, by collecting such combinations of simple ideas as are, by experience and observation of men's senses, taken notice of to exist together; and are therefore supposed to flow from the particular internal constitution, or unknown essence of that substance. [ECHU]

"It is the ordinary qualities observable" in an object "that make the true complex idea of those substances. . . . When we speak of any sort of substance we say it is a thing having such or such qualities; as body is a thing that is extended, figured and capable of motion; spirit, a thing capable of thinking; . . ." etc. With this remark Locke is sticking to his original thesis that knowledge is by observation (sensation) and that the *senses provided information about the objects* observed. The color observed (sensed) was *of* the object, the size observed (sensed) was *of* the object, on through all the sensations that was had *of* the object. The *object was known* by its characteristics revealed by the senses. There were "operations of the mind" involved, also, according to Locke. (We will see much made of this by Kant.) Originally he used matter and substance interchangeably, and was talking about what you and I would call a physical object. With that usage, there is no more mystery in "substance" than in "physical object" or "thing." But, in the same paragraph, he separates qualities from substance: "These, and the like fashions of speaking, intimate that the substance is supposed always something besides the extension, figure, solidity, motion, thinking or, other observable ideas, though we know not what it is." With this remark, Locke has divided physical objects in to two kinds: qualities, "the power to produce any idea in our mind," and substance with no power to produce an idea. It is as if he had "taken away" (Kant uses these very words, page 144) the qualities from the object leaving an unsensible something to be accounted for. These concepts had such a hold on Locke's thinking that he could not see their inadequacy. This method of having knowledge of things through qualities was limited in application to direct observation. If Locke had placed the object (substance, with all its qualities intact) in a suitable container of water as Archimedes did with the king's crown to determine its weight per given volume (specific gravity), he would have had evidence of bulk and weight not directly observed and not so easily thought of as something separate from the thing (substance) observed.

So, as Locke used the term qualities "to comply with the common way of speaking," he also appealed to common usage for the use of the term substance. Locke gives the same reason for our belief in the substance of spirit as for matter, namely that we suppose it to exist and "having no other idea" for it:

> It is evident that, having no other idea or notion of matter, but something wherein those many sensible qualities which affect our senses do subsist; by supposing a substance wherein thinking, knowing, doubting, and a power of moving, &c., do subsist, we have as clear a notion of the substance of spirit, as we have of body; the one being supposed to be (without knowing what it is) the substratum to those simple ideas we have from without; and the other supposed (with a like ignorance of what it is) to be the substratum to those operations we experiment in ourselves within. [ECHU]

It is interesting to note that Locke uses "matter" and "body" interchangeable with substance. He goes on to make the point that the "substance of matter" is no more mysterious than the "substance of spirit." Elsewhere (The *Essay*, Book IV, iii) he speculates that the substance of spirit might be matter.

> In respect of our notions, not much more remote from our comprehension to conceive that GOD can, if he pleases, superadd to matter a faculty of thinking, than that he should superadd to it another substance with a faculty of thinking; . . For I see no contradiction in it, that the first Eternal thinking Being, or Omnipotent Spirit, should, if he pleased, give to certain systems of created senseless matter, put together as he thinks fit, some degrees of sense, perception, and thought. . . He that considers how hardly sensation is, in our

> thoughts, reconcilable to extended matter; or existence to anything that has no extension at all, will confess that he is very far from certainly knowing what his soul is. It is a point which seems to me to be put out of the reach of our knowledge: and he who will give himself leave to consider freely, . . will scarce find his reason able to determine him fixedly for or against the soul's materiality.[ECHU]

Locke makes a valuable point that experience alone will teach us the meaning of some words. Locke emphasizes

> correctly, that there are certain words whose meaning cannot be adequately taught by means of verbal definitions, for they depend for their use on that direct inspection without a minimum of which no symbolism or language can describe the world at all. The use of such words can only be learnt "ostensively"--in the presence of the objects which they describe, with which their connection is conveyed by pointing, or some other effective method. An example of this is the impossibility of adequately teaching the meanings of color words to a blind man. It is obvious that verbal definitions--the substitution of one set of words for another--will not convey the meaning of "red" to those who cannot see.[AOE, 68]

After a lengthy investigation of "ideas" which we will follow no further, Locke determines the certainty and extent of human knowledge, naming four "sorts" of ideas and giving examples. He begins:

> Since the mind, in all its thoughts and reasonings, hath no other immediate object but its own ideas, which it alone does or can contemplate, it is evident that our knowledge is only conversant about them.
>
> Knowledge is the perception of the agreement or disagreement of two ideas. Knowledge then seems to me to be nothing but the perception of the connexion of and agreement, or disagreement and repugnancy of any of our ideas. In this alone it consists. . . . But to understand a little more distinctly wherein this agreement or disagreement consists, I think we may reduce it all to these four sorts: I. Identity, or diversity. II. Relation. III. Co-existence, or necessary connexion. IV. Real existence. . . . Within these four sorts of agreement or disagreement is, I suppose, contained all the knowledge we have, or are capable of. For all the inquiries we can make concerning any of our ideas, all that we know or can affirm concerning any of them, is, That it is, or is not, the same with some other [identity]; that it does or does not always coexist with some other idea in the same subject [relation]; that it has this or that relation with some other idea [necessary connection]; or that it has a real existence without the mind [real existence]. Thus, "blue is not yellow," is of identity. "Two

triangles upon equal bases between two parallels are equal," is of relation. "Iron is susceptible of magnetical impressions," is of co-existence. "God is," is of real existence. [ECHU]

This language creates a dilemma. If Locke has only the ideas and no external objects, how can he have knowledge of the external world? Ideas seem to have lost their meaning as information about things. He has been criticized for "creating two worlds--the subjective one, which we are free to investigate and describe but which contains within itself no guarantees of its objective truth; and the external world from which we are divided forever by the screen of our own 'ideas'."[AOE, 85] As he continues he is aware of the problem.

> It is evident the mind knows not things immediately, but only by the intervention of the ideas it has of them. Our knowledge, therefore is real only so far as there is a conformity between our ideas and the reality of things. But what shall be here the criterion? How shall the mind, when it perceives nothing but its own ideas, know that they agree with things themselves? This, though it seems not to want difficulty, yet, I think, there be two sorts of ideas that we may be assured agree with things. . . . I suggest, . . that morality is capable of demonstration as well as mathematics. [ECHU]

As to mathematical knowledge:

> I doubt not but it will be easily granted, that the knowledge we have of mathematical truths is not only certain, but real knowledge; . . and yet, if we will consider, we shall find that it is only of our own ideas. [ECHU]

Moral knowledge is certain, it being arrived at by deduction.

> For certainty being but the perception of the agreement or disagreement of our ideas, and demonstration nothing but the perception of such agreement, by the intervention of other ideas or mediums; our moral ideas, as well as mathematical, being archetypes themselves, and so adequate and complete ideas. [ECHU]

Locke did not follow up this rather strange statement with the deductions. Though urged to explain such demonstrative ethics, he did not do so. He seemed to be forced into this position by his declaration that moral ideas are not innate. These statements appeared early in his book:

> It may suffice that. . . moral rules are capable of demonstration: and therefore it is our own faults if we come not to a certain knowledge of them.

> But the ignorance wherein many men are of them, and the slowness of assent
> wherewith others receive them, are manifest proofs that they are not innate, .
> . .
>
> Whether there be any such moral principles, wherein all men do agree, I
> appeal to any who have been but moderately conversant in the history of
> mankind, and looked abroad beyond the smoke of their own chimneys. Where
> is that practical truth that is universally received, without doubt or question, as
> it must be if innate?
> So that the truth of all these moral rules plainly depends upon some other
> antecedent to them, and from which they must be deduced; which could not be
> if either they were innate or so much as self-evident.[ECHU]

Late in his book, Locke reneges on the demonstrativeness of morals with
a statement almost declaring them innate.

> I think it must be allowed that several moral rules may receive from mankind
> a very general approbation, without either knowing or admitting the true ground
> of morality; which can only be the will and law of a God, ...[ECHU]

Elsewhere he is ready to turn the task of proving truth in morality to
science: "I know not what may not pass for truth in morality, what may not
be introduced and proved in natural philosophy."
As to other kinds of knowledge we have, Locke's arguments are involved
and somewhat confused. We will not follow them further except to mention
what he calls degrees of knowledge.
(1) Intuitive knowledge, where the mind perceives the truth of the statement
immediately.
(2) Demonstrative [deductive] knowledge where each step is perceived
intuitively. This knowledge is inferior to intuitive "only so far as we are
obliged to rely upon memory in holding together the steps." This "despite
the fact that Locke's fame rests, rightly, on his victories over the great
seventeenth-century champions of infallible rational knowledge."[AOE, 105]
(3) Sensitive knowledge, knowledge of the existence of particular objects
outside us. Locke "admits that it does not reach perfectly to either of the
forgoing degrees of certainty; yet he claims that it goes beyond mere
probability."[AOE, 106] Thus, Locke belittled the principles with which he
began, experience and observation--that all knowledge comes from the
senses.
Where was the syllogism in all this critique of knowledge? He has little

use for it.

> He [God] has given them [people] a mind that can reason, without being instructed in methods of syllogizing: the understanding is not taught to reason by these rules; it has a native faculty to perceive the coherence or incoherence of its ideas, and can range them right, without any such perplexing repetitions.[ECHU]

And again:

> I readily own, that all right reasoning may be reduced to his [Aristotle's] forms of syllogism. But yet I think, without any diminution to him, I may truly say, that they are not the only nor the best way of reasoning.[ECHU]

It is incredible that Locke did not realize that many of his arguments were syllogistic. His arguments against innate ideas are mostly such. The fact that he did not state them formally does mean that they were not syllogistic. For example this statement: "There cannot any one moral rule be proposed whereof a man may not justly demand a reason: which would be perfectly ridiculous and absurd if they were innate; or so much as self-evident, which every innate principle must needs be." He is saying "Moral rules require a reason. The innate does not require a reason, therefore, moral rules are not innate."

Locke's theory of universals, or in his words, abstract general ideas, was not successful. He held several not-altogether compatible views as to how we form them. We will pass them by. His use of the inadequate concepts, current in his time and a holdover from the scholastics, of qualities and substance took him to a dead end. In time it "became clear that natural processes must be explained by laws of nature expressed in quantitative terms; . . . if nature is to be understood as the manifestation of mathematically precise natural laws, . . . the divisions into kinds by perceived qualitative differences becomes irrelevant and have no important place in the organization of scientific knowledge."[AOR, 12, 13]

Despite these faults and errors, "his merits are very great: he asked questions the answers to which by philosophers of greater genius created modern empiricism; he established the connection between philosophical criticism and action and scientific processes and thought; and he used intelligible language, destroying the magic of scholastic and rationalist terminology, which was the greatest of all obstacles to intellectual progress."[AOE, 112] For all its faults the *Essay* was one of the most influential book in modern psychology. It was a faltering step, but a very important one in the process of making psychology a science. Rationalism has not been the same since Locke.

By his insistence that knowledge was "conversant" only about our ideas, his arguments degenerated from a beginning as science to the verge of that abyss, idealism. It is but a small step from Locke's world of "all we have is ideas" (my words, not his, and a little exaggerated) to "ideas are everything" (again, my words), which is the next phase of empiricism. Talk about those scholastics arguing about how many angels could stand on the point of a needle. We haven't heard anything yet!

George Berkeley (1685-1753),

The second "great" empiricist is a philosopher I would like to skip as one whose philosophy is not part of the history of naturalism. If Descartes gave us a ghost in a machine, Berkeley gave us ghosts only.

But he did contribute to the importance of experience for knowledge, and thus to naturalism, in his first publication *An Essay towards a New Theory of Vision* (1709). In this book he made a brilliant contribution to psychology and optics. Given Locke's position that all ideas come from experience, the question arises, would a man born blind be able to distinguish a sphere from a cube, on recovering his sight. An associate posed this problem to Locke. Both agreed in the negative. Berkeley agreed with them and made his own analysis:

> A man born blind, being made to see, would at first have no idea of distance by sight; the sun and stars, the remotest objects as well as the nearer, would all seem to be in his eye, or rather in his mind. The objects intromitted by sight would seem to him (as in truth they are) no other than a new set of thoughts or sensations, each whereof is as near to him as the perceptions of pain or pleasure or the most inward passions of the soul. For judging objects perceived by sight to be at any distance, or without the mind, is entirely the effect of experience.

This was confirmed by the Royal Society (1709, 1728) when a congenitally blind person was surgically given sight. He could not judge the shape of objects nor determine their distance, believing they touched his eyes.

So much for Berkeley's contribution to science. His consuming passion was in the opposite direction. He was born and educated in Ireland where he spent the greater part of his life. A precocious student, at fifteen he entered Trinity College, Dublin. A few years later, convinced that matter did not exist, he expressed the idea which made him famous: that nothing exists except by being perceived, that therefore matter is a myth and mind is the only reality.

The following quotations, as noted, are from *A Treatise Concerning the Principles of Human Knowledge* (1710). It was from this book and *The Dialogues between Hylas and Philonous, in Opposition to Sceptics and Atheists* (1713) that Berkeley pursued his goal of eradicating the dratted materialism.

> As . . . the doctrine of Matter, or corporeal substance. . . [has] been the main pillar and support of skepticism, so likewise upon the same faith have been raised all the impious schemes of atheism and irreligion. . . How great a friend material substance hath been to atheists in all ages, were needless to relate. All their monstrous systems have so visible and necessary a dependance on it, that when this corner-stone is once removed, the whole fabric cannot choose but fall to the ground; insomuch that it is no longer worth while to bestow a particular consideration on the absurdities of every wretched sect of Atheists.[TCPH]

Berkeley did not find anything of substance in material substance. He pointed out that "Locke's hypothesis of the existence of material substance is such that it is logically impossible that any evidence could be found for or against it. . . ."[AOE, 146] For if qualities are the cause of ideas and ideas, our sole source of knowledge, are of qualities, substance cannot be detected.

He followed Locke on the origin of ideas:

> It is evident to any one who takes a survey of the objects of human knowledge, that they are either ideas actually imprinted on the senses; or else such as are perceived by attending to the passions and operations of the mind; or lastly, ideas formed by help of memory and imagination- either compounding, dividing, or barely representing those originally perceived in the aforesaid ways. By sight I have the ideas of light and colours, with their several degrees and variations. By touch I perceive hard and soft, heat and cold, motion and resistance, and of all these more and less either as to quantity or degree. Smelling furnishes me with odours; the palate with tastes; and hearing conveys

> sounds to the mind in all their variety of tone and composition. And as several of these are observed to accompany each other, they come to be marked by one name, and so to be reputed as one thing.[TCPH]

Here we see the central flaw in Berkeley's thinking (it can't be called reasoning) of confounding sensing with the things sensed. He did not say that the ideas were information or knowledge *of a thing* or that sensation brought knowledge to us via the ideas. He said that the ideas are reputed to be the thing as if appealing to common usage. He then defines the mind:

> But besides all that endless variety of ideas or objects of knowledge, there is likewise something which knows or perceives them, and exercises divers operations, as willing, imagining, remembering, about them. This perceiving, active being is what I call mind, spirit, soul, or myself. By which words I do not denote any one of my ideas, but a thing entirely distinct from them, wherein they exist, or, which is the same thing, whereby they are perceived- for the existence of an idea consists in being perceived . . . . To have an idea is all one as to perceive.[TCPH]

He identifies ideas with perception here and goes on to identify the idea with the thing sensed and insists that anything else is unintelligible.

> That neither our thoughts, nor passions, nor ideas formed by the imagination, exist without the mind, is what every body will allow. And it seems no less evident that the various sensations or ideas imprinted on the sense, however blended or combined together (that is, whatever objects they compose), cannot exist otherwise than in a mind perceiving them. . . .
>
> For as to what is said of the absolute existence of unthinking things without any relation to their being perceived, that is to me perfectly unintelligible. Their esse is percipi [their existence is to be perceived], nor is it possible they should have any existence out of the minds of thinking things which perceive them.[TCPH]

In my interpretation he is holding that it follows or has been demonstrated that the existence of a thing is in the perception of it. I will call this *the non sequitur* of the eighteenth century. He has confounded the thing sensed with the sensing or idea of it. It does not follow that because ideas are in the mind that the thing sensed is in the mind. He rules out the existence of the external world, as philosophers call it, by identifying things with ideas and declaring (rightly) that ideas can only be in the mind. He repeats his thesis over and over. We will quote him again.

It is indeed an opinion prevailing amongst men that houses, mountains, rivers, and in a word all sensible object have an existence, natural or real, distinct from their being perceived by the understanding. But with how great an assur-ance and acquiescence soever this Principle may be entertained in the world, yet whoever shall find in his heart to call it in question, may, if I mistake not, perceive it to involve a manifest contradiction. For what are the foremen-tioned objects but the things we perceive by sense? And what do we perceive besides our own ideas or sensations? and is it not plainly repugnant that any one of these or any combinations of them should exist unperceived?[TCPH]

And further,

> As it is impossible for me to see or feel any thing without an actual sensation of that thing, so it is impossible for me to conceive in my thoughts any sensible thing or object distinct from the sensation or perception of it.[TCPH]

This, of course, is not true. The whole world, except for a few idealists, believes (conceives in their thoughts) that the actual sensation of a thing is something other that the thing of which he/she has a sensation.

For those who insist that "there may be things like them [ideas] whereof they are copies or resemblances; which things exist without the mind," Berkeley answers "an idea can be like nothing but idea; . . ." If "those supposed originals or external things" are perceivable "then they are ideas." Thus he corrupts the word perceive to where it has no use in communication.

Locke held that primary qualities inhered in substance while secondary ones were only in the mind, somehow caused to be there by the primary ones. Berkeley argued that secondary qualities are only in the mind also. This exposed the weakness of Locke's theory, but did nothing to deal with the inadequacy of the concept of qualities for the problem of knowledge. He corrects Locke and disposes of the matter in a paragraph:

> Some there are who make a distinction betwixt primary and secondary qualities. By the former they mean extension, figure, motion, rest, solidity or impenetrability, and number; by the latter they denote all other sensible qualities, as colours, sounds, tastes, and so forth. The ideas we have of these they acknowledge not to be the resemblances of anything existing without the mind, or unperceived, but they will have our ideas of the primary qualities to be patterns or images of things which exist without the mind, in an unthinking substance which they call Matter. By Matter, therefore, we are to understand

> an inert, senseless substance, in which extension, figure, and motion do actually subsist. But it is evident from what we have already shown, that extension, figure, and motion are only ideas existing in the mind, and that an idea can be like nothing but another idea, and that consequently neither they nor their archetypes can exist in an unperceiving substance. Hence, it is plain that the very notion of what is called Matter or corporeal substance, involves a contradiction in it.[TCPH]

He does not say that qualities do not exist but that they only exist in the mind. They are what is perceived, and what is perceived is idea. As further proof that primary qualities exist only in the mind, he cites the dependency of the secondary ones on the primary ones. Locke had said that the secondary qualities were somehow brought to the mind with the primary ones. That God could annex the one to the other, he thought possible. Berkeley takes up the subject:

> Now if it be certain, that those original qualities are inseparably united with the other sensible qualities, and not, even in thought, capable of being abstracted from them, it plainly follows that they exist only in the mind. . . . I see evidently that it is not in my power to frame an idea of a body extended and moving but I must withal give it some color or other sensible quality which is acknowledged to exist only in the mind.[TCPH]

Locke cited qualities as the cause of ideas. For Berkeley qualities are just ideas and considering that he has shown that qualities are not the cause, he proceeds to tell us what it is:

> We perceive a continual succession of ideas, . . . There is, therefore, some cause of these ideas. . . . That this cause cannot be any quality or idea or combination of ideas, is clear from the preceding section. It must therefore be a substance; but it has been shown that there is no corporeal or material substance: it remains therefore that the cause of ideas is an incorporeal active substance or Spirit.[TCPH]

Berkeley assumed in the beginning that other minds exist. How does he know this? If he claimed that other minds were ideas they could not exist outside of Berkeley's mind. Thinking things, therefore have knowledge of other thinking things by some other method. Maybe having a "notion" will do the job.

> In a large sense indeed, we may be said to have an idea, or rather a notion of

spirit, [elsewhere he says that we have no idea of spirit] that is, we understand
the meaning of the word, otherwise we could not affirm or deny any thing of
it. [TCPH]

This in no way supports the existence of spirit. Berkeley, by the same
token, understands the meaning of the word, "matter;" otherwise he could
not affirm or deny anything of it. He does not consider that a reason for
believing in matter. We understand the word, Santa Claus, otherwise we
could not affirm or deny anything of him! Considering that he has shown
that spirits exist, Berkeley continues:

> Moreover, as we conceive the ideas that are in the mind of other spirits by
> means of our own, which we suppose to be resemblances of them; so we know
> other spirits by means of our own soul, which in that sense is the image or
> idea of them; it having a like respect to other spirits that blueness or heat by
> me perceived has to those ideas perceived by another. [Later (below) he says
> simply that we know of other spirits by experience.] [TCPH]

Here he jumps from "we suppose," an appeal to common usage, to "so we
know," and in doing so exhibits a double standard. He does not credit "we
suppose" that physical objects exist outside the mind, (where "we" is
everyone but Berkeley and a few other philosophers), as indicating that "so
we know" that physical objects exist outside of the mind. He uses a method
for knowing spirits exist that he denies valid to prove physical objects exist.

> There are spiritual substances, minds, or human souls, which will or excite
> ideas in themselves at pleasure but these are faint, weak, and unsteady in respect
> of others they perceive by sense- which being impressed upon them according
> to certain rules or laws of nature speak themselves [show themselves to be] the
> effects of a Mind more powerful and wise than human spirits. [TCPH]

And further,

> When I deny sensible things an existence out of the mind, I do not mean my
> mind in particular, but all minds. Now, it is plain they have an existence
> exterior to my mind; since I find them by experience to be independent of
> it. [AOE, 154]

So experience does tell him that there are things, thinking things, exterior
to his mind and it would seem that it would not strain Berkeley too much to
experience a thinking thing's body exterior to Berkeley's mind right along

with the thinking thing. Not so, but isn't perception the experience he has been talking about all the time? Does he not perceive other thinking things or rather infer their existence from what he does perceive?

To insure that an object does not cease to exist when no one is perceiving it, he has recourse to God. Locke had primary qualities as the cause of ideas, the secondary ones riding in piggyback on them (God could conceivably annex the secondary to the primary). Locke had given God a minor role. Berkeley gives him a major one.

> There is therefore some other Mind wherein they exist, during the intervals between the times of my perceiving them: as likewise they did before my birth, and would do after my supposed annihilation. And as the same is true with regard to all other finite created spirits, it necessarily follows there is an *omnipresent, eternal Mind* which knows and comprehends all things, and exhibits them to our view in such a manner, and according to such rules, as He Himself hath ordained, and are by us termed the *laws of nature.*[AOE, 154]

Thus, he brings God into the picture to insure that things exists when no person is observing them. "But this is not compatible with Berkeley's professed empiricism, and the introduction of God to rescue an otherwise untenable view of what material objects are is illegitimate."[AOE, 147]
At this point there is the question: Is Berkeley really an empiricist? His use of the word perception in the beginning seems to indicate that the origin or genesis of ideas is a natural process as in Locke, but his declaration that God "exhibits them [things] to our view" is a claim that God is the cause of ideas not that ideas originate from observation. Empiricism, in Berkeley's hands, is something quite different from empiricism in "empirical science" and "empirical evidence."
Berkeley "appears to deny the existence in the universe of anything except minds and 'ideas' in those minds. What we ordinarily call apples and trees and desks are not objects existing in their own right, external to and independent of minds; rather they are certain sorts of collections of ideas in the mind."[AOE, 144] But elsewhere he declares that

> I do not argue against the existence of any one thing that we can apprehend, either by sense or reflection. That the things I see with my eyes and touch with my hands do exist, really exist, I make not the lest question. The only thing whose existence we deny, is that which philosophers call Matter or corporeal substance.[TCPH]

But following this he repeats that the objects of sense exists only in the mind, so what he means by this is a mystery.

Berkeley's position that only minds and the contents of minds (ideas) exists makes him a pluralistic idealist, and he is so classified.[DOP, 53] His admission that other minds exist saves him from the charge of solipsism which "maintains that the individual self or the solipsistic philosopher is the whole of reality and that the external world and other persons are representations of that self having no independent existence."[DOP, 312] Still, Berkeley's world is not believable. There is no correlation between minds and bodies. For, if Berkeley feels, sees, smells, hears another person, he has only these ideas in his mind and according to Berkeley as quoted above, any and all persons perceived by Berkeley bodily exist only in Berkeley's mind. This leaves the perceived person's minds out there somewhere, "real" and independent, while that person's body is in Berkeley's mind (where it is safe from being matter). Even Berkeley's body exists only in his mind.

But, there is a question whether Berkeley's language consistently supports his contention that things exist only in the mind. Does it not also support things as existing, really existing, because they are perceived by minds, any minds? The logical consequence of perceived objects "existing in the mind" is that, if multi-observers perceive the same object, as many objects would exist as observers. Berkeley does not mention multiple existences (of a particular object) and at times seems to argue that an object exists when perceived by a person or persons and would continue to exist if they ceased to perceive it because God perceived it and it would all the time be one object. How then could it be conceived not to be public, that is, external to human minds? For an object perceived by God would, "existing only in a mind," in this case in Gods's mind, be inaccessible in the ordinary way of perceiving to other thinking things. He has said (page 91) as I interpret him, that we conceive the ideas that are in the mind of other spirits as resemblances which is the "image or idea" of those in our own. If God perceives all objects then they exist in God's mind (their *esse* is *percipi)*. If then, in the mind of other spirits, they are resemblances or images of those in God's mind they do not exist in the minds of other spirits. It is another thing if the objects are ideas in the minds of other spirits. As ideas they are the (perceived) object and therefore exist in the other spirit's mind as well as in God's according to Berkeley's definition, for to have an idea is all one as to perceive, and to be an idea (perceived) is to exist. In virtually identifying resemblances and images with ideas as quoted above, Berkeley seems to have violated his definition of idea (which can be like nothing but another idea).

  Once Berkeley brings God into the picture as perceiving all things and guaranteeing their existence, their being perceived by people is superfluous as to sustaining existence. How possibly could a thing already existing be made to exist again?

  If we complain that if things exist only in the mind, "we must be eating ideas, drinking ideas, clothing ourselves in ideas, etc., which is surely absurd,"[AOE, 159] Berkeley would point out (or perhaps did) that the absurdity is due to "reducing" food to "ideas" while leaving my body and my eating "unreduced" and "real."[AOE, 159] But Berkeley uses unreduced language throughout his argument, and for good reason, *it is necessary for communication.* In explaining what is meant by the term "exist" Berkeley writes,

> The table I write on, I say exists, that is, I see and feel it: and if I were out of my study I should say it existed, meaning thereby that if I was in my study I might perceive it, or that some other spirit actually does perceive it.[TCPH]

The "table I write on" is "unreduced" after which he confounds it with "I see and feel it," the experience of sensing it (the table reduced to idea). You and I are inclined to say that the later entails the former, that is, the table has to exist for Berkeley to see it, but it is not a reversible statement: the former does not entail the latter, that is, Berkeley does not have to see the table for it to exist. Berkeley thinks otherwise; he explains further (to repeat a quotation):

> It is indeed an opinion strangely prevailing amongst men that the houses, mountains, rivers, and in a word all sensible objects have an existence natural or real, distinct from their being perceived by the understanding.[TCPH]

Again, these "sensible" objects are "unreduced." A sensible object is one that can be sensed, not a sensed object. Berkeley insists that this strange opinion is a "manifest contradiction. For what are the fore-mentioned objects but the things we perceive by sense?"[TCPH]

The objects, things, are still "unreduced" and separate from the function of sensing. Berkeley thinks that this makes a point, but there is nothing in this sentence that so much as hints that the perception is the existence of the objects. Berkeley continues:

> and what do we perceive besides our own ideas or sensations? and is it not plainly repugnant that any one of these [objects] or any combination of them should exist unperceived?[TCPH]

For me this is the silliest question ever asked by a philosopher, but Berkeley's answer is yes, and in doing so he reduces objects to ideas by confounding the sensing with the thing sensed, the experience with the thing experienced, the "knowledge" with the thing known.

Is it possible for one philosopher to communicate to another about experience without speaking as if "sensible objects have an existence natural or real, distinct from their being perceived by the understanding?" Berkeley does not do so. I suggest that it is not possible. If Berkeley believes he perceives an apple where there is a "sensible object," apple, and does not expect to perceive an apple where there is no "sensible object" apple, then he must, to be consistent, believe he perceives an apple, a sensible object "natural or real, distinct from its being perceived by the understanding." If he believes he perceives an apple with no sensible "object apple" present, there may be help for him but his problem is not metaphysics.

Let us try to reduce all the physical objects in "I am sitting in a chair at a table eating an apple." Let us concede to Berkeley that "I" is mind (capable of having ideas) and does not need to be reduced, but this will not apply to his "physical" body. Our "reduction" must proceed thus: I (my mind) perceive the idea of my physical body sitting in my idea of a chair at my idea of a table eating my idea of an apple. But we have not reduced the objects (physical) body, chair, table, and apple. My ideas are *of* these things. Let us try again: I have the idea of an idea sitting in my idea at my idea eating my idea. But, sitting and eating are terms denoting a physical sitter and physical eater. Those dratted things have to be eliminated in order to speak in a "reduced" language, but how? And why, since our refined statement makes no sense?

Berkeley has been given credit for an important contribution to philosophy:

> Berkeley's contribution to logic, and to what is today called "linguistic analysis" is very great. But his abiding importance in the history of philosophy still lies in his unequivocal insistence that any statement purporting to be about physical objects in the external world must, if it is to be meaningful, be

somehow "reducible to," or "analyzable into," statements about the contents of immediate sense experience. [AOE, 160]

This was written in 1956. A. J. Ayer, who in 1936 held "that every factual proposition must refer to sense-experience,"[LTL, 71] wrote in 1982 "among those who believe that the concept of sense-data or something like them serves a useful purpose, there are few, if any, who believe that every empirical statement can be reformulated in their terms."[PTC, 140] There is further discussion of this on pages 220-222.

No one has shown that all empirical statements can be reduced to statements about sense-data. The reason, I suspect, is that it cannot be done. For it to be possible the mind would have to be Locke's blank paper, and sense data would have to be the sole producer of concepts. There is a mind that processes the data. There is a function in the brain when sensing takes place. In fairness to Locke, "blank paper" is not his entire theory of the mind. He speaks of the "operations of the mind", etc. (see page 78). This will get further treatment when we get to Immanuel Kant.

Both Locke and Berkeley are using only those sensations by which we detect physical objects as sense data and the basis of knowledge. (Berkeley does this despite his claim that the objects exist only in the mind.) But, we have to distinguish between (1) sensing a thing such as seeing the moon, which is sense data of a physical object and (2) sensing alleged information such as the moon is made of green cheese, which is not sense data of a physical object. Rather, it is sense data of someone expressing an opinion, and the hearer has to use something other than a sense datum of a physical object to determine if it is knowledge. Berkeley here has something to deal with that is not "in the mind." In (1) there is direct knowledge that there is a moon however little one knows about it. In (2) there is indeed sensation, but not direct knowledge. To determine that it is knowledge, if it is, the mind must function in a way that is not direct sensation of the moon's existence.

Was Berkeley arguing that things exist only in the mind or that they existed, "really existed," but only when they were perceived (and were perceived at all times by God)? He does neither consistently. Or, is he arguing that things exist as common sense tells us they do and function by natural law (he does use that term) but are spirit. If the latter, that is, if objects are as objects would be and nature does as nature would do, it boils down to an argument that the term for empirically known objects must be spelled with the letters s, p, i, r, i and t in that order and cannot be spelled with the letters m, a, t, t, e, and r, in that order, which is, of course, absurd.

No man ever surpassed Berkeley in promoting the unreality of the real. His arguments with which he tried to exorcise the Hobbesian materialism that was being taken seriously in England evolved in Hume and Kant into a critique of reason that left no basic dogma of Christianity unquestioned.

Why was Berkeley called a philosopher? It is a good question, but there is a good answer. Philosophy as we know it, that is, the literature of philosophy we have, has passed down to us as it has impressed philosophers, and Berkeley made an impression. The process of selecting what is called philosophy is mostly done in academia. To that extent it is the works of "schoolmen" as in the middle ages, and as such scholasticism is still with us, not as promoting the same ideas, but as the fact that what gets printed and taught is in the hands of "schoolmen."

Berkeley's impression was and is very great. Even today there are philosophers who have not quite made up their mind that the external world exists.

With one "great" empiricists to go, our enterprise has degenerated from naturalism, that brave start by Locke, to the metaphysics of spirit and ideas, in a word idealism. But there are more shocks ahead, with some that make sense, with our third "great" empiricist. There is some wheat in the chaff in David Hume's philosophy.

David Hume (1711-1776)

Hume agreed with some others of his time that Berkeley's arguments admit of no answer and produce no conviction, and that his writings in defense of religion tended more to teach skepticism than religion. Not that he had anything against the skepticism, which in this case was skepticism of the supernatural. Hume's philosophy is known for its skepticism concerning knowledge. Hume is

> one of the greatest and most iconoclastic philosophers of his own age or any age. . . . No man has influenced the history of philosophical thought to a deeper and more disturbing degree.[AOE, 163]

Hume's principal theme is the central thesis of all empiricism, namely, that all knowledge about the universe must be based on observation. And, he discounts the possibility of ever knowing the "ultimate principles" of human nature. He tells us:

> As the science of man is the only solid foundation of the other sciences, so the only solid foundation we can give to this science itself must be laid on experience and observation. . . .
> We must endeavor to render all our principles as universal as possible, by trac-ing up our experiments to the utmost, and explaining all effects from the simp-lest and fewest causes, 'tis still certain we cannot go beyond experience; and any hypothesis, that pretends to discover the ultimate original qualities of human nature, aught at first to be rejected as presumptuous and chimerical. . .
>
> But if this impossibility of explaining ultimate principles should be esteemed a defect in the science of man, I will venture to affirm, that 'tis a defect common to it with all the sciences, and all the arts, in which we can employ ourselves, whether they be such as are cultivated in the schools of the philosophers, or practiced in the shops of the meanest artisans. None of them can go beyond experience, or establish any principles which are not founded on that authority. [TOHN, xvi-xviii]

I get the feeling, as I read this, that science is only of the behavior of things, but nowhere does Hume say that. In these remarks we get a taste of his aversion to metaphysics about which he is more specific elsewhere. He raises, in his own words,

> the justest and most plausible objection against a considerable part of metaphysics; that they are not properly a science, but arise either from the fruitless efforts of human vanity, which would penetrate into subjects utterly inaccessible to the understanding; or from the craft of popular superstitions, which, being unable to defend themselves on fair ground, raise these entangling brambles to cover and protect their weakness. [FDTW, 123]

The "'observations' required for Hume's theory of knowledge are, apparently, to be conducted mainly in the field of introspective psychology." [AOE, 164] He discounts the possibility of doing moral philosophy--we will discuss this later--but as he begins he finds no problem with "natural" philosophy:

> When I am at a loss to know the effects of one body upon another in any situation I need only put them in that situation, and observe what results from

it. But should I endeavor to clear up after the same manner any doubt in moral philosophy, by placing myself in the same case with that which I consider, 'tis evident this reflection and premeditation would so disturb the operation of my natural principles, as must render it impossible to form any just conclusions from the phaenomenon. We must, therefore, glean up our experiments in this science from a cautious observation of human life, and take them as they appear in the common course of the world, by men's behavior in company, in affairs, and in their pleasures. Where experiments of this kind are judiciously collected and compared, we may hope to establish on them a science which will not be inferior in certainty, and will be much superior in utility, to any other of human comprehension. [TOHN, xix]

This must be the philosopher for a naturalist like myself! But, remember Locke's beginnings in this vein? Hume's result is much different from Locke's, but like Locke, in the end his philosophy is poor science. He exposes, so he believes, the very foundation of science (the very method he claims to be using), causation and induction, to doubt.

His philosophical masterpiece, the *Treatise of Human Nature* published in 1735, in his own words, "fell dead born from the press." In time it would get plenty of attention. In 1748 he published *An Enquiry Concerning the Human Understanding* which he thought an improvement over the *Treatise* which hadn't received much attention at that time. It contained a section "Of Miracles" that was originally a part of the *Treatise* which the publisher had refused to print. In 1751 he published *An Enquiry Concerning the Principles of Morals.* In 1752 he "began the publication of his celebrated *History of England.* The celebrity that eluded him as a philosopher came to him as an historian, and by the time he had finished his history--in 1761--he had become world famous."[AOE, 162]

Hume was born in Edinburgh, Scotland. His family,

all Presbyterian, gave the boy a strong infusion of Calvinist theology, which remained as determinism in David's philosophy. Every Sunday morning he attended church service three hours long, including two hours of preaching; every Sunday afternoon he returned to the kirk for an hour; to which were added morning prayers at home. If David had any character in him he was bound to react into heresy.[AOV, 140]

He said later that he had no belief in religion after reading Locke and Clarke. "He died as he had lived, an atheist."[AOE, 163]

In the interest of holding on to readers who are still with me, I suggest if this gets too tedious that he/she skip to my criticism of Hume on page 121, stopping on the way to read the paragraphs on induction, page 114. I plead that my heart and mind were in the right place. I have attempted to revise Hume's sketch downward in size, but each time it only got larger. I am quoting Hume that I may use his words against him.

Ideas, Their Origin and Composition

Hume divides "the contents of the mind," all labeled indiscriminately "ideas" by Locke and Berkeley, in two classes, "impressions" and "ideas." The impressions are intended to be the immediately given data of sense and introspection, while the ideas are images of memory and imagination. [AOE, 165, 166]

In Hume's own words,

All the perceptions of the human mind resolve themselves into two distinct kinds, which I shall call IMPRESSIONS and IDEAS. The difference betwixt these consist in the degrees of force and liveliness with which they strike upon the mind, and make their way into our thought or consciousness. Those perceptions which enter with most force and violence, we may name *impressions*; and under this name I comprehend all our sensations, passions, and emotions, as they make their first appearance in the soul. By *ideas*, I mean the faint images of these in thinking and reasoning [as memory?]; such as, for instance, are all the perceptions excited by the present discourse, excepting only those which arise from the sight and touch, and excepting the immediate pleasure or uneasiness it may occasion. [TOHN, 1]

Although Hume admits that this difference in force and liveliness is unsatisfactory, he counts that fact of no consequence:

In particular instances they may very nearly approach each other. Thus, in sleep, in a fever, in madness, or in any very violent emotions of the soul, our ideas may approach to our impressions: As, on the other hand, it sometimes happens that our impressions are so faint and low that we cannot distinguish them from our ideas. But notwithstanding this near resemblance in a few instances, they are in general so very different, that no-one can make a scruple to rank them under distinct heads, and assign to each a peculiar name to mark the difference. [TOHN, 2]

Further, he divides both impressions and ideas into simple and complex:

> Simple perceptions or impressions and ideas are such as admit of no distinction nor separation. . . .[TOHN, 2] [And] *all our simple ideas in their first appearance are deriv'd from simple impressions, which are correspondent to them, and which they exactly represent.*[TOHN, 4] The complex are contrary to these, and may be distinguished into parts. Tho' a particular colour, taste and smell, are qualities all united together in this apple, it is easy to perceive they are not the same, but are at least distinguishable from each other.[TOHN, 2]

Impressions are the cause of our simple ideas, and Hume provides proof:

> Our ideas upon their appearance produce not their correspondent impressions, nor do we perceive any colour, or feel any sensation merely upon thinking of them. On the other hand we find, that any impression either of the mind or body is constantly followed by an idea, which resembles it, and is only different in the degrees of force and liveliness, The constant conjunction of our resembling perceptions, is a convincing proof, that the one are the causes of the other; and this priority of the impressions is an equal proof, that our impressions are the causes of our ideas, not our ideas of our impressions.[TOHN, 5]

He is really making the case that we do not have ideas without experience, and he gives two examples of ideas which cannot occur without experience:

> To confirm this, I consider another plain and convincing phaenomenon; which is, that wher-ever, by any accident, the faculties which give rise to any impression are obstructed in their operations, as when one is born blind or deaf; not only the impressions are lost, but also their correspondent ideas; so that there never appear in the mind the lest traces of either of them. Nor is this only true where the organs of sensation are entirely destroy'd, but likewise where they have never been put in action to produce a particular impression. We cannot form to ourselves a just idea of the taste of a pineapple, without having actually tasted it.[TOHN, 5]

But ideas can produce the images of themselves in new ideas:

> As our ideas are images of our impressions, so we can form secondary ideas, which are images of the primary. . . . This is not, properly speaking, an exception to the rule so much as an explanation of it. Ideas produce the images of themselves in new ideas; but as the first ideas are supposed to be derived from impressions, it still remains true, that all our simple ideas proceed either mediately or immediately, from their correspondent impressions.[TOHN, 6, 7]

He concedes an exception to the rule that a simple idea does not occur without an impression and gives an example, that of an intermediate shade of blue between two shades that had been experience, but "the instance is so particular and singular that it is scarce worth our observing, and does not merit that for it alone, we should alter our general maxim."[TOHN 6]

This seeing (sensing) double with impressions and ideas is no problem for Hume, in fact it is the heart of his theory. However, in the case of a perception, which presumably owes its existence to the impression, which is object dependent (the impression of an apple requires an apple), and the object, he can find only one item. Two hundred and eleven pages into his book when he was losing his grip on science, he declared that "There are no principles either of the understanding or fancy, which lead us directly to embrace this opinion of the double existence of perceptions and objects."[TOHN, 211]

What are the causes of impressions? Does the object perceived have anything to do with it? Where Locke's ideas were caused by (the sensation of) qualities of the object (without an intermediary impression), surprisingly the cause of Hume's impressions are unknown.

> Impressions may be divided into two kinds, those of SENSATION and those of REFLECTION. The first kind arises in the soul originally from unknown causes. The second is derived in a great measure from our ideas, and that in the following order. An impression first strikes upon the senses, and makes us perceive heat or cold, thirst or hunger, pleasure or pain of some kind or other. Of this impression there is a copy taken by the mind, which remains after the impression ceases; and this we call idea. This idea of pleasure or pain, when it returns upon the soul [is remembered?], produces the new impressions of desire and aversion, hope and fear, which may properly be called impressions of reflection, because derived from it. These again are copied by the memory and imagination, and become ideas; which perhaps in their turn give rise to other impressions and ideas. So that the impressions of reflection are only antecedent to their correspondent ideas; but posterior to those of sensation and deriv'd from them.[TOHN, 7, 8]

It is important to understand here that Hume is not concerned with the sensation that originates or creates ideas or, in his terms, impressions and ideas; but only the finished product after it is in, or becomes part of, the mind. In his words: "The examination of our sensations belongs more to anatomists and natural philosophers than to moral; and shall not at present be enter'd upon."[TOHN, 8]   Not only is he not concerned with them, but 84 pages into his book he tells us that he believes they are inexplicable:

> As those *impressions*, which arise from the *senses*, their ultimate cause is, in my opinion, perfectly inexplicable by human reason, and 'twill always be impossible to decide with certainty, whether they arise immediately from the object, or are produc'd by the creative power of the mind, or are deriv'd from the author of our being. Nor is such a question any way material to our present purpose.[TOHN, 84]

Memory and Imagination

The mind has two faculties which presumably we can say process ideas. While it appeared that in the above explanation of impressions and ideas, ideas were remembered impressions, it is not so. In the memory we find ideas with a third level of vivacity intermediate between an impression and an idea.

Hume then tells us of two "species of ideas," memory and imagination. "When any impression has been present with the mind" and makes another appearance there and "retains a considerable degree of its first vivacity, and is somewhat intermediate betwixt an impression and idea," it is accomplished by a faculty called the memory. When an idea which makes another appearance and "entirely loses that vivacity, and is a perfect idea," it is [presumably a faculty] called imagination. This is a "sensible difference betwixt one species of ideas and another." The memory has no power of variation and preserves the idea as it appeared originally, or if it doesn't, it "proceeds from some defect or imperfection in that faculty." The imagination does not retain ideas as they originally appear but has the liberty to "*transpose and change its ideas.*"[TOHN, 8-10]

Hume finds yet another degree of vivacity in ideas which is weaker than those of the memory. In a discussion of the difference in a conception and a belief, he believes "that the ideas of memory are more *strong* and *lively* than those of the fancy."[TOHN, 628] And what is the fancy? Is it different from the "understanding?" If so, are the ideas in it of yet another degree of vivacity? I find no explanation of this.

Association of Ideas

Hume's next step in mapping out the workings of the mind is the association of ideas, a process by which the mind is conveyed from one idea to another by three qualities.

> As all simple ideas may be separated by the imagination, and may be united again in what form it pleases, nothing wou'd be more unaccountable than the operations of that faculty, were it not guided by some universal principles, which render it, in some measure, uniform with itself in all times and places. Were ideas entirely loose and unconnected, chance alone wou'd join them; and it is impossible the same simple ideas should fall regularly into complex ones (as they commonly do) without some bond of union among them, some associating quality, by which one idea naturally introduces another. This uniting principle . . . [is] a gentle force, which commonly prevails, and is the cause why, among other things, languages so nearly correspond to each other; nature in a manner, pointing out to every one those simple ideas, which are most proper to be united into a complex one. The qualities, from which this association arises, and by which the mind is, after this manner, convey'd from one idea to another, are three, *viz.* RESEMBLANCE, CONTIGUITY in time and place, and CAUSE and EFFECT. [TOHN, 10, 11]

We will skip his elaboration on these three "qualities," a much different use of the word than we found in Locke and Berkeley and which Hume uses elsewhere. He continues:

> These are therefore the principles of union or cohesion among our simple ideas, and in the imagination supply the place of that inseparable connection, by which they are united in our memory. Here is a kind of ATTRACTION, . . . Its effects are everywhere conspicuous; but as to its causes, they are mostly unknown, and must be resolved into original qualities of human nature, which I pretend not to explain. [TOHN, 12, 13]

No matter that he can't explain the causes, the result, he is certain[1], is complex ideas. Hume classifies them:

> Amongst the effects of this union or association of ideas, there are none more remarkable than those complex ideas, which are the common subject of our thoughts and reasoning, and generally arise from some principle of union among our simple ideas. These complex ideas may be divided into *Relations, Modes,*

and *Substances.*[TOHN, 13]

The foregoing with "some considerations concerning our *general* and *particular* ideas . . . may be considered as the elements of this philosophy."[TOHN, 13]

And what is a "relation?" "Those qualities, which make objects admit of comparison. . . . may be compriz'd under seven general heads, which may be considered as the source of all *philosophical* relation."[TOHN, 14] They are: resemblance, identity, space & time, quantity or number, degrees, contrariety, cause and effect.

If the reader has trouble thinking of these items as relations he is not alone. Perhaps further explanation will help. Hume explains that the word relation is used in two senses.

> Either for that quality by which two ideas are connected together in the imagination, and the one naturally introduces the other, after the manner above-explained; or for that particular circumstance, in which, even upon the arbitrary union of two ideas in the fancy, we may think proper to compare them. In common language the former is always the sense, in which we use the word, relation; . . in philosophy [we mean] any particular subject of comparison[TOHN, 13]

And what does he mean by substance and mode?

> The idea of a substance as well as that of a mode, is nothing but a collection of simple ideas, that are united by the imagination, and have a particular name assigned them, by which we are able to recall, either to ourselves or others, that collection. But the difference betwixt these ideas consists in this, that the particular qualities, which form a substance, are . . . closely and inseparably connected by the relations of contiguity and causation. The effect of this is, that whatever new simple quality we discover to have the same connexion with the rest, we immediately comprehend it among them, even tho' it did not enter into the first conception of the substance. Thus our idea of gold may at first be a yellow colour, weight, malleableness, fusibility; but upon the discovery of its dissolubility in *aqua regia*, we join that to the other qualities, and suppose it to belong to the substance as much as if its idea had from the beginning made a part of the compound one. The principal of union being regarded as the chief part of the complex idea, . . .[TOHN, 16]

Hume's "considerations concerning our *general* and *particular* ideas," is his answer to the problem of universals (interpreted).

The fallacy of ascribing independent being to characteristics springs from the fact that they can be distinguished from that which they characterize, and [therefore] whatever is distinguishable can exist separately. He argues against this that this distinguishing is one of "reason" only--that if we distinguish its characteristics from an object, nothing is left. In this sense we cannot, therefore, even distinguish. But we can compare objects--"view them in different aspects, according to the resemblances of which they are susceptible"--without distinguish -ing, i.e., splitting them into separate "ideas." These inseparable "aspects" and "resemblances" without which an object is nothing--which in a sense *are* the object--are symbolized by general terms [universals], and are mistakenly conceived as having existence--or some sort of being--in their own right.[AOE, 178]

Space and Time

Hume uses more than 40 pages to establish *"that the idea of space or extension is nothing but the idea of visible or tangible points distributed in a certain order;"*[TOHN, 53] and that we derive our idea of time from a succession of ideas and impressions.

"Upon opening my eyes, and turning them to the surrounding objects, I perceive many visible bodies; and upon shutting them again, and considering the distance betwixt these bodies, I acquire the idea of extension."[TOHN, 33] Therefore, Hume concludes, the senses are responsible for the idea of extension. How do the senses do this? They "convey to me only the impressions of colour'd points, dispos'd in a certain manner."[TOHN, 34] Therefore, "the idea of extension is nothing but a copy of these colour'd points, and of the manner of their appearance."[TOHN, 34] But Hume says that after viewing many colors we find "a resemblance in the disposition of colour'd points, of which they are compos'd, we omit the peculiarities of colour, as far as possible, and found an abstract idea merely on that disposition of points, or manner of appearance, in which they agree."[TOHN, 33, 34]

The idea of time, according to Hume, is

> deriv'd from the succession of our perceptions of every kind. . . . If you wheel about a burning coal with rapidity, it will present to the senses an image of a circle of fire; nor will there seem to be any interval of time betwixt its revolutions; merely because 'tis impossible for our perceptions to succeed each

other with the same rapidity, that motion may be communicated to external objects. Whenever we have no successive perceptions, we have no notion of time, even tho' there be a real succession in the objects. . . . [Time] is always discover'd by some *perceivable* succession of changeable objects.[TOHN, 34, 35]

Hume supports his position with further arguments too tiresome to repeat.

Idea of Existence

Hume next explains the ideas of existence and external existence.

> There is no impression nor idea of any kind, of which we have any consciousness or memory, that is not conceiv'd as existent; and 'tis evident, that from this consciousness the most perfect idea and assurance of being is deriv'd. From hence we may form a dilemma, the most clear and conclusive that can be imagin'd, *viz*, that since we never remember any idea or impression without attributing existence to it, the idea of existence must either be deriv'd from a distinct impression, conjoin'd with every perception or object of our thought, or must be the very same with the idea of the perception or object.[TOHN, 66]

Hume opts for the latter.

> To reflect on any thing simply, and to reflect on it as existent, are nothing different from each other. That idea, when conjoin'd with the idea of any object, makes no addition to it. Whatever we conceive, we conceive to be existent.[TOHN, 66, 67]

If we thought the forgoing covers the real world of external existences, we were wrong. He now extends perceptions to the "external" world.

> A like reasoning will account for the idea of *external existence*. We may observe, that 'tis universally allow'd by philosophers, and is besides pretty obvious of itself, that nothing is ever really present with the mind but its perceptions or impressions and ideas, and that external objects become known to us only by those perceptions they occasion.[TOHN, 67]

So far this position is sound. Hume seems on the verge of making Kant's discovery that "existence" is not an attribute, but he does not put it in those words. With the next paragraph, if it means what it says, Hume leaves the world of science and slips smoothly into idealism.

Now since nothing is ever present to the mind but perceptions, and since all ideas are deriv'd from something antecedently present to the mind; it follows, that 'tis impossible for us to so much as to conceive or form an idea of any thing specifically different from ideas and impressions. Let us fix our attention out of ourselves as much as possible: Let us chase our imagination to the heavens, or to the utmost limits of the universe; we never really advance a step beyond ourselves, nor can conceive any kind of existence, but those perceptions, which have appear'd in that narrow compass. This is the universe of the imagination, nor have we any idea but what is there produc'd.[TOHN, 67]

Of Knowledge

Hume returns to his "seven different kinds of philosophical relation," in a slightly different wording than when first mentioned (page 105). These relations (paraphrased) may be divided into two classes; into such as depend entirely on ideas, which we compare together, *resemblance, proportion in quantity and number, degrees in any quality and contrariety*, which he called "Relations of Ideas;" and such as may be changed without any change in the ideas; *identity, relation of time and place and causation*, which he called "Matters of Fact."[TOHN, 69] This is a revision, respectively, of Leibniz's "Truths of Reason" and "Truths of Fact."

In the interest of retaining our sanity, we will abandon Hume's elucidation of these terms which, by putting words, mostly Kant's, in Hume's mouth, are known by later philosophers as "Analytic" and "Synthetic." These terms apply to propositions. It is best to think of a proposition as a declarative sentence.

Analytic propositions are a priori, that is, known without experience; the negation of them leads to self-contradiction; they are true by definition; and they are necessarily true. In other words, they "are based on our own, ultimately arbitrary, rules and habits of using words and symbols."[AOE, 180]

Synthetic propositions are the opposite of analytic propositions. They are a posteriori, that is, known from experience (can be traced back to an impression, according to Hume); the negation of them does not lead to self-contradiction; and they are not true by definition. They can be true or false but never necessarily true.

Examples of analytic sentences (or propositions) are simple addition problems. Anyone who knows the definition of the terms, two, three, five, plus, and equal knows without experience (neglecting the experience of learning the definitions) that 2 + 3 = 5. Other examples of analytic sentences are: all bachelors are men, and all brothers are siblings which are true by definition. The negation of these, namely 2 + 3 does not = 5; bachelors are not men and brothers are not siblings is self contradictory.

Thus Hume is admitting that there is such a thing as a priori necessary truths, contrary to his empiricists premises (knowledge is from experience), but he deflates this by declaring them *tautological* (redundant, repetitive), providing no information about the world.

Examples of synthetic sentences are any statements of fact such as "there is an apple on the table." They can be true or false. If traceable back to an impressions (sense data) they are true. Never mind that they can be false; all knowledge about the world is based on observation.

If a proposition is neither analytic or synthetic, it is nonsense. "Propositions are either certain and uninformative, or informative and not certain. Metaphysical knowledge which claims to be both certain and informative is therefore in principle not possible."[AOE, 180] Hume expressed this in a famous statement.

> When we run over libraries, persuaded of these principles, what havoc must we make? If we take in our hand any volume, of divinity or school metaphysics, for instance; let us ask, Does it contain any abstract reasoning concerning quantity or number? No. Does it contain any experimental reasoning concerning matter of fact and existence? No. Commit it then to the flames, for it can contain nothing but sophistry and illusion.[AECH]

Causation and Induction

Hume examines the idea of cause and finds that it meets neither the analytic nor the synthetic test.

"Hume's analysis of causation, and his consequent posing of the problem of induction, is his most important, as it is his most celebrated, contribution to the theory of knowledge."[AOE, 185] He then proceeds to examines a single instance of cause and effect. For an example he uses one billiard ball striking another and thereby causing the second ball to move. What do we observe--what idea copied from what impression--do we have? Hume points out that we observe: (1) that the events were spatially contiguous, and (2) that the event of one ball striking the other occurred immediately before the event of the second ball moving. But he says that is not enough; that there has to be a necessary connection between the two events.[AOE, 185, 186]

Thus Hume "analyzed the idea of causation into its component ideas, those of contiguity, priority in time [or succession], and necessary connection."[AOE, 186] But, "Hume emphasizes, there is nothing observable in any one instance except the mere sequence of events. The one billiard ball rolls up to the other, the two are in contact, the second moves on; there is nothing observable here that can be called a necessary connection."[AOE, 187]

> As our senses shew us in one instance two bodies, or motions, or qualities, in certain relations of succession and contiguity; so our memory presents us only with a multitude of instances wherein we always find like bodies, motions, or qualities, in like relations. From the mere repetition of any past impression, even to infinity, there never will arise any new original idea, such as that of a necessary connection. . . .[TOHN, 88]

Having found contiguity and succession essential but inadequate to the idea of cause and effect, Hume found it "necessary for us to leave the direct survey of this question concerning the nature of *necessary connection* which enters into our idea of cause and effect and . . . beat about all the neighboring fields"[TOHN, 78] in hope of finding other components of the idea of causation. After doing so (we will not follow him through it) he concludes that when considering several instances of like objects always existing in like relations of contiguity and succession that by the repetition "the mind is *determin'd* [caused] by custom. . . . 'Tis this impression, then, or determination which affords me the idea of necessity."[TOHN, 156]

> The idea of necessity . . . must, therefore, be deriv'd from some internal impressions or impressions of reflection. There is no internal impression which has any relation to the present business, but that propensity, which custom produces, to pass from an object to the idea of its usual attendant. This therefore is the essence of necessity. Upon the whole, necessity is something that exists in the mind, not in objects; nor is it possible for us ever to form the most distinct idea of it, considered as a quality in bodies.[TOHN, 165, 167]

Having done what he could with the problem of necessity, he considers some other arguments for the proof of causation, which we will skip. He finds them wanting, except for "constance conjunction" which he discovered when he "least expected it." But, he deflates constant conjunction with "it implies no more than this, that like objects have always been plac'd in like relation of contiguity and succession. . . ."[TOHN, 88] And that produces no new idea:

> Thus, not only our reason fails us in the discovery of the *ultimate connection* of causes and effects, but even after experience has informed us of their *constant conjunction*, 'tis impossible for us to satisfy ourselves by our reason, why we should extend that experience beyond those particular instances, which have fallen under our observation. We suppose, but are never able to prove, that there must be a resemblance betwixt those objects, of which we have had experience, and those which lie beyond the reach of our discovery.[TOHN, 91, 92]

He now considers that "I have just now examin'd one of the most sublime questions in philosophy, *viz., that concerning the power and efficacy of causes*.[TOHN, 156] He then gives a definition of cause which is not so much a definition as the cause of the belief in cause. "A CAUSE is an object precedent and contiguous to another, and so united with it, that the idea of the one determines the mind to form the idea of the other, and the impression of the one to form a more lively idea of the other."[TOHN, 170]

Having analyzed cause, he next gives us a definition of reason which uses all these concepts. It is an instinct just like in the other animals.

> We are conscious, that we ourselves, in adapting means to ends, are guided by reason and design, and that 'tis not ignorantly nor casually we perform those actions, which tend to self-preservation, to the obtaining pleasures, and avoiding pain. When therefore we see other creatures, in millions of instances, perform like actions, and direct them to like ends, all our principles of reason and probability carry us with an invincible force to believe the existence of a like cause.[TOHN, 176]

However in making this comparison, we must consider only "those more extraordinary instances of sagacity, which they sometimes discover for their own preservation, and propagation of their species."[TOHN, 177]

> Beasts certainly never perceive any real connection among objects. 'Tis therefore by experience they infer one from another. They can never by any argument form a general conclusion, that those objects, of which they have had no experience, resemble those of which they have. 'Tis therefore by means of custom alone, that experience operates upon them. All this was sufficiently evident with respect to man. . . .

> To consider the matter aright, reason is nothing but a wonderful and unintelligible instinct in our souls, which carries us along a certain train of ideas, and endows them with particular qualities, according to their particular situations and relations. This instinct, 'tis true, arises from past observation and experience.[TOHN, 178, 179]

Hume makes no further use of instinct to support his position. In fact, he deprecates it: "There is a great difference betwixt such opinions as we form after a calm and profound reflection, [as Hume is doing!] and such as we embrace by a kind of instinct or natural impulse, on account of their suitableness and conformity to the mind."[TOHN, 214]

Hume next discusses skepticism and argues that reason degenerates into probability. He makes this assertion regarding even mathematics, contrary to his position on "analytic" knowledge.[TOHN, 180] He finds probability degenerating into uncertainty with arguments that make no sense to me and evidently not to himself, for suddenly he comes back to earth:

> Shou'd it here be ask'd me, whether I sincerely assent to this argument, which I seem to take such pains to inculcate, and whether I be really one of those sceptics, who hold that all is uncertain, and that our judgment is not in *any* thing possest of *any* measures of truth and falshood; I shou'd reply, that this question is entirely superfluous, and that neither I, nor any other person was ever sincerely and constantly of that opinion. Nature, by an absolute and uncontroulable necessity has determin'd us to judge as well as to breathe and feel; nor can we any more forbear viewing certain objects in a stronger and fuller light, upon account of their customary connexion with a present impression, than we can hinder ourselves from thinking as long, as we are awake, or seeing the surrounding bodies, when we turn our eyes towards them in broad sunshine. Whoever has taken the pains to refute the cavils of this total scepticism, has really disputed without an antagonist, and endeavour'd by arguments to establish a faculty, which nature has antecedently implanted in the mind, and render'd unavoidable.
>
> My intention then in displaying so carefully the arguments of that fantastic sect, is only to make the reader sensible of the truth of my hypothesis, *that all our reasonings concerning causes and effects are deriv'd from nothing but custom; and that belief is more properly an act of the, sensitive, than of the cogitative part of our natures.*[TOHN, 183]

His declaration that "an absolute and uncontrollable necessity has determin'd us" in these remarks would seem to repudiate his skepticism of induction, for an absolute necessity determining us ("us" being people in the past, present and future) would be the same in the future as in the past. He then returned to the same kind of arguments that he had just denounced.

It has been observed that Hume's arguments, many of which I have omitted (this much is tedious enough), are "not the whole truth" but this

> does not detract from the crucial importance of Hume's discovery, which consists in the uncovering of the problem of induction. If all our general statements about the world were causal (and they are not), and if the word "cause" stood for some metaphysically binding cement between events, such that the one not merely never did, but *could not*, happen without the other in any circumstances, there would be no problem of induction. Our general statements would be "metaphysically" guaranteed to the hilt for unobserved as for observed cases. But Hume shows that the word "cause" does not stand for any such impalpable entity, and thus reveals to the view a hitherto largely unnoticed problem, namely that we seem to claim to know, yet never in principle do know for certain, that any generalizations based upon observed instances of phenomena remain true when extrapolated to cover unobserved instances, whether in the past or in the future.[AOE, 189]

The Cause of the Concept of Cause

With "cause" having no basis in reason, it would seem that propositions using it are neither analytic nor synthetic and therefore, according to Hume, should have been called nonsense. Nevertheless he observed that we do believe there are causes and asks what causes (my term, not his) us to do so.

> Since it is not from knowledge or any scientific reasoning, that we derive the opinion of the necessity of a cause to every new production, that opinion must necessarily arise from [be caused by?] observation and experience. The next question, then, should naturally be, *how experience gives rise to such a principle. . . .* I find it will be more convenient to sink this question in the following, *Why we conclude that such particular causes must necessarily have such particular effects, and why we form and inference from one to another?*[TOHN, 82]

Hume, having concluded that "knowledge" and "scientific reasoning" are not the causes of our belief that there are causes, sets out to find the cause, indeed to seek the knowledge of the cause, of our belief in cause. He declares that

> there is no object which implies the existence of any other, if we consider these objects in themselves, and never look beyond the ideas which we form of them. Such an inference wou'd amount to knowledge, and would imply the absolute contradiction and impossibility of conceiving anything different. But as all distinct ideas are separable, 'tis evident there can be no impossibility of that kind. When we pass from a present impression to the idea of any object, we might possibly have separated the idea from the impression, and have substituted any other idea in its room.[TOHN, 86, 87]

This in spite of the fact that he has declared that simple ideas are exact copies of simple impressions.[TOHN, 4]

> 'Tis therefore by EXPERIENCE only, that we can [do?] infer the existence of one object from that of another. The nature of experience is this. We remember to have had frequent instances of the existence of one species of objects; and also remember, that the individuals of another species of objects have always attended them, and have existed in a regular order of contiguity and succession with regard to them. Thus we remember to have seen that species of object we call *flame*, and to have felt that species of sensation we call *heat*. We likewise call to mind their constant conjunction in all past instances. Without any farther ceremony, we call the one *cause*, and the other *effect*, and infer the existence of the one from that of the other. In all those instances from which we learn the conjunction of particular causes and effects, both the cause and effects have been perceiv'd by the senses, and are remember'd. But in all cases, wherein we reason concerning them, the is only one perceiv'd or remember'd, and the other is supplied in conformity to our past experience.[TOHN, 87]

Hume is here giving the natural history of our concept of cause and effect. We do believe in cause and it comes from experience. There is a natural cause for our belief in cause. We do not, indeed cannot, arrive at it by reason--a priori--without experience.

Probability Rests on Induction

One of Hume's most important discoveries is that we cannot obtain a guarantee of the principle of induction, "that unobserved instances resemble observed instances." . . . anywhere--that we neither know, nor can know, any principle which makes induction as certain as deduction.   Nor--and here he shows more perspicacity than many of his successors in this field--can we without circularity show such a principle to be even probable: "probability is founded on the presumption of a resemblance betwixt those objects of which we have had experience, and those of which we have had none; and, therefore, it is impossible that this presumption can arise from probability." Probability rests on the unbolsterable principle of induction, and cannot itself be used to bolster it up. This is the basis of the notorious 'skepticism' of Hume and later philosophers.[AOE, 189, 190]

The Conception of an Object and the Belief That it Exists

Hume considers the nature of idea and belief--how we distinguish the conception of an object and the belief that it exists:

> The idea of an object is an essential part of the belief of it, but not the whole. We conceive many things, which we do not believe. In order, then, to discover more fully the nature of belief, or the qualities of those ideas we assent to, let us weigh the following considerations.
>
> 'Tis evident that all reasonings from causes or effects terminate in conclusions concerning matter of fact; that is, concerning the existence of objects or of their qualities. T'is also evident that the idea of existence is nothing different from the idea of any object, and when after the simple conception of anything we wou'd conceive it as existent, we in reality make no addition to or alteration on our first idea. . . . I likewise maintain that belief of the existence join no new ideas to those, which compose the idea of the object. . . . But . . . there is a great difference betwixt the simple conception of the existence of an object and the belief of it.[TOHN, 94, 95]

He gives credit to feeling and vividness:

> Nothing is more evident than that those ideas to which we assent, are more strong, firm, and vivid than the loose reveries of a castle-builder.[TOHN, 97]
>
> I conclude, by an induction which seems to me very evident, that an opinion or belief is nothing but an idea, that is different from a fiction, not in the nature, or the order of its parts, but in the *manner* of its being conceived. . . . An idea assented to *feels* different from a fictitious idea, that the fancy alone presents to us. And this different feeling I endeavor to explain by calling it a superior

> *force*, of *vivacity*, or *solidity*, or *firmness*, or *steadiness*. . . . I confess that it is impossible to explain perfectly this feeling or manner of conception.[TOHN, 628, 629]

The "imagination" cannot be responsible for belief:

> The imagination has the command over all its ideas, and can join, and mix, and vary them in all the ways possible. It may conceive objects with all the circumstances of place and time. It may set them, in a manner, before our eyes in their true colors, just as they might have existed. But it is impossible, that that faculty can ever, of itself, reach belief, 'tis evident that belief consists not in the nature and order of our ideas, but in the manner of their conception, and in their feeling to the mind. . . . *belief*, . . . is something *felt* by the mind, which distinguishes the ideas of judgement from the fictions of the imagination.[TOHN, 629]

We have previously noted three degrees of vivacity in the ideas in Hume's theories (page 100). He does not tell us where this fourth one fits in with the others.

Our Belief in the Existence of Body

Hume tells us that concerning our belief in the existence of body we

> cannot pretend by any arguments of philosophy to maintain its veracity. Nature has not left this to his choice, and has doubtless steem'd it an affair of too great importance to be trusted to our uncertain reasonings and speculations. We may well ask, *What causes induce us to believe in the existence of body?* but 'tis in vain to ask, *Whether there be body or not?* That is a point which we must take for granted in all our reasonings.[TOHN, 187]

Hume divides the question of what causes us to believe in the existence of body into two questions:

> Why we attribute a CONTINU'D existence to objects, even when they are not present to the senses; and why we suppose them to have an existence DISTINCT from the mind and perception. Under this last head I comprehend their situation as well as relations, their *external* position as well as the *independence* of their existence and operation. . . . and shall consider, whether it be, the *senses*, *reason*, or the *imagination*, that produces the opinion of a *continu'd* or of a *distinct* existence. These are the only questions that are intelligible on the

present subject. For as to the notion of external existence, when taken for something specifically different from our perceptions, we have already shown its absurdity.[TOHN,188] [see page 108]

I will limit the following account mostly to his conclusions. First, it is not the senses that cause our opinion of a continued or of a distinct existence "because they convey to us nothing but a single perception, and never give us the least intimation of anything beyond."[TOHN, 189] "As far as the senses are judges, all perceptions are the same in the manner of their existence."[TOHN, 193]

And what about reason? If we

> take our perceptions and objects to be the same, we can never infer the existence of the one from the other. . . . Even after we distinguish our perceptions from our objects, 'twill appear presently, that we are still incapable of reasoning from the existence of one to that of the other: So that, upon the whole, our reason neither does, nor is it possible it ever shou'd, upon any supposition, give us an assurance of the continu'd and distinct existence of body.[TOHN, 193]

The senses and reason do not cause us to believe in body, so, what is left? Hume tells us "that opinion must be entirely owing to the IMAGINATION: which must now be the subject of our enquiry."[TOHN, 193] He gives his theory of how it happens:

> After a little examination, we shall find, that all those objects, to which we attribute a continu'd existence, have a peculiar *constancy*, which distinguishes them from the impressions, whose existence depends upon our perception. Those mountains, and houses, and trees, which lie at present under my eye, have always appear'd to me in the same order; and when I lose sight of them by shutting my eyes or turning my head, I soon after find them return upon me without the least alteration. . . .
>
> This constancy, however, is not so perfect as not to admit of very considerable exceptions. Bodies often change their position and qualities, and after a little absence or interruption may become hardly knowable. But here 'tis observable, that even in these changes they preserve a *coherence*, and have a regular dependence on each other; which is the foundation of a kind of reasoning from causation, and produces the opinion of their continu'd existence.[TOHN, 194, 195]

Hume has been interpreted as producing a philosophy of skepticism of the "identity" of material objects--those mountains, houses, and trees, in the quotation above--but in the quotation below he is skeptical only of reason and the senses.

> This skeptical doubt, both with respect to reason and the senses, is a malady, which can never be radically cur'd, but must return upon us every moment, however we may chace it away, and sometimes may seem entirely free from it. . . . As the skeptical doubt arises naturally from a profound and intense reflection on those subjects, . . . carelessness and in-attention alone can afford us any remedy.[TOHN, 218]

That is, a profound and intense reflection produces a skeptical doubt of reason and the senses, and it is only by carelessness and inattention that we will not be skeptical.

Mind

Hume does believe that his arguments produce a skepticism (which he disregards as soon as he lays down his pen). "We have no perfect idea of anything but a perception. A substance is entirely different from a perception. We have therefore no idea of a substance."[TOHN, 234] He accepts the position of Berkeley that we have no idea of external substance, distinct from the ideas of particular qualities and that the same is true as regards the mind which Berkeley said we have a "notion" of. The self [mind], he says, must by definition continue invariably the same, and we experience no such thing.

> If any impression gives rise to the idea of self, the impression must continue invariably the same, thro' the whole course of our lives; since self is suppos'd to exist after that manner. But there is no impression constant and invariable.[TOHN, 251]
>
> That what we call a *mind* is nothing but a heap or collection of different perceptions, united together by different relations, and suppos'd, tho' falsely, to be endow'd with a perfect simplicity and identity. . . .[TOHN, 207]
>
> For my part, when I enter most intimately into what I call *myself*, I always stumble on some particular perception or other, of heat or cold, light or shade, love or hatred, pain or pleasure, I never can catch *myself* at any time without a perception, and can never observe anything but the perception. When my perceptions are remov'd for any time, as by sound sleep, so long am I insensible to *myself*, and may truly be said to not exist. And were all my perceptions remov'd by death, and cou'd I neither think, nor feel, nor see, nor love, nor hate, after the dissolution of my body, I should be entirely annihilated; nor do

I conceive what is further requisite to name me a perfect non-entity. . . .

But setting aside some metaphysicians . . . I may venture to affirm of the rest of mankind that they are nothing but a bundle or collections of different perceptions, which succeed each other with inconceivable rapidity, and are in perpetual flux. . . . The successive perceptions . . . constitute the mind.[TOHN, 252, 253]

Hume did make a point about identity, and mind (above) is a case in point. "Perfect simplicity and identity" is the key term here. Let us consider an oak tree or a man. An oak tree is not exactly the same thing one year as it was the previous one. It is heaver, has more cells, some twigs and limbs die and fall off, etc. An old man may not have any of the cells he was born with, but you get the idea. Hume is right about identity, but we needn't get upset about it. We have no trouble with common usage in calling and old tree or a man the same *thing* all their lives even when the man's "mind is gone." Each has a unique history of changes that identifies them. This is the rationale for identity. But to give Hume his due, I will be in some agreement with him in my theory of the mind.

In the end Hume's philosophy left him melancholy. In the conclusion of Book I of the *Treatise* he wrote,

Most fortunately it happens, that since reason is incapable of dispelling these clouds, nature herself suffices to that purpose, and cures me of this philosophical melancholy and delirium, either by relaxing this bent of mind, or by some avocation, and lively impression of my senses, which obliterate all these chimeras. I dine, I play a game of back-gammon, I converse, and am merry with my friends; and when after three of four hours' amusement, I wou'd return to these speculations, they appear so cold, and strain'd and ridiculous, that I cannot find in my heart to enter into them any farther.[TOHN, 269]

However, this is not his last word. He still thinks his philosophy is valuable; better than superstition, for one thing.[TOHN, 271] In other writings he expressed a completely naturalistic outlook and abandoned the insistence that we can look no further into reality than our impressions and abandons or ignores his "skepticism" of induction, if in fact he was skeptical. We may infer that he embraces induction as the underlying principle of reason. This we see in the second paragraph below. Hume on miracles,

No testimony is sufficient to establish a miracle, unless the testimony be of such a kind that its falsehood would be more miraculous than the fact which it endeavors to establish. . . . When anyone tells me that he saw a dead man restored to life, I immediately consider with myself whether it be more probable that this person should either deceive or be deceived, or that the fact which he relates should really have happened. I weigh the one miracle against the other; and according to the superiority which I discover I . . . reject the greater miracle. There is not to be found in all history any miracle attested by a sufficient number of men, of such unquestioned good sense, education, and learning, as to secure us against all delusions in themselves; of such undoubted integrity as to place them beyond all suspicions of any design to deceive others; of such credit and reputation in the eyes of mankind as to have a great deal to lose in case of their being detected in any falsehood; and at the same time attesting facts performed in such a public manner, and in so celebrated a part of the world, as to render the detection unavoidable: all which circumstances are requisite to give us a full assurance in the testimony of men. . . .

The maxim by which we commonly conduct ourselves in our reasonings is that the objects of which we have no experience resemble those of which we have; that what we have found to be most usual is always most probable; and that where there is an opposition of arguments, we aught to give the preference to such as are founded on the greatest number of past observations. . . . It forms a strong presumption against all supernatural and miraculous relations, that they are observed chiefly to abound among ignorant and barbarous nations. . . . or [among civilized people] received. . . from ignorant and barbarous ancestors. . . . It is strange . . . that such prodigious events never happen in our days. But it is nothing strange . . . that men should lie in all ages.[AECH]

Morals

Hume argues that moral distinctions are not derived from reason and that virtue is not the same with what is natural and vice with what is unnatural. In a paragraph he poses the moral problem.

In every system of morality, which I have hitherto met with, I have always remark'd, that the author proceeds for some time in the ordinary way of reasoning, and establishes the being of a God, or makes observations concerning human affairs; when of a sudden I am surpriz'd to find, that instead of the usual copulations of propositions, *is*, and *is not*, I meet with no proposition that is not connected with an *ought*, or an *ought not*. This change is imperceptible; but is, however, of the last consequence. For as this *ought*, or *ought not*, expresses some new relation or affirmation, 'tis necessary that it shou'd be observ'd and explain'd; and at the same time that a reason should be given, for what seems altogether inconceivable, how this new relation can be a deduction from others, which are entirely different from it. . . . I shall presume to recommend it to the readers; and am persuaded, that this small attention wou'd subvert all the vulgar systems of morality.[TOHN, 469]

Hume held, quite rightly, I believe, that there is no deductive relation between an "is" and an "ought." This is sometimes known as Hume's law. I will have occasion to mention this again on page 215.

Criticism

Hume in the end (before he laid down his pen) could find neither mind nor body with his method of looking for an impression for verification. What can we make of Hume's analysis of the mind or of his analyzing it out of existence, for, as we have seen, in the beginning

> Hume seems to think of "the mind" as a real entity or agent experiencing, possessing, remembering, or judging impressions or ideas. As he proceeds, however, he denies the existence of any mind additional to the mental states--to the impressions, perceptions, idea, feeling, of desire occupying consciousness at the moment.[AOV, 143]

His road to a mindless mind begins with his division of the contents of the mind into impressions and ideas, the latter being an exact copy of the former. He has two methods, not entirely congruent, for distinguishing impressions and ideas: (1) The difference in force and liveliness with which they strike upon the mind, impressions having the greater force, and (2) The sequence in which they occur, impressions being those that make their first appearance in the "soul" [mind?], while ideas are the images of impressions that appear in thinking and reasoning.

This sensing double, an "impression" and an "idea," is no improvement over Locke's "idea." The impression has an unknown cause according to Hume, and disappears immediately after it occurs. It is hard to see any place for the it. Does he mean in the case of seeing, for example, that the impression is the sensation of light striking the eye plus the transmission of the image to the brain with the result being "idea"? If this is the case there would be no way Hume could distinguish a difference in force and liveliness between the two, for two reasons. (1) The idea that comes with seeing is for all practical purposes, the speed of light and electrons being what they are, immediate, and can be detected only as one sensation. (2) The function of the eye and nervous system, in the event of seeing, is below the level of consciousness. We are conscious only of the end product, the image or idea.

Or, does he mean that the impression is really an idea that makes a copy of itself and stores it in the mind? The idea is an exact copy of the impression, according to Hume; therefore, it is hard to see the impression as anything other than an idea. Would not an *exact copy* of an impression be another impression and, if an idea in one case, be an idea in the other? The interpretation that some have made, which seems to be supported by Hume's own words (page 100) that impressions are the immediately given data and that (the original) ideas are the images of memory, is contradicted by Hume's account of the memory (page 103). The memory is functioning, Hume tells us, when the impression makes another (second, third, etc.) appearance as an idea (so impressions are ideas) with a vivacity intermediate between an [original?] impression and an idea (and is an exact copy if there is no "defect or imperfection in that faculty"). Is this the original impression (of an unknown cause) which meanwhile had disappeared, (impressions are "perishing existences") reappearing on the scene, or is it another new impression, caused this time by the original idea? The first solution is a little spooky and the second does not occur, for Hume (page 101) has "proven" that the impression is the cause of the idea, not the other way around.

Even if the impressions and exact copy theory is valid, it is worthless in the analysis of knowledge for the simple reason that we do virtually all of our "thinking and reasoning" with what we remember--from the data of experience--plus whatever ideas or concepts past thinking and reasoning has produced. For, however vivid the experience that results in an idea, when we use it in thinking, it is history. However short the interval between the experience and the use of it, time has passed. If we use sitting on a tack as the paradigm of a possible exception and claim that the idea is instantaneous with the experience (Hume's impression) then we abandon Hume's claim that the idea is a copy of the impression. In any case, we have to abandon Hume's contention that our ideas are *exact* copies of original experience. When we remember having sat on a tack we remember just that, that we sat on the tack; we do not have the pain which would be an exact copy. Hume tell us this himself (page, 101). We do not "perceive any colour, or feel any sensation merely upon thinking of them." This poses the question, What is memory but "thinking of them?"

To repeat, *we do our thinking and reasoning from history--from data.* However well or poorly remembered, we use the record that remains in our mind (or computer or notebook). "Sense data" is the term often used by philosophers for this record. Our rejection of part of Hume's analysis does not, however, refute the thesis of empiricism that all knowledge is from experience, nor does this thesis rule out the existence of a substantial mind. More about this when we get to Immanuel Kant.

Is Hume's system of different degrees of vivacity credible as a means of telling the various types of ideas, four in all, apart? I think we can be sure that Hume experienced no such thing; that he never asked himself when he had an idea, "is this the right vivacity to be an original idea or a memory?" In the case of having an idea a second time, he could say accurately that I had this idea before, therefore this is a memory, but we can be sure that he didn't do that either. In the case of memory and the original experience or idea, no one needs such criteria to tell them apart. We can go back to Locke for a term. We do it "ostensively." The whole business of different degrees of vivacity to tell types of ideas apart is not credible.

In Hume's account of the origin of knowledge as caused by experience, his scenario of impressions and ideas is the detailed, step by step, history of how it occurs, and he says that it cannot happen any other way. If you cannot find an impression of a particular thing, you can be sure that you have no idea of it. Yet, he says we have the idea of cause and its principal component, necessary connection, although we observe no such thing (have no impression of it), contradicting himself. He them determines that we get the idea of causation from experience: the mind supplies it after the experience of observing constant conjunction and contiguity and succession in objects (events) (see page 114). Here he uses the word experience as if it were something that he had not been talking about all of the time.

He is dangerously close to abandoning his oft-expressed rule that every idea comes from an impression alone in his insistence that the idea of necessary connection comes from internal impressions or impressions of reflection. In this regard the use of the term "propensity" (page 110) takes him close to Kant's "Categories" (faculties of several kinds that are partners with experience in producing knowledge, discussed on page 145). Even if he has discovered an impression for the idea, it gives only the cause of the idea, according to Hume's theory, not that the idea is true. (It is his main contention that there is no proof of causation, however much we believe in it.) It does not prove that there is such a thing as causation.

Hume's "skepticism" of causation still holds, but there is a flaw in his words, namely, that there is no proof that unobserved instances resemble observed instances (or that the future will be like the past). There is the assumption in this statement that causation is working in observed cases, which is not consistent with his criteria. His criteria are that we have only observed constant conjunction and contiguity and succession, not causation, therefore, his position has to be, to be consistent, that we do not observe causation *anytime*. Neither reason nor experience prove causation *anytime*. He assumes causation to be valid in stating that we cannot validate it. He uses it as unquestioned in questioning it. He was believing in it while declaring that there is no reason to believe in it. Had he said that there is no proof that constant conjunction and succession will be the same in the future as in the past, there would be no error.

As to induction, of which causation is central, Hume held that we have no power to reason "a priori" that induction is valid, and we do not observe it. We observe only the sequence of events and constant conjunction. Not only did experience as pure (direct) observation fail, but experience as demonstration fails, for any attempt to prove induction by repeating an experiment assumes what you are trying to prove. You are assuming induction to prove induction. Philosophers have been so impressed with Hume's argument that it has been called the scandal of philosophy.

Although Hume found correctly that neither reason nor experience prove induction, he (and we) are still convinced of its validity. Induction was a basic assumption of Hume's empiricism, and furthermore, he assumes it in a quotation (on page 111). When he says "we suppose but are never able to prove," he did not say that we suppose once, nor that supposition has merely occurred; but as stated, it refers to all people of all time, an assumption that there is a resemblance between those instances of which we have experience and those of which we have not. I do not see any legitimate "skepticism" in this. If we cannot argue against induction without assuming it to be true we have no case against it.

Therefore, Hume did not make a skepticism of causation, rather, a skepticism of a method of proving it by reason. *He finally got it right*, if only in passing, when he said (page 111) that "reason is nothing but a wonderfull and unintelligible instinct in our souls, . ." In taking this position, he was saying that the basic assumption of science, namely that inductive reasoning is valid, is an instinct, and he leaves his narrowly constructed or radical empiricism, however briefly, and again takes a step in the direction of Kant's categories, which will soon be discussed. Custom, to which Hume attributes the cause of belief in causation and induction, is not an adequate term, for how do we come to accept it by custom but instinctively? It is an instinct or congenital faculty which is present when we have experience. I have found a use for some scholastic terms. The instinct is a *potential* that is *actualized* by experience. Hume was right that (the idea of) this instinct arises from past observation and experience (page 114), but it is not direct observation of the instinct. Rather, it is observation of behavior, and detecting the instinct (part of the mind) involves inference, a method he would not or did not use in the search for the (whole) mind. (We infer that animals, including the human, have instincts after our observing behavior we believe not to be cognitive.)

Having declared reason an instinct, he did not seem aware that this position undermined his skeptical arguments. Just as probability rest on induction, (as he has told us) the judgement that there are instincts involves the inductive process. At bottom what we are concerned with in making these judgements is universal natural law.

After declaring reason an instinct, Hume continued on with nearly 100 pages of his skepticism, leaving us neither mind nor body in its wake, and leaving it to Kant to fill in the specific instincts. His asking where is the impression for every idea, lead him to declare that we have no idea of the mind, nor, for that matter, body. He found no impression for either.

Somewhere in Hume's thinking, impressions lost their meaning as information *about* things impressed on, or given to, the mind. The terminology changed to "perceptions," which presumably was a synonym for impressions and/or ideas and he said that "we have no perfect idea of anything but a perception."[TOHN, 234] We do not observe a mind. He proceeded to claim that impressions revealed only a "heap or collection of different perceptions;" that the mind is "nothing but a bundle or collection of different perceptions which succeed each other with inconceivable rapidity, and are in perpetual flux"[TOHN, 253] and that the successive perceptions constitute the mind. Some job, bundling up those different perceptions which succeed each other with inconceivable rapidity. Hume trapped himself "within the sphere of his own experience without even the assurance of a self to whom that experience belongs."FDTW, 132

Given Hume's uncompromising insistence regarding causation, that we only observe constant conjunction and sequence of events, not causation, he is inconsistent in the case of the association of ideas (page 104). There he claimed that there is a "principle of union." His position should have been that he observed no such thing as a union only constant conjunction.

It is important to note that Hume, in laying out his theory of impressions and ideas (the contents of the mind), assumes quite a substantial mind other than, or in addition to, it being a bundle of impressions: that which has ideas as contents; that on which impressions strike with force and liveliness; that which uses ideas in thinking and reasoning; that which has passions and emotions; that which sleeps; and that which is conscious, page 100. There are the faculties which give rise to any impression, page 101; that which has creative powers, page 103; and that which associates ideas, page 104; that which recalls, page 105; that which beats about all the neighboring fields, page 110; that which supposes and infers, page 111; the necessity that exists in the mind, page 110; that which has instincts, page 111; that which reflects and has opinions, page 112; that which remembers, page 114; that which conceives and assents, page 115. There is the imagination which has command over all its ideas; that which has the simple conception of the existence of an object and that which has the belief that the object exists; that which feels the difference in vivacity and force, pages 115 & 116; There is that which makes a "profound and intense reflection" on certain subjects, and that which has "skeptical doubt, both with respect to reason and the senses", page 118. This does not attain to Kant's categories (listed on page 145) but what else but the mind could be doing these things? What else could this arsenal of faculties be but the mind? And, there is the fancy and the understanding.

Why could Hume not make the inference from all this that there is a mind? He had no trouble in inferring the "association of ideas." He points to no impression for it. Rather, he tells us (page 104) that "it is impossible the same simple ideas should fall regularly into complex ones (as they Commonly do) without . . . some associating quality," a universal principle. Thus, he is holding it to be a matter of logic, abandoning his rule that there has to be an impression for there to be an idea.

Hume was so close to his mind that he couldn't see it. In light of this, his skepticism of a mind, as other than impressions, is not credible and is even ridiculous.   However, I will salvage something from his "bundle of impressions" theory in my theory of the mind (page 193).

"Body" gets much the same treatment as mind. In contradiction to his empirical premises, he says that the senses do not inform us of the existence of body or in his words, a continued and distinct existence, "because they convey to us nothing but a single perception, and never give us the least intimation of anything beyond" (page 117). Perception, that is, experience, has lost its meaning as perception *of* things--as that from which knowledge comes.   He believes that he has shown the absurdity of the "notion of external existence when taken for something specifically different from our perceptions" (page 116). Shades of Berkeley! It is obvious that we (except for a few philosophers) do believe in "external existences." Hume admits this--and it is his *mind* that does the admitting--and, although he found that neither the senses nor reason cause us to believe in body, he found imagination doing the job, and it (imagination) found constancy and coherence which produced the opinion of continued existence.

Hume concluded, as we have seen (page 118), that "as a skeptical doubt arises naturally from a profound and intense reflection on those subjects [reason and the senses] . . . carelessness and inattention alone can afford them any remedy." He could not, consistent with the quote above, be skeptical of the existence of those bodies (persons) who reflect intensely and those that are careless and inattentive, bodies (objects) on a par with the mountains, houses, and trees. Some objects had to be assumed in order to raise the question. He could not produce a valid argument that they could not exist based on the assumption that they do.

I dismiss Hume's skepticism as to mind and body as perhaps due to carelessness and inattention. Empiricism, the theory that knowledge comes from experience, presupposes the existence of things, from humans to rocks, about which knowledge is acquired. We will find Kant arguing (page 146) that radical skepticism presupposes its own falsehood.

The analytic/synthetic distinction, has had a lot of attention by philosophers and has been considered a milestone in philosophy. It has been said (written in 1956) to be "of great importance in philosophy today,"[AOR, 148] but I suspect that it is worth little.   A. J. Ayer, who accepted it as a pillar of his early philosophy, wrote in 1982 that it had been put in question.[PTC, 140]

One philosopher who questions it is W. V. Quine. He calls it a dogma of empiricism and attacks the claim of logical identity in the cases of semantic propositions such as 'all bachelors are unmarried men'. "Quine's objection is that we lack any criterion for synonymity."[PTC, 245] Synonymous or not, it is of little importance. Semantic propositions arise or exist and get their authority by common usage. The fact that the subject is synonymous with the predicate is incidental to that fact (and nothing to make a fuss about), and it is a matter of experience to discover it--look it up in the dictionary, for example.

Is "Reason is an instinct" analytic or synthetic or nonsense? Assuming it to be true, as we are, we cannot call it nonsense. Hume has gone to great pains to show that we cannot prove it empirically or by reason, so it is not synthetic. It is not a tautology, as instinct is non-cognitive, and reason is cognitive.

There is something subversive of the intellect in saying that mathematics and definitions (analytic) are certain, known a priori. "The subject is in the predicate" leads the way in this subversion. This is so obvious in the "proposition" that $2 + 3 = 5$, or that "all single men are bachelors" that it seems safe to declare that such sentences are known without experience, are certain and give no knowledge about the world; the subject is in the predicate, therefore you already have the "answer" before you get it.

All of this is lost on school boys and girls struggling with algebra and unfamiliar terms. These "propositions" are obvious to almost everyone because before reading them here they had *learned by experience* the meaning that has been given to the terms in them--learned by experience either by hearing how the terms are used or by looking them up in a dictionary. Learning definitions is a constant process--experience--in an education which begins with a baby's first words. Learning language is to a significant degree having new terms put in familiar ones learned by experience or by other terms that have been defined for us in familiar terms the history of which leads back to experience. This is not to claim that all we learn by experiences has been or can be articulated.

That "1 and 1 and 1 and 1 and 1 = 5" and that "all single men are bachelors" are conventions, and conventions are learned by experience. We can say that 1 and 1 and 1 and 1 and 1 are collectively 5 be cause we have agreed to the word five and the symbol 5 to be used for that purpose.

Likewise we can say that all single men are bachelors because we have agreed to use that term for that purpose. To use a term or symbol in a way agreed to for the purpose of communication is not to know something a priori. We learn all our terms and symbols by experience. Therefore, it is my position that "knowing a priori" is not a distinguishing characteristic of so called analytic propositions.

The ridiculousness of the claim that mathematics is certain as opposed to "problematic science," is exposed by the fact that we are most accurate in mathematics when we use a computer, a product of "problematic" science. If Hume really believed that the predicate gives no information, it would have been sporting of him to declare it unnecessary.

And what about "non-contradiction" being the verifying characteristic of analyticity? As such, non-contradiction is, reputedly, the test for truth, but can a problem be simply and directly tested for contradiction? It may appear so in the case of $2 + 3 = 5$, but what about a long column of five digit numbers. To find if it contradicts, one must add the numbers to see if they are correct, and is not that what we do in the case of $2 + 3 = 5$, but so quickly there can be the illusion of checking for contradiction? Non-contradiction is a fact found only by the test of correctness or consistency (by the *experience* of testing, Hume forgive us!). It is derivative at best or synonymous (after the test) at worst, take your choice, not heuristic.

The reader now, I suspect, is asking, "But isn't it absurd to doubt that $2 + 3 = 5$?" Of course it is, and on a par with doubting that a baseball can be hit with a bat. Here we are at the point where "reason" begins. We assume that balls and bats and symbols for quantity will function in the future as in the past. If, instead of using such a simple example of the analytic, we use a complicated one from higher mathematics, one which only a computer can do in a relatively short time, and, if then we observe the problem and a *reputed* answer, and only the problem and the reputed answer, it would be absurd to say that it is true and absurd to say that it is false (for the simple reason that we cannot determine the answer). For those of us who could not work the problem, we can claim to know it to be true or false only on the testimony of a competent mathematician and we have to trust our experience in judging mathematicians. Here we have reached a point where we know something (by experience) about the world, namely, that there are people (something in the world) who do not know some propositions a priori of the type which Hume said are known a priori.

In the ordinary affairs of life, in the task of applying means to ends, in seeking answers to questions, mathematics and (tautological) definitions go hand in hand with experience.

Logic is not a self-contained metaphysical realm, separate from life. Logic is based on constants, experienced constants, in the universe, in nature. Those basics in traditional logic, "identity, contradiction, and excluded middle" and the "doctrine that these laws are in a special sense fundamental presuppositions of reasoning,"[DOP, 197] get their validity from intrinsic characteristics of the universe (nature). These three "elements" (propositions) of logic assume that (empirically identifiable) things exist, that things are what they are and not something else, and that a thing cannot both be a certain kind of thing and not be that certain kind of thing--no middle ground between "is" and "is not." Logic is simply a part, a guiding part, of naturalism--the intelligible rules of discourse.

I trust that I have sufficiently blurred the distinction between the analytic and synthetic, but there is another category of propositions in Hume's analysis, that of nonsense. We have seen that he (page 109) gave as examples of this category "any volume of divinity or school metaphysics" This reflects the fact that before and during Hume's time metaphysics was permeated with "divinity." Elsewhere, he had harsher words, a little too harsh perhaps: ". . . its [metaphysics'] rash arrogance, its lofty pretensions, and its superstitious credulity."[DH, 23] As one who has shed some theology, I empathize with Hume and agree that metaphysics is nonsense. This is not to say that metaphysical ideas do not have effects. In my theory of the mind, I will insist that they have the most profound ones.

Hume is correct about space and time. The concepts come directly from experience. We observe aspects of physical objects not space and time, although these are not his terms. More about this when we get to Kant.

Hume scored again with his discovery that probability rests on induction, a simple fact that is missed by philosophers who call science probabilistic.

Initially he seemed as perspicacious about existence as about space and time (page 107) but soon we see him retreating into his own mind. I have no problem with his saying that nothing is present to the mind except its perceptions, but in the next paragraph he makes one of his forays into idealism when he says that we cannot conceive any kind of existence but those perceptions.

Hume didn't get far in trying to determine the difference between the conception of an object and the belief that it exists. Subjectively we know in our own cases immediately, but, I would guess, we do not feel a difference in force as Hume suggests. I have what little I have to say about this in my theory of the mind.

Despite many shortcomings, Hume made important contributions to philosophy. Did he make a "scandal of philosophy?" It is an apt phrase, but only a scandal for a priorism. The real scandal is that philosophers have let Hume get away with so much faulty reasoning in other areas.

Empiricism, a Disappointment

For all its beginning as a science, the empiricism of Locke, Berkeley, and Hume was a big disappointment to me. Despite empiricism's victory over rationalism (what we might call the philosopher's conceit--that belief that wisdom can be pulled out of a hat with a metaphysicians head in it) empiricism fell short of it's early promise. As I see it, it was science aborted in the first trimester. After a respectable beginning, empiricism drifted in the direction of idealism. Among Locke's problems, was his use of the inadequate concepts, current in his time and a holdover from the scholastics, of qualities and substance. He missed the advice of Leucippus that "all qualitative differences in nature may be reduced to quantitative ones." It is clear (to repeat) "that natural processes must be explained by laws of nature expressed in quantitative terms; . . . if nature is to be understood as the manifestation of mathematically precise natural laws, . . . the divisions into kinds by perceived qualitative differences becomes irrelevant and have no important place in the organization of scientific knowledge."[AOR, 12, 13]

Locke's work lost all semblance of science when he reached the point of saying, "Since the mind in all its thoughts and reasonings hath no other immediate object but its own ideas . . . it is evident that our knowledge is only conversant about them." His arguments inevitably degenerated from a beginning as science to the verge of that abyss, idealism. In the end ideas, in the hands of the empiricists, become a screen which shields us from the "external world." It is a small step from Locke's world of "all we have is ideas" (my words, not his) to "ideas are everything" (again, my words), which is what empiricism becomes in the hands of Berkeley, who, with arguments too silly in my view to contemplate, confounds sensing with things sensed; and, to a degree with Hume, with his conclusion (to quote it again) that "we have no perfect idea of anything but a perception," and his claim that he had "shown the absurdity of the notion of external existence when taken for something specifically different from our perceptions." These remarks are as laughable as some of Berkeley's. All this came many pages after that brave beginning with science. Hume began with science in full flower and ended with an emasculated empiricism without known parents and with no hope of progeny.

Hume found the mind in the end to be only impressions. "Berkeley had demolished materialism by reducing matter to mind; Hume compounded the destruction by reducing mind to ideas. Neither 'matter' nor 'mind' exists. Forgivably the wits of the time dismissed both philosophers with 'no matter; never mind.' "[AOV, 143]

Hume found correctly that rationalism as well as empiricism could not prove the validity of induction, but he was using induction from the outset. There is nothing more fundamental in empiricism than induction. "Belief in experience is belief in nature, however vaguely nature may as yet be conceived, and every empiricists is a naturalist in principle, however hesitant his naturalism may be in practice."[SAAF, 142]

In the end, Hume's "impressions" revealed nothing but themselves, negating his original claim that they would make a science of man. It is disgusting to read his arguments that render experience impotent. "Experience, at its very inception, is a revelation of *things*."[SAAF, 189]

NATURALISM IN OTHER THAN PHILOSOPHY PROPER IN THE ENLIGHTENMENT

The European Enlightenment (roughly the eighteenth century), that philosophical movement that emphasized the use of reason to scrutinize previously accepted doctrines and traditions and brought about many humanitarian reforms, was not confined to the philosophers I have been quoting. It was a wide-spread movement among the educated. Christianity, the purveyor of the doctrines and traditions, bore the brunt of the attack. In England deism was a notable movement. I will quote only one.

Matthew Tindal (1657-1730)

In the first volume (a second was destroyed by a bishop) of *Christianity as Old as the Creation,* 1730,

Tindal ranged with no tender mercy through all the fantasies of theology. He asked why God should have given his revelation to one small people, the Jews, had let it remain their exclusive possession for four thousand years, and then had sent his son to them with another revelation that after seventeen hundred years was still confined to a minority of the human race. What sort of god could this be who used such clumsy methods with such tardy and inadequate results? What ogre of a god was this who punished Adam and Eve for seeking knowledge, and then punished all their posterity merely for being born? We are told that the absurdities in the Bible are due to God's adapting his speech to the language and ideas of his hearers. What nonsense! Why could he not speak the simple truth to them intelligibly? Why should he have used priests as his intermediaries instead of speaking directly to every man's soul? Why should he have allowed his specially revealed religion to become an engine of persecution, terror, and strife, leaving men no better morally, after centuries of this dispensation, than before?--making them, indeed, more fierce and cruel than under the pagan cults! Is there not a finer morality in Confucius or Cicero than in the Christianity of history? The real revelation is in Nature herself, and in man's God-given reason; the real God is the God that Newton revealed, the designer of a marvelous world operating majestically according to invariable law; and the real morality is the life of reason in harmony with nature.[AOV, 121]

The Philosophes

In France the *philosophes* (as distinguished from *philosopher*), namely those French philosophers who joined the attack upon Christianity, not only the dogma but the censorship and persecution, carried the principal part of the battle. What had begun as a campaign against superstition became a war against Christianity. Among the *Philosophes* was Voltaire who was the most prolific and influential writer of the century. But, for a sample of the attack, which was toward a more naturalistic outlook, we pass up these luminaries and turn to a catholic priest.

Jean Meslier (1678-1733)

One Catholic priest, Jean Meslier saw his church and its theology in naturalistic terms. To best understand his remarks we need to look at the Church at the time, and its relations with the people and the state.

In France the Church was a powerful organization owning a large share of the national wealth and soil, and yet bound by supreme allegiance to a foreign power. It seemed to be draining more wealth from secular into ecclesiastical hands through its role in the making of wills and the guidance of bequests, it refused to pay taxes beyond its occasional "gratuitous gift"; it held thousands of peasants in practical serfdom on its lands; it maintained monks in what seemed to be fruitless idleness. It had repeatedly profited from false documents and bogus miracles. It controlled nearly all schools and universities, through which it inoculated the minds of the young with stupefying absurdities. It denounced as heresy any teaching contrary to its own, and used the state to enforce its censorship over speech and press. It had done its best to choke the intellectual development of France. It had urged Louis XIV into the inhuman persecutions of the Huguenots, and the heartless destruction of Port-Royal. It had been guilty of barbarous campaigns against the Albigenses, and of sanctioning massacres like that of St. Bartholomew's Day; it had fomented religious wars that had almost ruined France. And amid all these crimes against the human spirit it had pretended, and had made millions of simple people believe, that it was above and beyond reason and questioning, that it had inherited a divine revelation, that it was the infallible and divinely inspired vicegerent of God, and that its crimes were as much the will of God as were its charities.[AOV, 608]

Jean Meslier was born in 1678 and became the parish priest "of Etrepigny in Champagne. . . . Devoted in all his duties, every year he gave what remained of his salary to the poor of his parishes; enthusiastic, and of rigid virtue, he was very temperate, . . . At his death. . . in 1733. . . he gave all he possessed, which was inconsiderable, to his parishioners, and desired to be buried in his garden."[SIAA, 27]

> They were greatly surprised to find in his house three manuscripts, each containing three hundred and sixty pages, all written by his hand, signed and entitled by him "*My Testament.*". . . [It] is a simple refutation of all the religious dogmas without excepting one. . . .
>
> Meslier had written upon a gray paper which enveloped the copy to his parishioners these remarkable words: "I have seen and recognized the errors, the abuses, the follies, and the wickedness of men. I have hated and despised them. I did not dare say it during my life, but I will say it at last in dying, and after my death; and it is that it may be known, that I write this present memorial in order that it may serve as a witness of truth to all those who may see and read it if they choose.". . . I do not sacrifice my belief to any vile interest. If I embraced a profession so directly opposed to my sentiments, it was not through cupidity. I obeyed my parents. . . .
>
> I call heaven to witness that I also thoroughly despised those who laughed at the simplicity of the blind people, those who furnished piously considerable sums of money to buy prayers. How horrible this monopoly! I do not blame the disdain which those who grow rich by your sweat and your pains, show for their mysteries and their superstitions; but I detest their insatiable cupidity and the signal pleasure such fellows take in railing at the ignorance of those whom they carefully keep in this state of blindness. . . .
>
> I carefully avoided exhorting you to bigotry, and I spoke to you as rarely as possible of our unfortunate dogmas. It was necessary that I should acquit myself as a priest of my ministry, but how often have not suffered within myself when I was forced to preach to those pious lies which I despised in my heart. What remorse I had for exciting your credulity. A thousand times upon the point of bursting forth publicly, I was going to open your eyes, but a fear superior to my strength restrained me and forced me to silence until my death.[SIAA, 29-31]

I think of Spinoza when I read this. Although he was a little more open about his beliefs than Meslier, he feared to publish in his lifetime the book that he had poured his heart and mind into. I think a little about myself, also. Meslier must have relieved his loneliness by sanctifying his thoughts in ink and paper. In all the campaign against Christianity, there was no attack so thoroughgoing and merciless, as his.

He dispenses with God. "Is it not more natural and more intelligent to deduce all which exists, from the bosom of matter, whose existence is demonstrated by all our senses, whose effects we feel at every moment. . . "[SIAA, 56] He will trust his reason, senses, and natural causation.

> I will not sacrifice my reason, because this reason alone enables me to distinguish between good and evil, the true and the false. . . . I will not give up experience, because it is a much better guide than imagination, or than the authority of the guides whom they wish to give me. . . . I will not distrust my senses. I do not ignore the fact that they can sometimes lead me into error; but on the other hand I know that they do not deceive me always; . . . my senses suffice to rectify the hasty judgements which they induced me to form.[SIAA, 180]

> The universe is not an effect; it is the cause of all effects; all the beings it embraces are the necessary effects of this cause. . . Men may use the word "chance" to cover their ignorance of the true causes; . . There is no effect with out a cause.[SIAA, 70, 71].

What are the causes of theology? "Men believe in God only upon the word of those who have no more idea of Him than they themselves. Our nurses are out first theologians; they talk to children of God as they talk to them of were-wolfs; they teach them from the most tender age."[SIAA, 61]

He criticized the Bible, pointing out the contradictions in the gospels, and quoting St. Jerome that they had been corrupted and falsified. "Those who maintain their Divinity are compelled to acknowledge that they have no certainty as a basis, if their faith did not assure them and oblige them to believe it. Now, as faith is but a principle of error and imposture, how can faith, that is to say, a blind belief, render the books reliable which are themselves the foundations of this blind belief."[SIAA, 292, 295]

Does the Bible have perfection suited to a God? Meslier says not.

> There is no erudition, no sublime thought, nor any production which surpasses the ordinary capacities of the human mind. On the contrary, we shall see on one side fabulous tales similar to that of a woman formed of a man's rib; of the pretended terrestrial Paradise; of a serpent which spoke, which reasoned, and which spoke, and reprimanded its master for ill-treating it; . . [We] see a mixture of laws and ordinances, of superstitious practices concerning sacrifices, the purifications of the old law the senseless distinction

in regard to animals, of which it supposes some to be pure and others to be impure. These laws are no more respectable than those of the most idolatrous nations.

Meslier did not see the conception of heaven as a consolation.

> The belief which delivers me from overwhelming fears in this world appears to me more desirable than the uncertainty in which I am left through belief in a God who, master of his favors, gives them but to his favorites, and permits all the others to render themselves worthy of eternal punishments.[SIAA, 146]

> Is there in nature a man so cruel as to wish in cold blood to torment, I do not say his fellow-beings, but any sentient being whatever? . . . Conclude, then, O theologians, that according to your own principles your God is infinitely more wicked than the most wicked of men. . .[SIAA, 95]

> The priests have made of God such a malicious, ferocious being . . . that there are few men in the world who do not wish at the bottom of their hearts that God did not Exist.[SIAA, 249] . . . What morals would we have if we should imitate this God![SIAA, 215]

What is called Providence is but a word void of sense.

> All the books are filled with the most flattering praises of Providence, whose attentive care is extolled. . . . However, . . . if I examine all parts of this globe, I see the uncivilized as well an the civilized man in a perpetual struggle with Providence; he is compelled to ward off the blows which it sends in the form of hurricanes, tempests, frost, hail, inundations, sterility, and the diverse accidents which so often render all man's labors useless. In a word, I see the human race continually occupied in protecting itself from the wicked tricks of this Providence, which is said to be busy with the care of their happiness.[SIAA, 80]

Is there a stranger and more incredible God than this?

> He is supposed to be infinitely wise, . . . We are assured that he sees everything, yet his presence remedies nothing. . . . everything in his universe is in a state of confusion and disorder. . . . He foresees everything, but his foresight prevents nothing. . . his works are full of imperfections and of little permanence. He is continually occupied in creating and destroying.[SIAA, 46]

Meslier does not spare even Jesus.

> Alas! we see Him but a God, or rather a fanatic, a misanthrope, who, preaching to the wretched, advises them to be poor, to combat and extinguish

nature, to hate pleasure, to seek sufferings, and to despise themselves. He tells them to leave father, mother, all the ties of life, in order to follow him. What beautiful morality! . . . It must be divine, because it is impracticable for men. . . .[SIAA, 217]

Religion, especially among modern people, in taking possession of morality, totally obscure its principles; it has rendered men unsocial from a sense of duty; it has forced them to be inhuman toward all those who did not think as they did. Theological disputes equally unintelligible for the parties already irritated against each other have unsettled empires, caused revolutions, ruined sovereigns, devastated the whole of Europe. These despicable quarrels could not be extinguished even in rivers of blood. . . . The votaries of a religion which preaches . . . charity, harmony, and peace have shown themselves more ferocious than cannibals or savages every time that their instructors have excited them to the destruction of their brethren. There is no crime men have not committed in the idea of pleasing the deity or appeasing his wrath,[SIAA, 208] or to sanction the knaveries of impostors on account of a being who exists only in their imagination.[SIAA, 38]

Religion is not necessary to morality and to virtue.

We are constantly told, . . that religion is necessary to restrain men; that without it there would be no check upon people; that morality and virtue are intimately connected with it. . . . But is it true that this dogma [of heaven and hell] renders men . . . more virtuous? The nations where this fiction is established, are they remarkable for the morality of their conduct? . . . To disabuse us . . . it is sufficient to open the eyes and to consider what are the morals of the most religious people. We see haughty tyrants, courtiers, countless extortioners, unscrupulous magistrates, impostors, adulterers, libertines, prostitutes, thieves, and rogues of all kinds, who have never doubted the existence of a vindictive God, or the punishments of hell, or the joys of Paradise.[SIAA, 188]

To discover the true principles of morality men have no need of theology, of revelation, or of Gods; they need but common sense; they have only to look within themselves, to reflect upon their own nature, to consult their obvious interests, to consider the object of society and of each of its members who compose it, and they will easily understand that virtue is advantage, and that vice is an injury, to beings of their species. . . . Men are unhappy only because they are ignorant; they are ignorant only because everything conspires to prevent them from being enlightened; and they are wicked only because their reason is not sufficiently developed.[SIAA, 42, 42]

Theology has dominated and ruined philosophy.

From the most remote periods theology alone regulated the march of philosophy. What aid has it lent it? It changed it into an unintelligible jargon, . . . with words void of sense, better suited to obscure than to enlighten. . . .[SIAA, 274, 275] How Descartes, Malebranche, Leibniz, and many others have been compelled to invent hypotheses and evasions in order to reconcile their discoveries with the reveries and the blunders which religion had rendered sacred! With what precautions have not the greatest philosophers guarded themselves, even at the risk of being absurd, inconsistent, and unintelligible, whenever their ideas did not correspond with the principles of theology! Vigilant priests were always ready to extinguish systems which could not be made to tally with their interests. . . . All that the most enlightened men could do was to speak and write with hidden meaning; and often, by a cowardly complaisance, to shamefully ally falsehood with truth. . . . How could modern philosophers, who, threatened with the most cruel persecution, were called upon to renounce reason and to submit to faith--that is, to priestly authority--I say, how could men thus fettered give free flight to their genius, perfect reason, or hasten human progress?[SIAA, 278, 279, 280]

Some ancient and modern philosophers have had the courage to accept experience and reason as their guides, and to shake off the chains of superstition--Leucippus, Democritus, Epicurus, . . . But their systems, too simple, too sensible, and too stripped of wonders for the lovers of fancy, were obliged to surrender to the fabulous conjectures of Plato, Socrates, and Zeno. Among the modern, Hobbes, Spinoza, Bayle, and others have followed the path of Epicurus. "[SIAA, 279]

Meslier pleaded for freedom of thought.

It is only by showing them the truth that they can know their best interests and the real motives that will lead them to happiness. Long enough have the instructors of the people fixed their eyes upon heaven; let them at last bring them back to earth. Tired of an incomprehensible theology, of ridiculous fables, the impenetrable mysteries, of puerile ceremonies, let the human mind occupy itself with natural things, intelligible objects, sensible truths, and useful knowledge.[SIAA, 41]

Materialism

Materialists would aptly describe some of the opponents of theology, but few were willing to call the mind matter. I quote one that was. Julien Offroy La Mettrie (1709-1751) thought that man is a machine. By that term he meant "a body whose actions are due entirely to physical or chemical causes and processes." His father gave him a good education and

> recommended the ecclesiastical profession . . . but a doctor friend of the father thought (as Frederick the Great put it) that "a mediocre physician would be better paid for his remedies that a good priest for his absolutions." So Julien turned his zeal to anatomy and medicine, received the doctor's degree at Reims, studied under Boerhaave at Leiden, wrote several medical treatises, served as surgeon in the French army, and saw "one percent glory and ninety-nine per cent diarrhea" + on the fields of Dettingen and Fontenoy. Himself bedded with violent fever, he claimed, on recovery, that the clearness of his thinking had varied with the height of his fever; from this he concluded that thought is a function of the brain. He published these and allied ideas in 1745 in *Histoire naturelle de l'ame.*
>
> We cannot know what the soul is (ran the argument), and we do not know what matter is; we do know, however, that we never find a soul without a body. To study the soul we must study the body, and to study the body we must investigate the laws of matter. Matter is not mere extension, it is also a capacity for motion; it contains an active principle, which takes more and more complex forms in different bodies. We do not know that matter has of itself the power to feel, but we see evidences of that power in even the lowest animals. It is more logical to believe that this sensitivity is a development from some kindred potentiality in matter than to ascribe it to some mysterious soul infused into bodies by a supernatural agency. So the "active principle" in matter evolves through plants and animals until in man it enables the heart to beat, the stomach to digest, and the brain to think. This is the natural history of the soul.[AOV, 617]

Science in the Eighteenth Century

While philosophy "proper" was in as much turmoil as ever at the end of the 18th century, natural philosophy, which was now classified as science as we use the word today, continued to advance knowledge.

It is customary to rank the eighteenth century below the seventeenth in scientific achievements; and certainly there are no figures here to tower like Galileo or Newton, no accomplishments commensurate with the enlargement of the known universe of the cosmic extension of gravitation, of the formulation of calculus, or the discovery of the circulation of the blood. And, yet, what a galaxy of stars brightens the scientific scene in the eighteenth century!--Euler and Lagrange in Mathematics, Herschel and Laplace in astronomy, d'Alembert, Franklin, Galvani, and Volta in physics, Priestley and Lavoisier in chemistry, Linnaeus in botany, Buffon and Lamarck in biology, Haller in physiology, John Hunter in anatomy, Condillac in psychology, Jenner and Boerhaave in medicine. The multiplying academies gave more and more of their time and funds to scientific research. . . . Not until our own explosive times did science enjoy such popularity and honor.[AOV, 507, 508]

The discoveries in these fields in the eighteenth century make too long a story to include here, but I will indulge one quotations from Priestley, although it has nothing to do with his discovery of oxygen or his other discoveries. It is the ultimate in naturalism. In the Book *Disquisitions Relating to Matter and Spirit* (1777) he invoked the support of the "ancients" for a material theory of the mind.

It being well known to the learned . . . that what the ancients meant by an immaterial being was only a *finer kind* of what we should now call matter; something like air or breath, which first supplied a name for the *soul*. . . . Consequently the ancients did not exclude from mind the property of *extension* and local pressure. It had, in their idea, some common properties with matter, was capable of being united with it, of acting and being acted upon by it. . . . It was therefore seen that . . . the power of sensation or thought . . . might be imparted to the very grossest matter, . . . and that the *soul* and *body*, being in reality the same kind of substance, must die together.[ECB, 177]

And be investigated together, (by the same method), say by a chemist, I might add.

IMMANUEL KANT, IDEALISM
AND THE REACTION

Despite Hume's disclaimers, his philosophy was considered devastating to "philosophy." The job of giving back mind and causation and science to philosophy fell to Immanuel Kant (1724-1804). He realized that Hume's argument undermined everything most philosophers believed and felt it necessary that Hume's skeptical arguments be refuted. In the end Kant thought he had made a "copernican revolution" in philosophy. He has been called the greatest philosopher since Aristotle.

Kant lived all of his life in Konigsberg in the northeastern corner of Prussia (today, Russia). He was a bachelor and a respected professor of the university. Most commentators on Kant tell us that he was so methodical that his neighbors set their clock by his afternoon walks. He had been trained in rationalists metaphysics about which he had no doubts until he discovered Hume's *Enquiry.* Hume's position "that the indubitably knowable, a priori, truths [the analytic] are based on our own, ultimately arbitrary, rules or habits of using words and symbols, and give no information about the world" awakened Kant from his (in his own words) "dogmatic slumber."[AOE, 180] Kant refuted Hume's skeptical arguments in *Critique of Pure Reason,* eleven or twelve years in the writing, and published in 1781. He reclaimed the mind and body from Hume's destruction (interpreted):

> The mind of man . . . is not passive wax upon which experience and sensation write their absolute and yet whimsical will; nor is it a mere abstract name for the series or group of mental states; it is an active organ which moulds and coordinates sensation into ideas, an organ which transforms the chaotic multiplicity of experience into the ordered unity of thought.[SOP, 202]

It is told that "when Kant gave the MS. of the *Critique* to his friend Herz, a man much versed in speculation, Herz returned it half read, saying he feared insanity if he went on with it."[SOP, 192, 193] With this in mind, I have not ventured into the book much past the introduction which seems at times to be hemorrhaging *a prioris.* His blending of the synthetic with a principal ingredient of Hume's analytic, the a priori, accounts for much of this.

Kant settles Locke's dilemma concerning substance with "a priori," a solution not available to Locke, given his empiricist premises. In Kant's own words,

> Not only in judgements, however, but even in conceptions, is an *a priori* origin manifest. For example, if we take away by degrees from our conceptions of a body all that can be referred to mere sensuous experience--color, hardness or softness, weight, even impenetrability--the body will then vanish; but the space which it occupied still remains, and this it is utterly impossible to annihilate in thought. Again, if we take away, in like manner, from our empirical conception of any object, corporeal or incorporeal, all properties which mere experience has taught us to connect with it, still we cannot think away those through which we cogitate it as substance, or adhering to substance, although our conception of substance is more determined than that of an object. Compelled, therefore, by that necessity with which the conception of substance forces itself upon us, we must confess that it has its seat in our faculty of cognition *a priori*.[CPR, 46]

Kant accepted Hume's analytic/synthetic distinction as the key philosophical tool of analysis, but disagreed with Hume's strict empiricism. He held that there are meaningful statement about reality whose truth is known independently of observation, and dubbed them "synthetic a priori." These "truths" then form the proper subject matter of philosophy. The principal question of philosophy for Kant became "How are synthetic judgements *a priori* possible?"[CPR, 56]

> How is pure mathematical science possible? How is pure natural science possible? Respecting these sciences, as they do certainly exist, it may with propriety be asked, *how* they are possible?--for that they must be possible, is shown by the fact of their really existing. But as to metaphysics, the miserable progress it has hitherto made, and the fact that of no one system yet brought forward, as far as its true aim, can it be said that this science really exists, leaves any one at liberty to doubt with reason the very possibility of its existence. [CPR, 56, 57]

"These synthetic *a priori* truths, since they cannot be established empirically, are justifiable, if at all, through reflection, and reflection will confer on them the only kind of truth that is within its gift: necessary truth."[FDTW, 139, 140] His answer to that question (or method of solving it) he called "transcendental idealism."

There is an immediate intellectual difficulty of which Kant was aware, and which provides the explanation of the word 'transcendental'. . . . if the synthetic a priori principles of the understanding are as fundamental to thought as Kant asserted, then the very attempt to establish their validity must at the same time assume it. It was for this reason that Kant called his philosophical method 'transcendental', since it contained an attempt to transcend through argument what argument must presuppose. Not surprisingly, the possibility of such 'transcendental argument' has been the object of continual scepticism.[FDTW, 140]

Nevertheless we will examine (or study) Kant's argument.

Kant believed that neither the empiricists nor the rationalists could provide a coherent theory of knowledge. . . . Knowledge is achieved through a synthesis of concept and experience, and Kant called this synthesis 'transcendental', meaning that it could not be observed as a process, but must always be presupposed as a result. Synthetic *a priori* knowledge is possible because we can establish that experience, if it is subject to this synthesis, must conform to the 'categories' of the understanding. The categories are the basic forms of thought, or *a priori* concepts, under which all merely empirical concepts are subsumed.[FDTW, 140, 141]

Whether "concepts" is the correct interpretation of Kant's a priori element in knowledge is not certain to me, "principle" is also used. I do not believe that Kant in using the term synthetic a priori was claiming that we have ready-made ideas in the mind.   Rather, ideas or concepts are produced by the analysis of the data of experience--information supplied by the senses-- with ready-made or inborn faculties or principles. We might compare these faculties to the program in a computer which processes data fed into it.

Whatever the correct interpretation, Kant categories are, namely: three categories of quantity--unity, plurality, and totality; three categories of quality--reality, negation, and limitation; three twin categories of relation-- substance and quality, cause and effect, activity and passivity; and three twin categories of modality--possibility and impossibility, existence and nonexistence, necessity and contingency.

Kant makes the case against skepticism (of having knowledge) by recognizing that "there is contained in the idea of a thought, as of every mental content, the notion of a subject [person having the thought]. Moreover, this subject has an immediate and intuitive apprehension of its own unity [that it exists as a separate entity from other things]; I know immediately of my present mental states that they are mine and in the normal case I cannot be wrong about this."[FDTW, 142]   Example: If I am having pain, It is impossible that I would not know it is mine. I would not say that there is pain in the room somewhere, but that I do not know where it is. This unity consists "in the existence of a thing (the subject), which bears its mental states not as adjuncts but as properties. The very idea of self knowledge leads us therefore to the unity of the self, as an entity over and above the totality of its mental contents. It follows that there is more to the self than present self-knowledge can offer."[FDTW, 142]   And while I may have immediate knowledge of my present thoughts and feelings, there are other aspects of myself which I may have to discover, such as the truth about my past or future. "Hence the self as subject presupposes the self as object. . . . Radical skepticism, which can be stated only from the premise of self-knowledge, therefore presupposes its own falsehood."[FDTW, 142]

> Having shown that no knowledge is possible, not even self-knowledge, without the general concept of an object, we can at once conclude that experience must conform to the strictures which that concept contains. In other words, experience must conform to the categories; for these are nothing more than a working out in detail of all that is contained in the abstract concept of objectivity. Thus I cannot think in terms of objects without thinking of entities that endure through change; this requires that I apply to my experience the concept of substance. But substance, in its turn, involves the idea of something that sustains itself in being and that idea involves the notion of causality (or causal explanation). Causality in turn requires the idea of a law of nature, and hence the notions of necessity, possibility and actuality. And so on. Thus we see that, from the assumption that experience falls under the concept of an object, we arrive at the conclusion that it must fall under all the categories in turn. [FDTW, 143]

This, according to Kant, is the Transcendental Deduction of the Categories.

> Having shown (as he thinks) that experience conforms to the categories, he feels that he must show that the categories conform to experience. [They] . . . have their primary application in experience; and that means . . . in space and time [which are not listed in the categories]. . . . The idea of experience is inseparable from that of time, and the idea of experienced *world* is inseparable from that of space. . . .   Through the process of 'fit' between concept and experience, Kant argues, the whole of scientific knowledge is generated.[FDTW, 143]

This, according to Kant, explains the natural world, the world known to the senses, but what about concepts devoid of content from the senses such as God, soul, immortality, and justice? The categories do not apply to them. Space, time, and causality, for example, apply only to the observable world. Traditional metaphysics which has illegitimately applied these concepts to the noumenal world is impossible. This, needless to say, was upsetting to theologians and metaphysicians of the time.

This is pure naturalism; applying the categories to experience produces the only knowledge we have, and that is of the natural world. Knowledge is defined as in the realm of science; the categories are natural attributes. Having taken this position, it is a mystery why Kant referred to his philosophy as a form of idealism, specifically "transcendental idealism" a form of "empirical realism." He contrasts this with Berkeley's philosophy which he opposed and called "empirical idealism." His use of idealism to categorize his philosophy is even more puzzling as he appended a chapter entitled "The Refutation of Idealism" to the second edition of the *Critique*.

Whatever Kant's intentions, there is much in his philosophy that dilutes the apparent completeness of the categories and their inherent naturalism as regards knowledge. It is said of Kant's dictum (interpreted), "without the categories there could be no knowledge or experience of nature," that "just therein and only therein lies their validity."[DOP, 175] Here it seems with the word "only" there is a relegating of the doctrine of the categories to a minor role. Further, Kant insists that the categories "are not deduced by the mind from reality; on the contrary, the mind brings them to reality." I interpret this to mean, as discussed above, that the faculties are there (in or as part of the mind) and determine how we see reality. (Since they do function to deal with reality, there is no justification to deprecate them) However, "brings them to the mind" lends itself to the interpretation that the categories are illegitimate or are invented, not the stuff of reality. Indeed, according to Kant, the categories apply only to "the phenomenal world," that is, the world as conceived and interpreted through or by experience in space and time. "Ultimate reality" is something beyond this which common sense and science cannot penetrate. Nothing can be said about it except that it exists.

Ultimate reality he called "the Noumenal world" or "thing-in-itself." And science is further limited by what Kant called antinomies which are

> the insoluble dilemmas born of a science that tries to over leap experience. So,
> for example, when knowledge attempts to decide whether the world is finite or

infinite in space, thought rebels against either supposition: beyond any limit, we are driven to conceive something further, endlessly; and yet infinity is itself inconceivable. Again: did the world have a beginning in time? We cannot conceive eternity; but then, too, we cannot conceive any point in the past without feeling at once that before that, something was. Or has that chain of causes which science studies, a beginning, a First Cause? Yes, for an endless chain is inconceivable; no, for a first cause uncaused is inconceivable as well. Is there any exit from these blind alleys of thought? There is, says Kant, if we remember that space, time and cause are modes of perception and conception, which must enter into all our experience, since they are the web and structure for experience; these dilemmas arise from supposing that space, time and cause are external things independent of perception. We shall never have any experience which we shall not interpret in terms of space and time and cause; but we shall never have any philosophy if we forget that these are not things, but modes of interpretation and understanding.[SOP, 207, 208]

Will Durant sums up Kant's philosophy of the first critique in a colorful paragraph:

> Here was a tremendous book, eight hundred pages long; weighted beyond bearing, almost, with ponderous terminology; proposing to solve all the problems of metaphysics, and incidentally to save the absoluteness of science and the essential truth of religion. What had the book really done? It had destroyed the naive world of science, and limited it, if not in degree, certainly in scope,-- and to a world confessedly of mere surface and appearance, beyond which it could issue only in farcical "antinomies"; so science was "saved"! The most eloquent and incisive portions of the book had argued that the objects of faith--a free and immortal soul, a benevolent creator--could never be proved by reason; so religion was "saved"! No wonder the priests of Germany protested madly against this salvation, and revenged themselves by calling their dogs Immanuel Kant.[SOP, 208]

We may say that our first interpretation of Kant's philosophy (pages 144-147) has been naturalistic. We are now seeing another interpretation. Kant, as we have seen used both "empirical realism" and "transcendental idealism" for his philosophy. It is now apparent, however, that there are two interpretations. One emphasizes "empirical realism [naturalism]" which may be called the objective interpretation. Another emphasizes "transcendental idealism" which may be called the subjective. It deprecates the concept of "experience" holding that it gives us only the world of appearances. (This brief statement necessarily over simplifies it). I agree with one philosopher who writes, "It seems to me that only the objective interpretation of the first *Critique* allows us to think of Kant's enterprise as either worthwhile or significant."[FDTW, 146]   The subjective was far more widely accepted until recently. Now there is a tendency to accept the objective.

Despite the impossibility of proving the existence of God, free will, and morality, Kant found a way; a very old and very human way: when reason fails to give us what we want, we rationalize. So, despite his dictum that there is no logical necessity for the terms God, immortality, justice, and freedom, believing in them is a moral necessity. Without these concepts man would despair of living, We are justified in believing in them to make us better and happier persons. If we cannot prove these concepts to be valid, we can, nevertheless, believe in them. In Kant's own words:

> Now it is true that I cannot, by means of speculative reason, and still less by empirical observation, *cognize* my soul as a thing in its self, [as real] and consequently, cannot cognize liberty as a property of a being to which I ascribe effects in the world of sense [observable world]. For, to do so, I must cognize this being as existing, and yet not in time, which--since I cannot support my conception by any intuition--is impossible. At the same time, while I cannot *cognize*, I can quite well *think* freedom.[CPR, 32]

And *think* he did. For this Kant has been accused of kicking God out the front door and letting him in the back door.

Having found that we have a right to believe in God and morality, Kant proceeded in a second critique, *Critique of Practical Reason*, 1788, to find the moral law, the categorical imperative within us, and, from the moral law, the existence of God. "We find, in fact, that practical reason leads precisely to those crucial metaphysical doctrines that the first *Critique* had purported to refute: the existence of a noumenal realm, the immortality of the soul, the affirmation of positive freedom, and the existence of God."[FDTW, 158]   Access to this transempirical world of things in themselves is through the postulates of practical reason which we may interpret as meaning opinion not proof. One interpreter puts us squarely in this unknowable realm:

> As *phenomenal* beings we are subject to the laws of nature and reason; but as pure rational wills we move in the free, *noumenal* or intelligible realm, bound only by the self-imposed rational law "to treat humanity in every case as an end, never as a means only.[DOP, 175]

This brings us to the categorical imperative. Kant declared that all men have a moral consciousness, a tribunal if you will, that is part of them, that commands them unconditionally to do what is right as an end in itself, not as a reward. In Kant's own words in two translations: (1) "Act as if the maxim of your action were to become through your will a general natural law." (2) "Act so that the maxim [determining motive of the will] may be capable of becoming a universal law for all rational beings." If it seems that some interpretation would help, we will indulge two: (1) "Act so that the maxim of thy will can always hold good as a principle of universal legislation.". (2) "So act as to treat humanity, whether in thine own person or in that of any other, in every case as an end, never only as a means."

In either case morality is duty. Kant was so concerned to base morality on duty that he accorded no value to the natural tendency or inclination to behave well. If you are naturally a "moral person," if nature imposed good behavior on you, you deserved less credit than a person who was not so constituted but managed out of a sense of duty to be "morally good."

Kant felt that we cannot reach moral perfection here on earth, but as we have this inborn moral sense to try, practical reason tells us that we are justified in believing their is life after death in which we will be granted moral fulfillment. Further, we are justified in believing that we have free will. Morality makes no sense without it. This also assumes that a just God exists. Philosophers have traditionally derived the moral sense from God. Kant inverted the procedure.

Criticism

As I have observed, empiricism, after a beginning as science, degenerated to the verge of idealism in the case of Locke and Hume, and *was* idealism in the case of Berkeley, and to repeat, I considered it science aborted in the first trimester. Kant gave us some of the most profound naturalism in all philosophy, yet seemed to lead us to the brink of idealism.

Hume robbed philosophy of mind and Kant gave it (a quite natural one) back, namely the "principles" or "faculties" which are there waiting for sense data, information of whatever kind, to process as it arrives (here I am using the interpretation of the categories as discussed on page 145). This is quite different from the mind being a bundle of impressions as in Hume. But, what about using the term "a priori" for these "faculties" or "principles"? Let us consider Berkeley's contention (page 86) that a man blind from birth, made to see, would have no conception of distance. This was confirmed (to repeat) by the Royal Society (1709, 1728) when a congenitally blind person was given sight. He could not judge the shape of objects nor determine their distance, believing they touched his eyes.

The concepts in this case were not prior in time to the regaining of sight, for *at first* the man had no concepts of distance, etc. Presumably he did in time obtain these concepts, the faculties for them coming into action *with* experience.

Experience is said of minds; experience presupposes mind. Knowledge comes when the twain meet.   Kant, I presume, is using a priori to say that the faculties for processing sense data exist and that they exist prior to receiving sense data. I do not see this as refuting Hume's skepticism which in this case is skepticism of a faculty of reason capable of coming up with knowledge without experience. I, therefore, interpret Kant's usage of "a priori" as a different word than Hume's; and as Kant used it, it does not militate against the central thesis of empiricism, that all knowledge must be, or is, based on experience.

If Kant means that his categories are concepts or ideas, then my analysis does not hold (the interpretation I use has the ambiguity of "concepts" and "faculties"), but my position is that "faculties" is the correct term and that they are instincts. If we say they are a priori, we would, to be consistent, have to apply the term to the weaver finch for its faculties for nest building. As instincts they belong to science not philosophy.

Thus far this all seems pure naturalism. The categories are the natural faculties with which we deal scientifically with the natural, substantive world of real things, real physical objects. We might suspect that Kant is saying that we must use these categories to survive because they reflect the structure of the world (nature). If the science of genetics had been developed in his time we could suspect that he was saying that we are genetically determined to have these categories because natural selection gave them to us to deal with the world as it is. We survive by using them, which is tantamount to evidence that the world is structured that way. But discouragingly and disgustingly for a naturalist, the world of things is quite something else according to Kant. At first blush, it appeared that we have a mind that we can be proud of, but the categories are restricted in their application to the world of experiencable phenomena, and phenomena, it turns out, are "things as they are" for human experience, and as such are little more than a shadow (my term) of the real things--mere appearances of the real things. The real things are "things in themselves" or noumena and cannot be known.

I suggest it would make more sense to put this in the scientific terms of heredity and environment. The mind, the mechanism, the faculties that process the data of experience are genetically determined and vary in capacity from individual to individual. The materials or information or data received is from the environment. The state of the science of genetics today dictates that we attribute the existence of our faculties, Kant's categories, to their survival value. They exist because they reflect the world as it is and enable us to deal with the world as it is. This contrasts with Kant's apparent position that we bring the world to our mind.

It is irrelevant to talk about an idea or a concept being either a priori or a posteriori. We are considering two kinds of determinism, and the one statement that can be made without exception regarding the origin of concepts is simply this: *Heredity is such that the environment caused the concept.* It is never one or the other.

What about Kant's Transcendental Deduction of the Categories. Did he really do it? The process essentially found that one concept suggests or entails another, the new concept another, then again, etc., until it runs full circle. There is nothing wrong with a perfect circle, unless we make a claim of logic for it, but, it seems, the term deduction makes that claim. There is something other than logic at work here. If, for example, "we cannot think in terms of objects without thinking of entities that endure through change," isn't it a matter of observation to know that we know this; and therefore more empirical than transcendental? Indeed, since Kant's time science has made this an empirical study.

If the Transcendental Deduction fails, as I believe it does, Kant had certainty[1] in the matter, and did not arrive at certainty[2]. This failure, however, does not make a case for mindless, purely empirical, learning. The educational systems the world over testify that we learn from experience and implicit in "learn" is "learning thing." If this does not satisfy the reader, let us consider aptitude tests, which show great variation in ability to learn. If experience alone taught, all would learn the same. Kant was right that neither the empiricists nor rationalists were entirely correct. There are faculties that function with experience, and we call them the mind; but, it is an empirical matter that we know this, not a matter of logic (deducing transcendentally).   In Kant's efforts to correct the shortcomings of empiricism he became more of a rationalist than an empiricist.

Although we can thank Kant for reclaiming the mind from Hume's skepticism, there is more to the mind than the categories, namely whatever produces metaphysics. Kant himself is an example despite his finding that metaphysics is impossible because there are no synthetic a priori foundations for it. Traditional metaphysics was impossible according to Kant, because it requires applying the notions of space, time, and causality to the noumenal world when in fact these concepts can only be applied to the observable world (page 147). But, this can only mean that metaphysics was worthless as knowledge (as Hume had claimed) not impossible, for all history testifies to the fact that there is metaphysics. If the epistemologist can ignore metaphysics, the psychologist cannot. Metaphysical ideas, concepts, thoughts, are natural events and have far reaching effects. Over all history they have used much human energy; having some utility, as well as being a great burden.

How is metaphysics done then, if there are no faculties for it? The wellsprings for much of it are in the mind's desire for things that the categories cannot produce which is to say, for answers that science cannot supply. I will pursue this in my theory of the mind (page 197).

I accept Kant's view that metaphysical entities, including God, cannot be proven to exist with "pure" reason, which is about where Hume left metaphysics, but Kant amended this by bringing God in the back door in a later book. Rejecting the proofs of Anselm and Aquinas, he found proof of, or at least the "right" to believe in, the existence of God in man's moral sense. Just as Berkeley abandoned his empiricist premises, after pursuing them to the point of solipsism, to bring God into the picture to insure the existence of objects (as ideas) when no person was viewing (having an idea of them) them, Kant abandoned his empiricism and found God in the moral sense. Although in use since the ancients, his terminology of "practical" for reason in the second book and "theoretical" for it in the first is just the opposite of what I would have used. I would use practical as Descartes uses it on page 57, but philosophers create their own jargon.

What are we to make of the interpretation of getting access to the transempirical world of things in themselves and as pure rational wills moving in the free noumenal or intelligible realm (page 149). He told us in the beginning that we reason with the categories about the natural properties of things and that they do not provide access to the noumenon. Every thing, which we can know only as appearance, is really a "thing in itself" that is inaccessible, and that this applies to every physical object. This would include baseballs. So, we are to believe that starting with morality (page 149) he deduced God and free will, or he may have gotten all three from the concept of "Justice," which would not be possible, according to Kant, without God and free will, and from there gain knowledge of the noumenon in a baseball. How could this unknown "thing in itself" in a baseball possibly be equated with moving around in a transempirical world or realm? Of course, we are dealing with an interpretation of Kant, and it may not be what he meant. This interpretation of gaining access to the noumenal realm was cherished by those idealist philosophers who were a spin off from Kant, which, except for a brief note, I will ignore.

There is a similarity between Kant's treatment of substance and noumenon. I was surprised to find his use of the term substance as a constituent part of things, namely what is left when all that we can detect by "mere sensuous experience," Locke's qualities, are "taken away" (page 144). No interpretation of Kant that I had read mentioned it. My criticism of Kant's substance is that it is only in fantasy that we extract the experiencable characteristics of things from things, and it makes no sense in the real world to talk about what is left after these so called qualities are removed. In common usage substance is a kind of thing where it is useful to refer to something by one or more of its characteristics; glue is a sticky substance; lead is a heavy substance; steel is a strong substance; rubber is an elastic substance, etc. As a general term, substance simply means thing. As a philosophical term, separate or separable from its attributes, it is an illusion. While Kant was "taking away" from the conception of the thing, not from the thing itself, it makes no sense to talk of taking away from the conception of a thing if one cannot "take away" from the thing.

The noumenon has much the same status as substance. The noumenon is what is left over (Kant's words in the case of substance, but not in the case of the noumenon) after accounting for the experiencable attributes of things with the categories. I can only wonder if Kant's conception of substance, which Locke had said was an unknown something, metamorphosed in Kant's hands, into noumenon, something we cannot know.

In my view, noumenon and thing-in-itself are terms which philosophy could well have done without.   For one thing, they lent themselves to the drift in Kant's philosophy toward idealism.   Secondly, they do not tell us anything useful in our pursuit of knowledge.   I presume that for Kant there is a one-to-one correspondence between the appearance of a thing and the real thing--a phenomenon and its noumenon; that everywhere an appearance went its real thing was with it.   Kant "knew" that there was a real unknowable thing where he observed a phenomenon, and presumably he never knew, did not even suspect, that there was a real unknowable thing where he did not observe a phenomenon.   If we do not "know" the noumenon, we at least know something about its behavior, namely that everywhere (like Mary's little lamb) the phenomenon goes the noumenon tags along.   When a baseball goes over the fence on a home run, the noumenon goes over the fence with the phenomenon, and in doing so, has the same relation to space and time, contrary to Kant's dictum, as the phenomenon.   We are at all times dependent on observing the phenomenon to know where the noumenon is. If I swing a hammer to drive a nail, am I not allowed to suppose that the real hammer drove the nail? even though I must say that the phenomenon is only the appearance of driving a nail.   Kant, would, I believe, say that my categories (the necessary principles) prepared me to drive the nail and that I did drive the nail and that I, the nail and the hammer were real.   He was not, I believe, an idealist however much his philosophy lent itself to idealism.

He held, as I understand him, that my categories prepare me to function *only* in nature, in what he called the phenomenal world.   In saying that we do not know things, in Kant's terms, things in themselves, or noumena, it is implicit, having given this second world a name, that there is something to be known if only we had a faculty for it.   But, what this knowing could be we have not the slightest clue, nor that there is something to be known.   If we only have faculties for dealing with the phenomenon, it appears that Kant (being one of us) has no faculty to know that there is a noumenal world.   It is time to discard the terms, they do not clarify.   While we are throwing "qualities and "substance" (as Locke used them) in the waste basket, let us do the same with "phenomenon" and "noumenon."

Yet this analysis by Kant almost makes a valid point.   I propose that beyond the basic assumptions of science, observation is of the behavior of things: we do not know things beyond their behavior, and the specific laws, and principles we declare, but do not observe, are derived by the faculties--Kant's categories--from the behavior we observe. I am accepting Kant's position that the categories deal only with the natural world. In saying this I give "behavior" the broadest possible meaning. In support of this view, I quote Galileo on gravity. Simplicio in a dialogue "gravely explains that there is nothing strange or interesting about what makes bodies fall: 'everyone knows that it is Gravity'; but Galileo is in a position to reprove him gently:"

> You are out, my dear Simplicio, you should say that everyone knows that it is *called* Gravity: but I do not question you about the name, but about the essence of the thing, of which essence you know not a little more than you know the essence of the mover of the stars in gyration: unless it be the name that has been put to this, and made familiar and domestical, by the many experiences which we see thereof every hour of the day: but not as if we really understood any more what principle of vertue that is, than when we say the stars are moved by "intelligences."[AOAv, 20]

When after many experiences, the names or terms of things become "familiar and domestical," there is the illusion that we know the "essence" of them, but we only know things by their behavior and instinctively derive laws and terminology for thinking and communication. Behavior reveals no such thing as a "thing in itself;" nevertheless behavior is revealing. I suggest that *behavior is revelation itself--of things, natural things, the only things.* Kant's position points up this fact that we do not know such an essence, but he overruns the mark and declares that there is one (the noumenon) however unknown. Whether observation is of behavior of things or more than behavior, always it is *things* that philosophy and science are about. "Things" is implicit in "behavior."

To say that knowledge as derived from observation is only of the behavior of things is to say that knowledge is not and cannot be about anything else; therefore to say that there is some reality such as a noumenon would be to abandon the position.

Are time and space real? Kant says that they are not, but are, nevertheless, indispensable concepts. I agree, there are no entities, time and space; but they (time and space) are concepts concerning real entities encompassed in their use, namely, the measurable aspects of physical objects. Let us consider Hume's billiard balls. At any instant they are a measurable distance (space) apart. If Hume wants to change that distance it requires successive events (time) such as revolutions of the ball if he rolls it. Any change in space requires time. Any time in moving the ball changes the space. Time and space are inseparable concepts, but not being things, the experienced reality they communicate or denote is not theirs, but is of physical objects. Time and space are nouns that are not the name of a person, place or thing, grammarians notwithstanding. For the lack of a better term, I will call them incorporating or incorporative nouns. They incorporate the properties and functions of things and communicate them with one word.

As to those insoluble dilemmas that Kant called antinomies, I think his treatment of them, as I understand it, is correct. The categories are for dealing with things, natural and observable. There are no faculties for demystifying the antinomies. Knowledge is limited to science. It is at this point that I am inclined to see the knowledge of things as of their behavior.

For Kant's ethics I will use a criticism that is a naturalistic view and holds that there are no absolutes in ethics, a position I will defend in my discussion of the subject on page 209-218.

> The nineteenth century dealt rather harshly with Kant's ethics, his theory of an innate, *a priori*, absolute moral sense. The philosophy of evolution suggested irresistibly that the sense of duty is a social deposit in the individual. The content of conscience is acquired, though the vague disposition to social behavior is innate.   The moral self, the social man, is no "special creation" coming mysteriously from the hand of God, but the late product of a leisurely evolution. Morals are not absolute; they are a code of conduct more or less haphazardly developed for group survival, and varying with the nature and circumstances of the group: . . No action is good in itself, as Kant supposes. [SOP, 218]

Kant's ethical conclusions were those of his Lutheran upbringing, the ethics he had known all his life. He imposed his cultural heritage upon his philosophy. It is interesting to note that he remained a philosopher (as opposed to theologian) in doing so. He reached his position from reason rather than from divine commandment. After years of wakeful reasoning in the first *Critique*, Kant resumed his dogmatic slumbers.

The contrast between "natural philosophy" and "philosophy proper" in this era is striking. The former filled volumes that were building blocks to greater accomplishments while the latter, Kant's "Copernican revolution" not withstanding, was poised to flounder into idealism.

G. W. F. Hegel (1770-1831), a Brief Note

Kant, as we have seen, despite his rehabilitation of the mind, left philosophy about where he found it, with one foot in idealism. Both feet were soon to go in, propelled by other philosophers. Idealism was a long dry spell for a naturalist. Mill has been quoted as saying that he could not read Hegel without becoming nauseated. I was spared the nausea because it was too obscure and odd for me to read. The obscurity may have convinced some philosophers that it was profound for he had no trouble attracting followers. A quote from Schopenhauer (1788-1864) fits in well with my prejudice against metaphysics, but I am not qualified to confirm it.

> The height of audacity in serving up pure nonsense, in stringing together senseless and extravagant mazes of words, such as had previously been known only in madhouses, was finally reached in Hegel, and became the instrument of the most bare-faced general mystification that has ever taken place, with a result which will appear fabulous to posterity.[SOP, 221]

Hegel's philosophy is a "philosophy of history." "Briefly put, Hegel regards all change as historical, and history itself as the dialectic deployed in time. As such, it is, in effect, a great waltz-like movement, from thesis through antitheses to synthesis, with each step representing a still higher stage in the self-development of the Absolute."[AOI, 76] Since I have no idea what this means, I will stop with this paragraph. I presume that Hegel's philosophy has little to do with naturalism in the sense of respecting science as the method to knowledge.

For me, idealism was the dark age of modern philosophy. To be an idealist, one need only to be capable of believing that George Washington's picture is the real George Washington.

Positivism

The idealists were ideological conservatives who sought to preserve, although on a modified basis, what they took to be the primary values of the Christian tradition. In the meantime, however, the intransigent secularistic spirit of the Enlightenment still remained alive, and in the age which followed there were many Philosophers who were opposed to even such attenuated reinterpretations of the Christian world-view as the idealists had proposed. There were many philosophers, particularly in France and England, who continued to insist upon a more radical break with the tradition than the idealists were prepared to countenance, and they sought to provide the basis for a new scientifically oriented ideology which would replace altogether what remained of the outlook of medieval Christendom. What they aspired to was a completely humanistic culture, securely based on the foundation of modern science, and purged of the double-talking equivocations and evasions of idealism. Among them Auguste Comte [1798-1857] occupies a place of pre-eminence.[AOI, 115, 116]

This naturalistic philosophy Comte called "positivism" that is, it was a positive as opposed to a critical attitude toward science. He refused "to go outside science in order to provide it with a critical justification as the only form of human knowledge. His only standard of rationality, from the outset, is that of science, and his refusal to regard theology or metaphysics as domains of knowledge is based merely on the fact that their cognitive claims cannot be justified by scientific methods of inquiry."[AOI, 116] He did not use psychology in his rationale such as the British empiricist's method of tracing our ideas to impressions of sensation and reflection or feeling. For him a statement had to be verified by the methods of empirical science to be worthy of belief and he "refused to regard the human mind as a unique sphere of inquiry which is unaccessible to public inter-subjective modes of analysis and observation."[AOI, 122] As an idealogue his aim was "to inculcate a mentality which simply will not think in unscientific terms, and which will reject the propositions of traditional theology and metaphysics simply on the ground that they are unscientific."[AOI, 116, 117]

For him there are, at bottom, only two basic sciences of human behavior, physiology and sociology. Any third discipline which purports to deal with some special 'psychical' phenomena Comte regards as pure mythology. It should be added here that Comte himself coined the bastard word 'sociology' in order to designate an as yet non-existent science of human society, in terms of whose laws alone, as he believed, the economic, political, and moral behavior of men can be understood.[AOI, 122]

Comte was right about sociology becoming a science, but when attempting to be scientific with a theory about the development of the human mind, he failed badly in my view. He had apparently looked at all history (thus, theorized from observation) and found three stages of development. He tells us,

> From the study of the development of human intelligence, in all directions, and through all times, the discovery arises of a great fundamental law, to which it is necessarily subject, and which has a solid foundation of proof, both in the facts of our organization and in our historical experience. The law is this--that each of our leading conceptions,--each branch of our knowledge,--passes successively through three different Theoretical conditions: the Theological, or fictitious; the Metaphysical, or abstract; and the Scientific, or positive. . . . The first is the necessary point of departure of the human understanding; and the third is its fixed and definitive state. The second is merely a state of transition.[AOI, 124, 125]

He elaborates on the three stages:

> *First stage*--In the theological state, the human mind seeking the essential nature of beings, the first and final cases (the origin and purpose) of all effects,--in short, Absolute knowledge,--supposes all phenomena to be produced by the immediate action of supernatural beings.
>
> *Second stage*--In the metaphysical state, which is only a modification of the first, the mind supposes, instead of supernatural beings, abstract forces, veritable entities (that is, personified abstractions) inherent in all beings, and capable of producing all phenomena. What is called the explanation of phenomena is, in this stage, a mere reference of each to its proper entity.
>
> *Third stage*--In the final, the positive state, the mind has given over the vain search after Absolute notions, the origin and destination of the universe, and the cause of phenomena, and applies itself to the study of their laws--that is, their invariable relations of succession and resemblance. Reasoning and observation, duly combined, are the means of this knowledge. What is now understood when we speak of an explanation of facts is simply the establishment of a connection between single phenomena and some general facts, the number of which continually diminishes with the progress of science.[AOI, 125]

Comte's theory entails a naive psychology although he seems to be saying that a science of psychology is impossible. There is just one thing wrong with Comte's theory: it simply isn't true. I will try to make the case that the behavior Comte puts in stages exists in all ages side by side; that they function as parallel activities (my theory of the mind, pages 193, 194).

There is more to Comte's philosophy, which I will omit. "In his later writings, Comte came more and more to regard his philosophy as providing a basis for a new 'religion of humanity', which alone, he thought, was suitable to the mentality of human beings in an age of science."[AOI, 122] He furnished it "with an elaborate ritual, which became an object of ridicule on the part of his critics."[AOI, 123] In doing this he became more of an ideologue than a philosopher. However, for all his faults he is "the forerunner of much that is most alive in the empiricist and naturalistic philosophies of our own age."[AOI, 123]

Analysis

If philosophy lost its charm for me in idealism, it was hardly revived by analysis. Their tendency to "think of philosophy not as a rival of science but rather as an activity which is partly devoted to clarifying it"[AOA, 190] had an appeal initially, but it soon became apparent that my philosophy could not find a home in analysis. What is worth saving in analysis will, I believe, eventually be classified as science and lose its status as philosophy. I do, however, share their evaluation of metaphysics.

Bertrand Russell (1872-1970) was the acknowledged leader in analysis.[AOA, 17] We will indulge one example of his analysis. Idealism, in particular Hegelianism, was in decline. "Hegel held that the universe reveals the workings, the development, the realization, the unfolding of a World Spirit or Absolute Idea (sometimes called the Absolute for short). On his view the universe is not unlike an animate being that has a soul, desires, aims, intentions, and goals."[AOA, 13] Philosophers who had rejected this one big queer entity were filling the universe with many small queer entities. "Some of them, like Alexius Meinong [1853-1920], were driven to supposing that there must be some unusual entity whose existence is implied when we say (truly) that the golden mountain does not exist. It cannot be the golden mountain, of course, for *it* is said not to exist, and so it must be something whose exact nature is quite puzzling."[AOA, 24] Meinong's puzzle is just the kind of thing that spurred Russell to analysis. He called his solution the "theory of descriptions."

By a "description" he meant a phrase such as "The prime minister of Canada" (not the example he gave, but analogous to it). Such a phrase contains no name, but rather a "description," that is, a person or thing is designated by some property which is supposed or known to be peculiar to him or it." Such phrases, according to Russell, have been troublesome. To clear this up he analyzed not a phrase such as this--it was to make clear to the reader what a "description" is--but a sentence containing a description, for example, Meinong's "The golden mountain does not exist" which seemed, to Meinong and Russell, to attribute some kind of existence to the golden mountain. When Russell's analysis, namely the "theory of descriptions," is performed on a statement containing a "description," the "description" disappears and the puzzle as to what is meant when we say "The golden mountain does not exist" disappears. According to this theory, in Russell own words (*A History of Western Philosophy*): "when a statement containing a phrase of the form 'the so-and-so' is rightly analyzed, the phrase 'the so-and-so' disappears. . . . The golden mountain does not exists" means: "There is no entity c such that 'x is golden and mountainous' is true when x is c, but not otherwise." Russell thought that his analysis cleared up two millennia of muddle-head-edness about "existence."

Other philosophers, including his ally in analysis, G. E. Moore (1873-1958), have made objections to the theory of descriptions. Moore pointed out that it does not apply to all statements of the grammatical form "the so-and-so"[PALA, 65] and gave the example "The whale is a mammal." Russell admitted this and said, "The blame lies on the English language, in which the word 'the' is capable of various different meanings"[PALA, 65] but provided no "criterion for distinguishing between the different meanings."[PALA, 66] There is not much to distinguish.

Further criticism that has been made of the theory of descriptions is rather tedious. I will pursue it no further as I have my own criticism of "the golden mountain."

There is the illusion that this sentence is a complete thought or commun-ication and therefore worthy of analysis. That it has a subject and predicate is all that can be said for it in that regard. "The golden mountain does not exist" lacks that status because it is in no context whatsoever. "The" is a designating article, but "the" in itself does not designate. There has to be a context. The golden mountain of some assertion or allegation is what must apply here. It would have status as an intelligible proposition only as *part* of some conversation or discourse, in which case the designating or specifying article "the" designates, or refers to, a declared or alleged golden mountain in the other part of a complete thought.

I dare say that it is only in a philosopher's world that a mystery can be seen here. In the real world, the sentence would be in some context such as this: One person remarks that "I read of a golden mountain in a novel." To which another person replied "The golden mountain does not exist." Here the article "the" specifies the fictitious golden mountain, therefore, the reply means that "The fictitious mountain does not exist." It is a tautology that needs no analysis (or it is analyzed into a tautology) and does not attribute some sort of existence to the golden mountain.

Another example of the sentence being in context would be this: if one person alleges that a golden mountain exists in Missouri and another person replies that "The golden mountain does not exist." In this case "the" specifies the *alleged* golden mountain. The reply would mean "The alleged golden mountain does not exist," which does not attribute some sort of existence to the golden mountain.

If it is objected that "the" in the sentence "The golden mountain does not exist" does have a context, namely, a golden mountain said not to exist, then "the" means "the non-existent golden mountain," and the sentence means "The non-existent golden mountain does not exist." It is resolved into a redundancy. If rather it is claimed that "the" has the context of an existing golden mountain, then the sentence means "The existing golden mountain does not exist" and may be discarded as nonsense.

My position is that these two examples do not apply; that context is missing in the sentence "The golden mountain does not exist," therefore it is pointless to analyze it. It was a waste of time for so august a philosopher as Russell.

Moore, although a "common-sense" philosopher, was in the forefront of analysis with Russell (more about Moore and common sense later). Early on both came under the influence of the idealists M. E. McTaggart (1866-1925) and F. H. Bradley (1846-1924 and together they rebelled against them. "Bradley argued that everything common sense believes in is mere appearance,[AOA, 23] while Moore and Russell, in rebellion, took the opposite view, and "thought that *everything* is real that common sense, uninfluenced by philosophy or theology, supposes real."[AOA, 23] As a result, they and others were called realist, however, there were "two distinct elements within . . . [this] realism. One is represented by its common-sense belief that physical objects like the sun and stars exist independently of the mind, and the other by its highly uncommonsensical belief that there are such things as platonic ideas or universals that also exist independently."[AOA, 23] For me this distorts the term "realism" to the point where it is useless. It has slept with too many philosophies to have any credibility left.

The philosophical school of "New Realism" that resulted is, on the surface, pure naturalism. There is, however, so much disagreement between "New Realism's" various advocates, that I can say only that I agree with its "salient features":

> The first characteristic of the new [written in 1928] philosophy is that it abandons the claim to a special philosophic method or peculiar brand of knowledge to be obtained by its means. It regards philosophy as essentially one with science, differing from the special sciences merely by the generality of its problems, and by the fact that it is concerned with the formation of hypotheses where empirical evidence is still lacking. It conceives that all knowledge is scientific knowledge, to be ascertained and proved by the methods of science.[SE, 48]

In time, Moore and Russell held widely divergent views. For example, "Russell was . . . willing to say that all one sees when one looks at a thing is part of one's own brain, and that we do not know for certain the truth of any statement about a material thing, while Moore vehemently denied both of these contentions in the name of common sense." Moore was therefore forced "to argue against his old realistic and analytic comrade Russell in a vein similar to that in which he (Moore) argued against their common enemy the idealists."[AOA, 192] Unlike Russell, Moore, had no interest in science and mathematics. His common-sense philosophy made the basic assumptions of science up to a point, yet in spite of this, he held views on ethics in the name of common sense which could not be a science. I discuss this in the section on ethics. There is a contrast in Moore's common sense philosophy and his analysis. The former is presented as knowledge pure and simple too basic to need analyzing but after taking his stand on it he was for the greater part engaged in uncommon analysis.

Although Russell commented on all philosophical problems, his first love was logic. One chapter in one of his books was entitled "Logic as the

Essence of Philosophy." In it (*Our Knowledge of the External World*) he termed the facts of sense-perception atomic facts, and remarked that "if we knew all atomic facts, and knew that there were none except those we knew, we should, theoretically, be able to infer all truths of whatever form."[OKEW, 48, 49] As far as I know he had no illusions about obtaining all atomic facts. It was the logical positivists who took up the subject.

Hume's distinction between the mathematical and empirical was disregarded for most of the nineteenth century because it was contradicted by Kant. By the twentieth there was a revival. From Russell's and Moore's beginnings in analysis, a group of European philosophers took Hume's analysis seriously that there are only three kinds of propositions; and since there are only the analytic, synthetic, and nonsense, nothing was left for philosophy but analysis. This group, originated in 1923 and called "The Vienna Circle," grew "out of a seminar conducted by Moritz Schlick (1882-1936) who had become professor of philosophy at Vienna in 1922. Its original members were mainly ex-scientists who had become philosophers and practicing scientists with an interest in philosophy"[AOA, 204] Their philosophy was a merger of empiricism and logic and was at first called Logical Positivism but was later, at least part of the time, Logical Empiricism. It has two sides,

> a negative, militant, critical, almost contemptuous attitude toward the previous history of philosophy, which expresses itself in hostility toward the traditional disciplines of metaphysics and ethics, and a positive, admiring attitude toward logic and the sciences. Together they led to the view that philosophy is nothing but the logic of science.[AOA, 205]

The Unity of Science movement was taken up by the Logical Positivists. It was the position that the "different branches of science are not of fundamentally different kinds but belong to one coherent system." It is or was the aim to develop "a simple set of connected, fundamental laws from which the special laws in the different branches of science, including the social sciences, can be deduced."[DOP, 303] Gilbert Ryle (1900-1976) is quoted as "characteristically" asking what purpose the unity of science would serve.[PTC, 140]

Schlick held that the meaning of a proposition is its method of verification. The language of verification would have to be in sentences that expressed the basic simple verifiable facts and these would be the starting points of all knowledge. Failing to get the desired results, he and his associates tried modifying and reducing the sentences still further but they were not successful. Disagreements arose which were never satisfactorily settled. It is thought by some that they only managed to proved themselves wrong.

They stated their claims as to what they were trying to do, but were they really doing something else? For them the analytic was certain and needed no further perfection. Were they trying to make the synthetic certain also, against their avowed logic that it could not be? Perhaps the lesson is "Do not analyze beyond necessity."

Rudolf Carnap (1891-1970) expressed the view of the Vienna Circle that logical analysis renders all metaphysics including all philosophy of value and normative theory, meaningless. He found there to be two functions to language, the expressive which is in art and metaphysics, and the representative which is found in the sciences and logic. A. J. Ayer (1810-1989) found moral propositions, which Carnap put in the "expressive," to be emotive. In his words, "in so far as statements of value are significant, they are ordinary 'scientific' statements; and that in so far as they are not scientific, they are not in the literal sense significant, but are simple expressions of emotion which can be neither true or false.[LTL, 102, 103]

> There can be no way of determining the validity of any ethical system, and, indeed, no sense in asking whether any such system is true. All that one may legitimately enquire in this connection is, What are the moral habits of a given person or group of people, and what causes them to have precisely those habits and feelings? And this enquiry falls wholly within the scope of the existing social sciences.[LTL, 112]

An example of a "scientific" statement is "A good diet is valuable for your health." An example of one not "scientific" (normative) is "A good diet is right."

Ayer's book *Language, Truth and Logic* has been considered something of a text book on logical positivism. He states that his views are derived from the doctrines of Russell and Wittgenstein but that Moore takes a "rather different view of philosophical analysis." He states that he (Ayer) is in closest agreement to the "Viennese circle" which indicates that he did not consider himself a member of that group.[LTL, 31, 32] He writes of the relationship of logical positivism to science:

> Philosophy does not in any way compete with the sciences. It does not make

any speculative assertions which could conflict with the speculative assertions of science, nor does it profess to venture into fields which lie beyond the scope of scientific investigations.   Only the metaphysician does that, and produces nonsense as a result. And we have also pointed out that it is impossible merely by philosophizing to determine the validity of a coherent system of scientific propositions. For the question whether such system is valid is always a question of empirical fact; and, therefore, the propositions of philosophy, since they are purely linguistic propositions, can have no bearing upon it. Thus the philosopher is not, *qua* philosopher, in a position to assess the value of any scientific theory; his function is simply to elucidate the theory by defining the symbols which occur in it.[LTL, 151, 152]

Ayer adopted

what may be called a modified verification principle.   For I require of an empirical hypothesis, not indeed that it should be conclusively verifiable, but that some possible sense-experience should be relevant to the determination of its truth or falsehood. If a putative proposition fails to satisfy this principle, and is not a tautology, then I hold that it is metaphysical, and . . . senseless.[LTL, 31]

And there has been criticism of the analytic, synthetic, or nonsense, classification of propositions, for indeed, the proposition that states the classification, namely "All propositions are either analytic, synthetic, or nonsense" seems itself not to come under one of the classifications. If it is analytic, it is a mere tautology and tells us nothing about the world. This was Ayer's view. If it is synthetic (Carnap's view), it can be verified empirically. But this cannot be done. If neither, is it nonsense? This was Wittgenstein's view.

I suspect that the problem was in not recognizing that there are four categories of propositions, the analytic, the synthetic, nonsense, and the one which named the four kinds of propositions. Could we call it the protocol proposition?--there must be a better term. It reads, There are four kinds of propositions, the analytic, the synthetic, nonsense, and the protocol (or whatever).   However, I am not pushing this;   I have argued that the distinction is not worth much (page 127-130), so why salvage it?

Ludwig Wittgenstein (1889-1951), whose book *Tractatus Logico-Philosophicus* had an influence on the Vienna Circle, stayed aloof from them. The book was about 100 pages in length and each bit of wisdom expressed in it was numbered. It contained such diverse remarks as (2.04) "The totality of existent atomic facts is the world." (4.112) The object of philosophy is the logical clarification of thoughts; and (6.53) "The right method of philosophy would be this: To say nothing except what can be said--i.e., the propositions of natural science--i.e., something that has nothing to do with philosophy: and then always, when someone else wished to say something metaphysical, to demonstrate to him that he had given no meaning to certain signs in his propositions. This . . . would be the only strictly correct method." and, the most memorable in my view, (6.54) "My propositions are elucidatory in the this way: he who understands me finally recognizes them as senseless, when he has climbed out through them, on them, over them (He must, so to speak, throw away the ladder, after he has climbed up on it.) He must surmount these propositions; and then he will see the world rightly." Number 7: "Whereof one cannot speak, thereof one must be silent,"[TL] though ideal, would put an intolerable burden on philosophers. I did not get far up the ladder and evidently Wittgenstein climbed back down it for he later repudiated the *Tractatus* and in *Philosophical Investigations,* a collection of his notes published after his death, he claimed that the meaning of a word is its use, and his philosophy became "ordinary language philosophy," which put some distance between him and the logical positivists and "atomic facts." He asked,

> But what are the simple constituent parts of which reality is composed?--What are the simple constituent parts of a chair?--The bits of wood of which it is made? or the molecules, or the atoms?--"Simple" means: not composite. And here the point is: In what sense "composite"? It makes no sense at all to speak absolutely of the "simple parts of a chair."

He called attention to the problem of precise definitions, using "games" as an example. He pointed out that there is not something that is common to all, but similarities and relationships. He characterized the similarities as "family resemblances." His aim "was not to *solve* philosophical problems but to *dissolve* them, by showing that they were the result of deviating from the path of everyday language." According to him, "philosophy can in no way interfere with the actual use of language; it can in the end only describe it. For it cannot give it any foundation either. It leaves everything just as it is." If logical positivism is dead or dying, I suggest this for its epitaph. Whatever the status of logical positivism, it should be noted that there is still much interest in logic and analysis in philosophy today.

I presume that Wittgenstein would approve of my figure "No certificate from heaven" (see page 2). This seems the appropriate place for me to try to make the point that language is for communication. When it serves that purpose well, it is as good as it is going to get. Even flawed language communicates; when Johnnie says, "I ain't got no apples," Teacher knows what he means or else she could not correct him.

One philosopher has this understanding of the "later" Wittgenstein:

> He believed, as I understand him, that philosophical puzzlement can be eliminated by careful, scrupulous description of language as we actually use it. It is only when we study it in this way and see how it works that we can disengage ourselves from the traps of traditional philosophies like platonism and cartesianism. (These are not Wittgenstein's terms.) By platonism I mean the view that there are abstract entities called meanings which exist above and over the words that express them and the people who utter them; by cartesianism I mean what Gilbert Ryle has called the doctrine of the ghost in the machine, a purely spiritual soul joined mysteriously with a purely material body. Wittgenstein also objected to the view that there are special, momentary or relatively short, inner *acts* of understanding in which cartesian souls grasp platonic meanings. [AOA, 227]

This is naturalism where, by contrast, the logical positivists admired science from a position within shouting distance and held ground somewhere below, beside or above it.

Others interpret the later Wittgenstein differently. We are told "despite the attack on the method and metaphysics of phenomenology, [which we have not covered] Wittgenstein shares with the phenomenologists the sense that there is a mystery in human things that will not yield to scientific investigation." [FDTW, 284] He has also been called a mystic. Whatever the case, we leave him at this point to work a richer ore of naturalism.

UNABASHED NATURALISM

The naturalism of other philosophers was more direct than that of the analysts in a growing trend after idealism's heyday. Santayana is notably quotable. "This effort to be skeptically strict in doubting the veracity of experience has been carried by the Germans [Kant and Hegel were German] to the point of disease, like a madman forever washing his hands to clean away the dirt that is not there. But even these philosophers 'who look for the foundations of the universe in their own minds' do not live as if they really believe that things cease to exist when not perceived."[SOP, 368, 369]

> We are not asked to abolish our conceptions of the natural world, nor even in our daily life, to cease to believe in it; we are to be idealists only north-northwest, or transcendentally; when the wind is southerly we are to remain realists. . . . I should be ashamed to countenance opinions which, when not arguing, I did not believe. It would seem to me dishonest and cowardly to militate under other colors than those under which I live. . . . I have frankly taken nature by the hand, accepting as a rule, in my farthest speculations, the animal faith I live by from day to day.[SAAF, 298, 305, 308]
>
> In natural philosophy, I am a decided materialist--apparently the only one living. . . . But I do not profess to know what matter is in itself. . . . I wait for the men of science to tell me. . . . But whatever matter may be, I call it matter boldly, as I call my acquaintances Smith and Jones without knowing their secrets.[SAAF, vii, viii]
>
> Mechanism is probably universal; and though "physics cannot account for that minute motion and pullulation in the earth's crust of which human affairs are a portion," the best method in psychology is to suppose that mechanism prevails even in the inmost recesses of the soul. Psychology graduates from literature into science only when it seeks the mechanical and material basis of every mental event.[SOP, 370, 371]

When I read the line which begins "I have frankly taken nature by the hand," I got goose bumps. Here at last, I thought, is the philosopher I have been looking for, so I hurried to buy his book, *Skepticism and Animal Faith*, from which the quotation was taken. But I was a bit disappointed; in some of it he read like a scholastic, a scholastic without theology, of course. Reading a philosopher's whole works is like reading a poet's. Somewhere along the line, one wishes he had not started it and just remembered him for the gems. There were gems in Santayana, and I accept his position on psychology as is obvious from my definition of naturalism.

There are objections to this 100% determinism, the most prominent of which are made in moral philosophy. I discuss this below in my section on ethics and esthetics on page 209. Indeterminists, however, take heart most avidly from "quantum indeterminacy" of science itself. I let another explain:

> It is known that for measurements in the domain of subatomic dimensions, the Heisenberg Uncertainty Relation comes into play. This relation states that for a given uncertainty or vagueness in the value of an observable quantity like position, there is a definite limit, imposed by the laws of nature, on the accuracy with which the simultaneous value of another empirical quantity like velocity can be known, and that this limit is independent of the particular apparatus or method used in the determination. Since the apparatus used in measurement disturbs the system under observation, it would seem that the possibilities of refining measurements are not unlimited and that the dream of classical physics can therefore never come true. No refinement of experimental technique could ascertain the present values of the observables of a physical system accurately enough to enable us to make a *precise* prediction of the future values. Consequently, the new quantum mechanics is content to specify the frequencies or probabilities with which different values will be found in a given set of measurements.[CRGP, 335]

Further:

> Bohr gives several reasons for supposing that the most precise experimentally ascertainable knowledge of the momentary state of the constituent particles of the nervous system and of the external stimuli affecting it permits only a statistical prediction and not a completely detailed prediction of the fate of these stimuli in the nervous system.[CRGP, 335]

The writer quoted makes the point that a statistical prediction, that is, those cases in which we have to be content with specifying probabilities, which he calls statistico-deterministic, holds no refuge for indeterminism. I will not go into his argument, as I have shown elsewhere that probability rests on induction, that is, on laws of nature--natural determinism--in the future being like the past. Therefore when quantum mechanics is specifying probabilities, it has not abandoned science. This is not the argument the writer makes, but it is reasonable enough to convince us that the mysteries in the atom hold no refuge for the gods. These unpredictables have no bearing on determinism, in what I will call, for the want of a better term, other levels of determinism.

On the level of baseball the unpredictables in the atoms in a baseball, all millions of them, unpredictables and predictables alike, predictably go over the fence on a home run. Kant's "thing in itself" in a baseball likewise goes over the fence with the "thing" on a home run. The physicist and the "thing in itself" philosopher confirm their belief in determinism at other levels when they set their alarm clock to get up by; turn the doorknob to go out the door and turn the key to start their car.

I discuss the problem of free will on page 203 following my theory of the mind; against the odds, I have a solution.

The great difference of views of philosophers who agree on science is exasperating. For example, Russell and Dewey, "despite their not inconsiderable differences," agreed that "*All knowledge that men have is scientific knowledge.*"[TQFB, 214] Russell thought that philosophy should be done like science, but he was far afield at times. It was not that he put the cart before the horse, rather he appeared to want to pull the cart with the harness (logic) and eliminate the horse (science). Although he was often a clever and interesting writer, I suffered considerable conceptual indigestion reading his *Our Knowledge of the External World.* Anyone's external world is everything but his/her mind, and for those who hold that the mind is something separate from the brain, it includes his/her brain.

The question arises, can one reasonably ask if the external world exists? Even if we just ask, does it exist when no one is perceiving it (and does exist when someone is perceiving it)? Can that be reasonable? Russell asks these questions. Dewey did not think much of them. He quotes Russell's from his book: Can we "know that objects of sense . . . exist at times when we are not perceiving them?" Or, in another mode of statement: "Can the existence of anything other than our own hard data be inferred from the existence of those data?"[EIEL, 282]

And Dewey quotes Russell's position: "I think it must be admitted as probable that the immediate objects of sense depend for their existence upon physiological conditions in ourselves, and that for example, the colored surfaces which we see cease to exist when we shut our eyes."[EIEL, 283]
Dewey's criticism was this:

> I have not quoted the passage for the sake of gaining an easy victory by pointing out that this statement involves the existence of physiological conditions.
> For Mr. Russell himself affirms that fact. As he points out, such arguments

assume precisely the "common-sense world of stable objects" professedly put in doubt. . . . My purpose is to ask what justification there is for calling immediate data "objects of sense." Statements of this type always call color visual, sound auditory, and so on. . . . That color is visual in the sense of being an object of vision is certainly admitted in the common-sense world, but this is the world we have left. That color is visual is a proposition about color and it is a proposition which color itself does not utter. Visible or visual color is already a "synthetic" proposition, not a term nor an analysis of a single term. That color is seen, or is visible, I do not call in question; but I insist that fact already assumes an answer to the question which Mr. Russell has put. It presupposes existence beyond the color itself.[EIEL, 283, 284]

And that is the "external world." Dewey has considerably more criticism than this but it is a little tedious, so I will make this much do. I agree with Dewey that Russell's position presupposes the existence of the external world. But then so does his questions; take "our own hard data:" "Our" denotes ownership and can only mean Russell and all others that have "hard" sense data. All others are in Russell's external world. Each philosopher occupies the external world of all other philosophers. I believe that the language of philosophy--of any reasonable discourse whatever--belies anyone's disclaimer of the existence of things other than minds.

Durant remarked that Russell "emphasized the virtues of logic, and made a divinity of mathematics" and, after quoting him on the subject, wrote, "It is remarkable that after writing several volumes of this learned moonshine, Bertrand Russell should suddenly come down upon the surface of this planet, and begin to reason very passionately about war, and government, and socialism, and revolution,--and never once make use of the impeccable formulae piled like Pelion upon Ossa in his *Principia Mathematica*. Nor has anyone else, observably, made use of them."[SOP, 358, 360] I make no pretense of understanding *Principia Mathematica*, but I doubt that, if I could, it would change my mind that logic is only a guide, not the foundation of science.

Mathematics is language--the language of measurement and quantity--an efficient and manipulable language. It owes no more to logic than the written word, both of which get their authority from the fact that they reflect a natural universe. That the written word is also used to create and disseminate nonsense does not militate against the fact that its basis is natural law. It would not communicate if it were not, and would never have been developed.

Dewey came down upon the surface of this planet after being schooled in Hegelian idealism.   One of his books, *Experience and Nature* is, as one would expect from the title, naturalistic empiricism.   I was surprised to find the term metaphysics used in conjunction with naturalism in the book. Sidney Hook relates that Dewey "wrote in his ninetieth year that 'nothing can be farther from the facts of the case' than 'that I use the word metaphysical in the sense it bears in the classic tradition based on Aristotle.' He vowed at that time (as if he had all eternity before him) 'never to use the words [*metaphysics* and *metaphysical*] again in connection with any aspect of any part of my own position'."[TQFB, 160]

I could quote Dewey in defense of much of my position, but I will quote Sidney Hook, who was in Dewey's philosophical camp.   Hook on naturalism,

> There is only one reliable method of reaching the truth about the nature of things anywhere and at any time, that this reliable method come to full fruition in the methods of science, and that a man's normal behavior in adapting means to ends belies his words whenever he denies it. Naturalism as a philosophy not only accepts this method but also the broad generalizations which are established by the use of it; *viz*, that the occurrence of all qualities or events depends upon the organization of a material system in space-time, and that their emergence, development and disappearance are determined by changes in such organization.
>
> Common sense takes the word "material" as loosely equivalent to the *materials* with which men deal as they go from problem to problem; naturalism as a philosophy takes it to refer to the subject matter of the physical sciences. Neither the one nor the other asserts that only what can be observed exists, for many things may be legitimately inferred to exist (electrons, the expanding universe, the past, the other side of the moon) from what is observed; but both hold that there is no evidence for the assertion of the existence of anything which does not rest upon some observable effects.[TQFB, 185, 186]

Hook further insists that

> all human beings in their everyday experience are guided by the conception of knowledge as scientific knowledge. To deny this is palpably insincere. A Platonist might invidiously dub all empirical knowledge as "opinion," but no matter what one calls such knowledge, one acts on it, and to achieve one's ends one must necessarily act on it. The burden of proof rests entirely upon those who assert that there exists another kind of knowledge over and above technological, common-sense, empirical knowledge, and the scientific knowledge

which is an outgrowth and development of it.[TQFB, 217]

Hook remarks that "some traditional forms of materialism are in actuality species of idealism which have adopted the fighting word 'materialism' as a strategic masquerade in their struggle against other varieties of idealism. Orthodox dialectical materialism is a philosophy of this kind."[TQFB, 236, 137] I put a slightly different emphasis on common sense and science from that of Hook. For me, technological, common-sense, empirical knowledge, *is* science. *Advanced science* of calipers and test tube, and complicated mathematical formula are an outgrowth of it.

> Indeed there is no difference in kind between them. The superiority of the scientific hypothesis consists merely in its being more abstract, more precise, and more fruitful. And although scientific objects such as atoms and electrons seem to be fictitious in a way that chairs and tables are not, here too, the distinction is only a distinction of degree. For both these kinds of objects are known only by their sensible manifestations and are definable in terms of them. [LTL, 49]

Common sense in common parlance is naturalism, that is to say, it is naturalism to the majority. Common expressions and old adages tend to creep in; therefore, it is necessary to distinguish between the concepts of naturalistic common sense and common metaphysical concepts. To consider the subject further, and point up some hazards in defining the term, we turn to a Common-Sense philosopher, G. E. Moore.

He made a list of things he claimed to "know" (was certain[1] they were certain[2]--I would have said, rather, it was not reasonable to doubt them) which was a return (from idealism) to sanity in philosophy. Here are some examples from his essay, "A Defense of Common Sense":

A. There exists at present a living human body, which is my body.
B. This body was much smaller when it was born than it is now.
C. Ever since it was born it has been in contact with, or not far from, the surface of the earth.
D. Ever since it was born it has been at various distances from a great number of physical objects.
E. The earth had existed many years before my body was born.
F. Many other human bodies had existed before my body was born, and many of them had already died before my birth.[PP]

This list is a long and tedious one, as Moore was aware. He held that somewhere, sometime, in the history of philosophy, each of these statements has been denied. I believe it is Moore's position that it is absurd to deny these statements. I, of course, agree; I use the absurdity of denial as the criteria for using the term "knowledge," page 188. Moore's Common Sense, however, does not remain this common as he pursues the subject further.

He does so in his book, *Some Main Problems of Philosophy*, from which the following account is taken except as otherwise noted. In this book he attempted to give a description of the whole range of philosophy. Regarding common sense, he held that views held by almost everybody, those views so universally held, may be called the views of common sense. However, he counts neither the belief in God nor an after life as common sense despite the almost universal belief in God. Great numbers of people, he says, are not sure and this rules it out as a common sense belief. This confines common sense to apply to the natural universe. Elsewhere he includes ethics in common sense and holds that right and wrong are known intuitively. This is discussed on page 213. To recapitulate, common sense, according to Moore, is views of the natural universe universally held, including ethical ones held intuitively.

He then names the views that are so universally held as to make them common sense. According to Moore the most important things we are sure exist in the natural universe by common sense are material objects in space, acts of consciousness of men and animals, space and time, and appearances of material objects. We are sure of these although there may be other things. As to "appearances of material objects," Moore cites various views of physical objects at different distances and gives the example of a church steeple. There are two views about them: (1) The appearances, some of them at least, are really part of the church which is really situated in space and continue to exist when we are not conscious of them. (2) None of the appearances are in space and exist only so long as they appear to some one. Both, he says, are consistent with common sense but are not held by common sense. All common sense insists on is that the appearances are of material objects in space that exist when we are not viewing them.

Whatever Moore thinks about these two views--we will skip his comments on them--*he accepts the reality of "appearances. "* Elsewhere he pursues the subject using an envelope that he holds up before an audience and calling attention to the different appearances it presents. Moore uses terms like "it seems to me" and "I think" in presenting his case for common sense. In a like vein, it seems to me that when we say "the church steeple appears," common sense tells us that it means "The church staple is seen." There is no ghostly, queer entity "appearance" involved. To say so is to nominalize (make a noun of) a verb, and therefore multiply entities beyond necessity. I do not believe philosophy has any such magic.

Although Moore accepts the reality of appearances, he believes they disappear when he is not looking at the object of which it is the appearance. I cannot find where he says this in so many words, but we can determine this to be his position by what he said about seeing the church steeple. The appearance appeared (if you will) only when he saw the steeple. This would be the case when he looked at the steeple a second time. It could not be claimed that it just appeared at the moment he looked at the steeple if it continued to exist between times.

As to what ceases to exist when we are not seeing the steeple, I believe common sense tell us that (1) The light rays which are reflecting the (surface of) the steeple to our eyes ceases to function in that capacity when the eyes are directed away from the steeple. (2) The idea, to use Locke's and Hume's term (the reader may substitute his own) resulting from seeing the church ceases to exist when the memory can no longer recall it, but exists even when we are not conscious of it (do not recall it) as long as it is there to be recalled. I will argue in my theory of the mind that these ideas or images exist as a function within brain cells.

To return to his position on the existence of God, he held that those who assert that there certainly is a God go beyond the view of common sense, and make an important addition to it, while not contradicting it. I can't understand how a view that goes beyond common sense could be an addition to it. If that were the case, every conceivable view on any subject would be an addition.

Moore's criteria for assigning common sense to a belief or concept are that they "are so universally held," are things that "we all commonly assume to be true about the Universe" and that "we are sure that we know to be true about it." On this view, what is commonly believed is common sense, and as such, it seems to be an absolute starting point for knowledge, not derived or deducted from anything--something congenital, something "known" by all normal persons.

Even neglecting the part about appearances, Moore's treatment of common sense is not adequate. We need some refinement here. We saw that Hook, page 176, lumped "technological, common sense, empirical knowledge" together, but let us go back to Kant's categories, page 145, those faculties with which we deal with the experienced world. The definition of common sense from a dictionary is "having and exhibiting native good intelligence." This is virtually the native intelligence in Kant's categories. It is with these that we function. It is the resulting basic naturalistic concepts, which make the basic assumptions of science, that are common. In my theory of the mind, I will call these the constant elements in our minds. I believe this is common usage for "common sense." Still, common usage is not 100%; Moore is an example. Therefore, to be strictly accurate, I must say only that this is my definition of common sense. This is the way I use it, as, in fact, I have.

Moore had little interest in science, and I do not believe he was aware of the consequences of common-sense philosophy as regards science; he did not seem to consider its presuppositions, which are those of science. He put this queer entity, appearance, between the mind and the object seen and takes one faltering step toward the idealism that he detests. I believe he thinks he disassociates himself from idealism by saying that the appearance is of a real material object that exists and continues to exist when we are not looking at it.

Moore made other arguments besides common sense for the existence of material objects. He argued (paraphrased) "that if the thesis that there are none is true, no philosopher has ever held it; for philosophers are themselves embodied persons."[PTC, 61] He surely meant that "no philosopher has reasonably held it" for the whole purpose of Moore's common-sense argument is that some philosophers have held these views that contradict common sense. He further argues that there is a contradiction by "those who argue that we do not know that there are material objects. He finds the contradiction in the use of the word 'we' which he takes as implying the claim to know that the speaker and other persons exist."[PTC, 61, 62] We can use the same logic against Moore regarding the church steeple. Having said "steeple" he implied that he was seeing the steeple not an appearance of it. It should be added here that Moore missed an important element in common sense, that of perspective in viewing physical objects. Common sense tells us that when we see different views of a steeple we are seeing the steeple.

With this I bring the history of naturalism to an end. The reader has suffered long enough. Hereafter, philosophers will be quoted only as their philosophy pertains to subjects discussed. The history of naturalism in philosophy as presented here, as brief and incomplete as it is, suffices, I believe, to show the great importance of naturalism in the advance of knowledge and the relative unimportance of "philosophy proper."

POSITIONS AND DEFINITIONS

Having written disparagingly about philosophy in general and metaphysics and epistemology in particular, I must now give further treatment of these subjects. Also, I now give my conclusions concerning induction and the body-mind "problems," or if they have been fairly covered in the forgoing, a recapitulation. I want to be thoroughly understood on these subjects before I attempt a theory of the mind.

Metaphysics, My Definition

It has been said that metaphysics is "the art of befuddling one's self methodically."[SOP, 276] This fits in well with my point of view. But more respectfully, to quote Will Durant, "metaphysics, as William James said, is nothing but an attempt to think things out clearly to their ultimate significance, to find their substantial essence in the scheme of reality,--or, as Spinoza puts it, their essential substance; and thereby to unify all truth and reach that 'highest of all generalizations' which, even to the practical Englishman, constitutes philosophy."[SOP, 131] Thinking things out clearly is, I suspect, what the Scholastics thought they were doing, and we have seen (page 52) what the philosophers who followed them thought of their metaphysics.

"The classification of metaphysics as a separate branch of study is due to Aristotle whose term for it was 'First Philosophy'"[GTP, 158] Later it was the "arbitrary title given by Andronicus of Rhodes, circa 70 B.C. to a certain collection of Aristotelian writings,"[DOP, 212] namely those *other than* his physics.

Having expressed my distrust of metaphysics, it is time I defined the word as I use it. Early on, I got the impression that it meant "other than physics," but in fact, it is used very loosely, almost as a synonym for philosophy, as in the quote from James above and in the paragraph below. It is necessary, therefore, to define it as one uses it.

One metaphysician tells us that in one respect metaphysics

> is to be distinguished from the sciences, which deliberately confine their attention
> to some special department of what is--physics to the world of matter, biology

> to living organisms, geology to rocks, botany to plants, and so forth. . . . The metaphysician will have to consider the ultimate grounds which underlie all these special branches of study and the assumptions on which they proceed. . . . Metaphysics . . . examines the presuppositions of the sciences. Its enquiries leave off where theirs begin. From another point of view, its enquiries begin where theirs leave off. . . . the significance of the title metaphysics is that it denotes the branch of study which comes *after* physics, in the sense that its interests begin at the point at which those of physics stop.[GTP, 159]

This philosopher further states that "while metaphysical systems may and do differ in the most bewildering fashion, they are all or almost all unanimous in denying the title of full reality to the worlds affirmed by common sense and explored by science."[GTP, 160] I would reserve all of this except the last sentence for a definition of philosophy, and agree that the "branch of study which comes after physics" in the last sentence is metaphysics.

Here is a definition given in a dictionary:

> Traditionally given by the oracular phrase: "The science of being as such." To be distinguished from the study of being under some particular aspect; hence opposed to such sciences as are concerned with *ens mobile, ens quantum,* etc, The term, "science", is here used in its classic sense of "knowledge by causes", where "knowledge" is contrasted with "opinion" and the term cause has the full signification of the Greek aitia. The "causes" which are the objects of metaphysical cognition are said to be "first" in the natural order (first principles), as being founded in no higher or more complete generalizations available to the human intellect by means of its own natural powers.[DOP, 212]

I find "science of being" unintelligible. Can being mean anything other than existence? Surely philosophy is about things which exist, therefore, when you are doing philosophy, your subject from the outset is that which exists, and, as Kant has taught us, existence is not a predicate. Perhaps I am mistaken about this. Perhaps being is "be" that "ings" or something like that but, it leaves me in the dark.

The science to which it is opposed I understand to be physical science (as in the previous quotation from GTP). I can buy that. I also feel certain (certainty[1]) that I fathom metaphysics's "knowledge" and "opinion" as defined here. The former is my certainty[2] and the latter is my certainty[1]. But the most interesting part of the definition is the last. The method of arriving at certainty[2] is by the means of the intellect's "own natural powers."

Historically, more often than not, these powers have been held to be reason, deductive and a priori. As we have seen, the latter received a devastating blow from Hume, and Kant tried to resurrect it.

But this is not all of the definition. We are given "secondary and derivative meanings:"

> (a) Anything concerned with the supra-physical. Thus "metaphysical healing, metaphysical poetry", . . . etc.
>
> (b) Any scheme of explanation which transcends the inadequacies or inaccuracies of ordinary thought.[DOP, 212]

In (a) I find my "other than physical" definition, but I find (b) contradictory. I can only conceive, for example, that when Copernicus discovered that the earth moved, it was by a scheme of explanation which transcended the inadequacies and inaccuracies of ordinary thought of his time and was concerned with the physical, not the supra-physical; and further that the church's thought that the earth did not move was inadequate, inaccurate, and very ordinary thought, and, as it was based on "holy scripture," it was "supra-physical."

Carnap called those propositions *metaphysical* which claimed to be knowledge about that which is over or beyond experience such as the Absolute, Things in them selves, and real essence. His "over and beyond" is roughly equivalent to my "other than" and his "experience" is close to my "physical," as the physical must ultimately be defined as that which can be known or inferred to exist by experience. In saying this, I am not subscribing to the classical empiricist dogma that any statement purporting to be about physical objects in the external world can be reducible to or analyzable into sense data. (see page 95)

Kant gives us the subject matter of metaphysics:

> And just in this transcendental or supersensible sphere, where experience affords us neither instruction nor guidance, lie the investigations of *Reason*, which on account of their importance, we consider far preferable to, and as having a far more elevated aim than, all that the understanding can achieve within the sphere of sensuous phenomena. So high a value do we set upon these investigations, that even at the risk of error, we persist in following them out, and permit neither doubt nor disregard nor indifference to restrain us from the pursuit. These unavoidable problems of mere pure reason are GOD, FREEDOM (of will) and IMMORTALITY. The science which, with all its preliminaries, has for

its especial object the solution of these problems is named metaphysics.[CPR, 47]

I disagree that we have any such power of reason a priori, but what Kant calls metaphysics fits in my definition. I will hold to my definition of metaphysics as "other than physical." Since this is not exactly how the word is used by many philosophers, when I use the word I will write it "metaphysics[t]." The superscripted "t" is to indicate "metaphysics defined, or as used, by Tichenor." The "t" is a lower case "t" to indicate that Tichenor is a very small philosopher. If I call myself a philosopher, albeit an insignificant one, what is my definition of philosophy? This concerns us next.

Philosophy, an Evaluation of the Term

It would be nice if one could use common usage for a definition, but this has varied over the centuries. We can only use the definition of our own age. Philosophy once included "natural philosophy." "Until the death of Newton, and even later there was no generally recognized, clear line of distinction between philosophy and the natural sciences."[AOR, 14] Philosophers are now content to leave science to scientists. This may be sound philosophy, but they had no choice.   The scientific knowledge explosion made it impossible for philosophers to have competency in "natural philosophy." So great is the knowledge that one can hope to master only a specialty or a specialty within a specialty. Leibniz, it has been said, "was the last man who could hope to master the whole range of modern knowledge, and to be an encyclopedia in himself."[AOR, 143]

I will define philosophy as all those thoughts, ideas, concepts, whatever, as well as questions and their answers about the mysteries of the universe which lie "outside" of science and the formal disciplines. And while this includes what has historically been called metaphysics and metaphysics[t], I hold that metaphysics[t] is philosophically worthless however valuable it may be in other respects. One philosopher explains,

> Philosophical questions cannot be answered by adducing the results of observation or experience, as empirical questions, whether of science of common sense, are answered. Such questions as: "What is the supreme good?" Or How can I be sure that your sensations are similar to mine? Or that I ever genuinely understand what you are saying, and do not merely seem

to myself to do so?" cannot be, on the face of it, answered by either of the two great instruments of human knowledge: empirical investigation on the one hand, and deductive reasoning as it is used in the formal disciplines on the other--the kind of argument which occurs, for example, in mathematics or logic or grammar.

Indeed it might almost be said that the history of philosophy in its relation to the sciences consists, in part, in the disentangling of those questions which are either empirical (and inductive), or formal (and deductive), from the mass of problems which fill the minds of men, and the sorting out of these under the heads of the empirical or formal sciences concerned with them. It is in this way that, for instance, astronomy, mathematics, psychology, biology, etc., became divorced from the general corpus of philosophy (of which they once formed a part), and embarked upon fruitful careers of their own as independent disciplines. They remained within the province of philosophy only as long as the kinds of way in which their problems were to be settled remained unclear, and so were liable to be confused with other problems with which they had relatively little in common, and from which their differences had not been sufficiently concerned. The advance both of the sciences and of philosophy seems bound up with this progressive allocation of the empirical and formal elements, each to its own proper sphere; always, however, leaving behind a nucleus of unresolved (and largely unanalyzed) questions, whose generality, obscurity, and above all, apparent (or real) insolubility by empirical or formal methods, gives them a status of their own which we tend to call philosophical. [AOE, 12, 13]

It is interesting that our philosopher has said "philosophical questions cannot be answered by adducing the results of observations or experience, as empirical questions, whether of science or of common sense, are answered" and that he also says that questions "remain within the province of philosophy only as long as the kinds of way in which their problems were to be settled remained unclear." These remarks are presented as facts; thus, he holds that clear answers are science and that questions that have no clear answers are philosophy. But, it is simply a matter of definition. We define those answers that are clearly supported with evidence as scientific and those that are not clear, in the sense that evidence makes answers clear, as philosophical. This is, therefore, by common usage (or majority usage, for there are dissenters) the definition of philosophy. I add that when evidence is only considered valid when it assumes natural law, one's philosophy is naturalism, and that is my position.

The philosopher gives us only such wisdom as he can muster while sitting and thinking or perhaps walking around; I do not want to rule out the peripatetic. If he leaves this posture to experiment and investigate by other means than his reason, we classify him as a scientist or at least a natural philosopher. But, notwithstanding this fact, he brings experience to his trade; such experience as he had in life and what he has learned of science. So he reasons, making do with what experience he has had up to the time he became a philosopher. However pure a metaphysician[t] any philosopher thinks he is, his work is tainted with naturalism.

We are doomed to be philosophers because of our limitations; the questions are there because we don't have ready-made answers. Likewise for the scientist; we use the scientific method because of our limitations; we are not endowed with an unerring capacity to know without it.

I have expressed my view that knowledge is scientific knowledge and I have dismissed metaphysics[t] (I remind the reader that this is not everyone's definition of metaphysics) as nonsense. I have further stated that I abandon epistemology for psychology (one branch of philosophy for one branch of science). What then is left of philosophy for me? More than may appear; one does not escape philosophy so easily. These statements reveal a philosophical position, that of naturalism. Within the general position of naturalism there are specific items long held to be philosophical positions, "monism," to name one, my position that all "things" are of one kind, my physicalism. One neither escapes from philosophy in general nor epistemology in particular by insisting that knowledge is scientific knowledge, for that is a philosophical position.

There is a gray line or overlapping area between philosophy and science. Theories, however fanciful, are naturalistic when natural law is assumed regarding them and potentially scientific. They are science when there is evidence to support them. The ubiquity of science is often not recognized. There are philosophers who miss this important fact. I think I have made the point on the preceding pages that every instance of applying means to ends in the everyday functions of life makes the fundamental assumptions of science. Everyone, including those who cite quantum indeterminacy in the Heisenberg Uncertainty Relation to disparage science, begins the day assuming that when his/her feet hit the floor it will function to hold him up as in the past, that his breakfast will give him energy, that the latch on the door will let him out the door, that his car will furnish transportation, that the accelerator, brakes, steering wheel, and door latches will function as in the past. If they do not, he takes a purely naturalistic approach to the problem when he expects science, both investigative and applied, to repair them.

To epitomize the "philosophy or science first" predicament, we think of philosophy as first when considering ideas which, as Kant taught us, lie outside of the province of science as well as those supposedly within it but for which science does not yet have the answers. But, once science does have the answers we consider them--that is to say, the pronouncements of those who base their findings on evidence and reasoning--superior (i.e. first) to the pronouncements of those who have based their "knowledge" on reading the philosophers plus such reasoning as they can muster. Although the latter do not reason without interjecting some matter from experience, they keep their hands clean of whole-hearted empirical investigation (otherwise they would be classified as scientists and lose their status as philosophers). Science touches every facet of our lives; therefore, its very ubiquity, as a matter of fact, is overwhelmingly first in our lives. Therefore, our philosophy however tacitly or subconsciously held, even when denying it, is naturalism.

Philosophers, as we have seen, hold widely varying views. Our environment, the ideas to which we have been exposed, surely has something to do with it, but I think we have to consider that there could be a genetic factor also. If I had a different gene I might not be so interested in the view I hold and be saying something quite different. And if the reader would hold this against me (as showing that I do not have a mind of my own), I remind him that he is using a naturalistic theory which fits in well with my position and in no way diminishes it.

Epistemology Displaced, Almost

The empiricists insisted that knowledge comes from experience. Their theories were descriptive of how we obtain ideas or concepts. There are those who would say, "So that is how we come by ideas, but are they true--are they knowledge?" Therefore, the question arises, *should epistemological theories of knowledge encompass theories of learning?* It does seem so. If we can demonstrate that some method has taught, then someone has learned, and by definition they have some knowledge. But we are told that

> The epistemologist must . . . guard against a particularly insidious form of the genetic fallacy: viz. the supposition that the psychological origin of an item of knowledge prejudices either favorably or unfavorably its cognitive validity--a fallacy which is psychologism at its worst.[DOP, 109]

But, if a man's house is on fire, and we insist that the genesis of his believing it is burning is his observation of it burning, and if we insist that he does not merely believe it is burning but has knowledge that it is burning, we are insisting that the psychological origin of his belief prejudices favorably its cognitive validity.

Thus in the beginning, prior to the facts of life, holding that knowledge is certainty^2, we cannot answer the epistemological question. In the thick of experience, which I epitomize with the bit about the man witnessing his house burning, epistemological skepticism becomes absurd, and we are naturalists in assigning truth to propositions, and knowledge is scientific knowledge if the word is to have any meaning in our language. I have called this (page 3) a predicament, not a paradox.

The moment of truth, then, comes (naturally) in experience--in a specific situation. With certainty^2 elusive; with no help from heaven or from the philosophers, we are on our own and the judge of "knowledge." *The absurdity of denial is our critique of knowledge.* I have made my case on page 129 that the so-called analytic as applied science is no exception.

In holding such a view one has abandoned epistemology for psychology, almost. Almost, for within psychology, empiricism is one's epistemology.

Induction, the Heart of Reason

When Francis Bacon told the world that "nature, to be commanded, must be obeyed" and emphasized the importance of induction, it was already in extensive use. As Macaulay later thought, (to quote Will Durant) "Induction as described by Bacon is a very old-fashioned affair, over which there is no need of raising any commotion, much less a monument. 'Induction has been practiced from morning till night by every human being since the world began.' "[SOP, 106]

It has been said that Hume ceased to be skeptical of induction when he laid down his pen, but this misses the fact that he was not skeptical, at least subconsciously, while using it. As he was in the process of putting his thoughts on paper, he trusted the "future to be like the past." As he used his pen to write one word, he confidently assumed the pen would function to write the next one (in the future). He trusted the characteristics of paper to be the same in the future as in the past and to hold the ink in the position in which he put it. He expected publishers of books to function as in the past.

Induction is not an option, for to function is to use it. Every step we take, every plan we make, every judgement in applying means to ends assumes it, however subconscious it may be. There has been some mention of it in Western philosophy beginning with the Greeks, but its importance was largely lost in centuries of theology-ridden philosophy until Francis Bacon.

Hume was right. There is no rational proof of the principle of induction and causation before the fact--a priori; nor can we deduce it. We cannot promote our belief that they are valid beyond certainty[1] to certainty[2], but, contrary to Hume, who evidently thought that he had made a legitimate (rational) skepticism, it only shows our limitations. And these limitations prevent us from being "rationally" skeptical. The same is true of evidence and observation, which are concomitant concepts to induction and causation and are not really separate "problems." Natural law is the root concept of each. Kant was right, our categories, our *rational faculties*, are limited to natural philosophy.

The question then, "Is induction valid?" given our limitations, is not a pertinent question. We cannot prove a priori or by deduction, prior to all experience that, if fire has burned one minute, nature will function in the future as in the past, and that the fire will burn the next minute and the next. The answerable question in real life is "Is it reasonable to doubt induction?" The answer is, "It is not." No rational person is skeptical of induction when his house is on fire. If he is not so emotionally unstrung that he cannot think, he thinks inductively. He *reasonably* thinks inductively. *Reason begins with inductive thinking.*

We come by induction instinctually, which is to say genetically, as do all the other animals, because it has survival value. When we become conscious of it, as the other animals do not, and hold that concept as the operation of things by inviolate law and give it a name, it becomes part of us. The resulting concepts we develop with the many inductions we live by are inseparable from our minds, indeed are part of our minds. When our science reaches the point where "survival value" explains the genesis of the concept, *we divest ourselves of it only in fantasy* or philosophy, which are often the same thing, to ask the questions "Does the external world exist?" and "Is induction valid?" and consequently involve ourselves in absurdities. At this point *Hume's skepticism of induction becomes just so much sophistry.* This position will not satisfy everyone; even Wittgenstein's "pulling the ladder up behind us" may be preferred, but there can be no rational support for natural law because there is no more fundamental concept than induction in the reasoning process. It and the deduction that is based on it is reason itself. The "problem of induction" is only a scandal within that philosophy which has only deduction and a priorism as its canon (for other than the formal disciplines).

We have a craving for a rational support or proof, nevertheless. It is another instinct which causes us to waste paper and ink in philosophy.

In my theory of the mind, I will argue that induction (the capacity or propensity to use it) is a congenital faculty or characteristic. Any definition of the "mind" must include it. This is no longer a matter of philosophical speculation. That the mind functions as if natural law is universal is now established by psychologists, notably in the work of Elizabeth Spelke of Harvard. She has shown that children as young as three months old interpret the world as predictable; they expect objects to obey laws. Fortunately for psychologists, babies are uncontaminated by the babble of philosophers.

Body-Mind

The two areas where arguments are most often urged against naturalism (conceived as materialism) are the body-mind problem and ethics. The presentation of naturalism would not be complete without a discussion of them.

Locke reluctantly accepted the dualism of corporeal body and incorporeal mind, but suggests that 'mind' might be a form of 'matter' basing his judgement of what God could do. It is (to repeat from page 81)

not much more remote from our comprehension to conceive that God can, if He pleases, superadd to matter a *faculty of thinking*, than that He should add to *it another substance with the faculty of thinking.* . . . He who will give himself leave to consider freely . . . will scarce find his reason able to determine him fixedly for or against the soul's materiality.

I suggest that it may have been Locke's position that mind was a form of matter, and that he pussyfooted around it because in his day men were still hanged or burned for saying the wrong (unauthorized) thing about the soul. It is a good statement; our "reason" cannot establish that there is a metaphysical[t] "soul" and/or "mind," a separate entity from the body, a ghost in the machine. It is just as conceivable that mind is body stuff as that it is a metaphysical[t] ghost.

Hobbes had no trouble in saying (paraphrased) that the soul and mind are not immaterial; they are names for the vital processes of the body and operations of the brain. We have seen that La Mettrie (page 140) and Priestley (page 141), had material theories of the mind. More anciently Democritus (page 10) and the Epicureans (page 20), did also. Anaxagoras "was the first philosopher who attributed mind to matter."[EGP, 138] I will pass over more recent philosophers with a like bent, with whose theories I am only vaguely familiar. I wish, however, if any of my theory of the mind, soon to follow, has been proposed by any of them, to relinquish it to the rightful owner. I will mention only Gilbert Ryle whose memorable and apt phrase "Ghost in the Machine"[COM, 15] I have quoted. While I enthusiastically adopt the phrase, our methods, as I understand his, are quite different. The physical theory of the mind is an old idea that has gone nowhere in philosophy. The Emots (see page 198) in us have collectively squelched it. I believe, however, that the sciences of genetics and the brain are quietly taking the subject away from philosophy. I hope that my two cents worth, soon to follow, which is neither of these, will nevertheless be considered scientific. If the reader will not allow this, I will have to be content with calling it a naturalistic theory.

I quote Hook again for moral support for my theory:

> If the production of mind by material changes and *only* by material changes is a mystery, then the production or creation of things by mental activity . . . is no less mysterious. The argument that the disparity between mind and matter is so great that there is no common determinable under which their specific qualitative differences may intelligibly be subsumed--an argument derived from the old

superstition that "only like can affect like"--would make causal explanation of any qualitative change within any one realm, mental or material, impossible, so that even if the argument were valid, it operates equally against the materialist and idealist.[TQFB, 234]

The first step in reason (my position, page 189) is the acceptance of induction and the concomitant acceptance of evidence that it entails; and the evidence is that we do our thinking with the brain, which is "body." Thinking stops when the function of the brain stops. If the brain owes its existence to food we eat and the air we breathe, corporeal stuff all, if the brain ceases to function when that supply is cut off, then we have no reason to believe that the "mind" is any other type of entity. There is no evidence for a ghost, it not bothering to wear its sheet. Further, we have no reason to believe that thoughts are not comprised of those constituents of food.

A THEORY OF THE MIND

I theorize, therefore, that some functions within the brain constitute the mind, and that the function of the mind is in all cases some *disposition* (to choose a word not yet corrupted by philosophers) of physical entities; something changes in some brain cells when we have thoughts. I presume that this function is on the chemical or physical level. These terms are still useful but a clear distinction between them was wiped out about a century ago. We say chemical in reference to elements and compounds and physical as regards atomic particles. But as the elementary particles of matter gave up their secrets, "the borderland between physics and chemistry was obliterated."[CTSOC, 197] I think of chemistry as the chemistry of physics and hereafter use the latter to cover both. I use the word disposition as it is general enough to cover both, a "chemical" and a physical entity, that is, the brain forming compounds and/or making use of atomic particles beneath that level of organization in a way not now known and by particles known or not now known. I make an uneducated guess that it is both, but it is not necessary to know this for the physical theory of the mind to be believable. Just as it was reasonable to believe that apples were food long before their chemical analysis was known, it is reasonable to believe in the physical composition of the "mind."

The "vital force" theory of elements comes to mind as I try to explain my position. Before Friedrich Woehler synthesized urea, it was believed that there was a vital force present in animal and vegetable compounds that was not in mineral substances and that these compounds could not be made up from mineral compounds in the laboratory.[CTSOC, 129] Something similar prevails in most quarters today concerning the mind. It is believed that the mind cannot, is not, comprised of ordinary elements such as in the food we eat. But those ghostly things, whatever they are conceived to be, (again) cannot be detected if they will not wear a sheet.

Ideas, to use the elemental term of the classical empiricists, are not, I theorize, metaphysical[t] entities floating around between a philosopher's ears, scalp and palate. Rather they are something physical happening within a cell or cells in the brain; something that would not be if the idea did not occur; ideas, all ideas, thoughts, both cognitive and subconscious, whether of conviction or skepticism; even metaphysical[t] ideas. Further, these are not something the mind has but, among other things, *are* the mind. It may make sense to say the brain *has* these, but not that the mind has them. Language in this regard presents a problem--for example, in the expression, "I have knowledge." Rather than go into some Russellesque analysis, I prefer to say simply that when I say, "have/has knowledge," I do not mean that the knowledge (concept) is not part of the mind any more than I mean that the fingers are not part of the hand when I say "the hand has five fingers."

We were perhaps a little incensed with Hume's analysis of the mind as a "bundle of perceptions" and his argument that the mind is not "endowed with a perfect simplicity and identity," (page 118) that the self is not an "invariable and uninterrupted existence."[AOE, 246] But (if my theory is correct) perceptions--ideas, concepts--do constitute part of the mind. I have made the point (page 189) that we cannot divest ourselves of the assumption of the validity of induction. Here I insist that it is physically impossible, because it is part of us. Hume's problem was in not seeing that perceptions *among other things*, including the faculties Kant put back in the mind, are the mind. (In saying this, I am not claiming that Kant had the last word concerning the faculties of the mind). Hume could not envision the mind being a function of the brain, because he found "body," which included the brain, was also a bundle of impressions. And Hume had a point about identity. He meant that we are different as we grow. We are not exactly the same "thing" in both mind or body year after year. After years of education the mind is quite different from before. Psychologists now have evidence that experience not only teaches but that it makes physical changes in the brain (mind) which increases the brain's ability to learn. This is another reason for deflating "a priori" as Kant used it in "synthetic a priori."

I suggest that the first law (if not law, then initial step) of concepts in general is that sensing is believing (certainty[1]), and that this holds for hearsay (propositions) as for direct experience. Our sole powers (or causes) of resisting believing any proposition are having a previously acquired belief to the contrary or conceiving it to be contrary to self interest. The "incoming" belief is some disposition of physical entities in the brain. If there are no impeding physical entities (concepts), the conviction is immediate and complete. If there is a previous opposing disposition of physical entities (concept), it is rejected or there is doubt. After the experience of receiving much misinformation as eventually happens to everyone, a degree of skepticism sets in, varying from individual to individual (due to genetic factors); and the immediate acceptance of secondhand information (propositions, testimony) is eroded. This would seem to obscure the first law step, that is, that experience is believing. But the metaphysics[t] we hear including religion especially early in life, persists with little erosion, resulting in a great body of concepts being passed down from generation to generation, for which there is no good reason to believe. It owes its existence to the first law or step except for being reinforced by being emotionally rewarding. This is a process akin to imprinting. By contrast, "experience is believing" makes change possible in naturalistic beliefs and fosters the advancement of knowledge.

It should be obvious that my theory is opposed to and does not use the following theories:

(1) Occasionalism of Malebranche and others that attempts to make sense of the Cartesian dualism (the ghost in the machine). According to this theory, mind and matter are non interactive, but events in one realm occur in correspondence with events in the other realm. Thus, God sees to it that an idea of noise occurs in a mind on the occasion of the occurrence of a physical noise. It throws bad money after bad and puts the gods to a lot of unnecessary trouble.

(2) Psychophysical parallelism, which appears in Spinoza (page 67), but under different terms. It holds that there is a correlation between the system of physical events in nature and the system of psychical events in the mind. There is disagreement as to whether the correlation is complete one-to-one or partial.

(3) Leibniz's preestablished harmony, which was thought to refute or improve on the above two; and which keeps mind and body separate but equal--equal, that is, in synchronized clock work. According to Leibniz, "matter and spirit, body and soul, the physical and the moral, each a 'windowless,' perfect monad [an elemental metaphysical unit]. . . in itself, are once and for all not only corresponding realities, but they are also synchronized by God in their changes like two clocks, thus rendering the assumption of any mutual or other influences nugatory."[DOP, 264]

(4) Epiphenomenalism. It is thought to be more "scientific" than the others, it holds, as I understand it, that consciousness is only appearance or a by-product of the brain with no effects--a kind of nothing at all.

(5) Emergent mentalism, held by some naturalists to mean "Mind is a novel quality emerging from the non-mental when the latter attains a certain

complexity of organization."[DOP, 104]   What is novel about it?   There are billions of them and they are nurtured by the same blood stream that feeds the muscles of the body.   And, what is a quality?   Emerging?   "Attains a certain complexity of organization" I can accept.   To us the brain and those functions of it which we call the mind *are* complex organization; complex enough we haven't comprehended much of it yet.   But to nature, one degree of "complexity" is as "natural" as another.

(6) Emergent materialism.   In something C. D. Broad (1887-1971) calls materialistic emergency, "everything happens by the blind combination of the elements of matter or energy, without any guidance, excluding the assumption of a non-material component."   Primary qualities are physical emergents.   Secondary qualities such as color, taste, and smell are transphysical emergents.   There is "emergence of laws, qualities and classes.   Psyche, physical in nature, combines with other material factors to make the life of the mind. . . . Psyche persists after death for some time, floats about in cosmic space indefinitely, ready to combine with a material body under suitable conditions."[DOP, 57]   This theory begins as physicalism, but loses its way.   Primary and secondary qualities should have been dropped from philosophy a century ago.

(7) Neutral monism, which came into play in the contemplation of mind. It is another theory held by naturalists who were at one stroke opposing idealism and a dualism.   Even Russell with his insistence on science in philosophy flirted with it.   He attributes this concept to James and explains it as "that the fundamental stuff of the world is neither mental nor material but, something simpler and more fundamental, out of which both mind and matter are constructed."[SE, 47, 48]

For all the knowledge we have in physics, what is still unknown may be greater than what is known.   To say that "matter" cannot be mind--to say with Pascal "that nothing is so inconceivable as that matter should be conscious of itself"--is to lack imagination in contemplating the possibilities in that mysterious domain, and it puts unjustified limits on speculation.   It holds a stagnant, limited, myopic view, and is equivalent to that wisdom that warns not to sail too far from land's end.

For moral support, I use Francis Crick, co-discoverer of DNA and a Nobel laureate.   He has a book entitled *The Astonishing Hypothesis: The Scientific Search for the Soul.*   Crick declares that all of our interior states, joys and sorrows, our memories and ambitions, even our personal identity and the cherished notion of freewill, are no more than the behavior of a vast assembly of nerve cells. He is more specific than I am with my "some disposition of physical entities," but he is in a position to be so. My conclusion is, then, that the body-mind "problem" is no problem for naturalism, and that naturalism is the only avenue for obtaining more understanding of the "mind."

Having taken the position that we are congenital naturalists, that regarding induction, to function is to use it, the question arises: How does a naturalist explain the obvious widespread belief in the metaphysical[t]? Explain, for example, how a person, say a primitive farmer, who believes that he must sow, tend, and reap to have food (his naturalism), also has faith in the magic rituals he uses to insure a good harvest (his metaphysics[t]). My answer is that metaphysics[t] (in this case the tendency to satisfy emotional needs) is also congenital, but by contrast with naturalism its contents are *variables* which are culturally determined; one variable having the same claim (or lack of it) to the truth as another. *Faith is a slave to its culture.* For the handling of these two "worlds" there is a *division of labor in the mind.* One part of the mind supervises the everyday practical functions of life, the naturalism; while another part takes care of the emotional needs, the metaphysics[t]. I have called the making of the basic assumptions of science a *constant* in people's actions, although not necessarily conscious. Often it is so instinctive and subconscious that our primitive farmer is able to ignore it and believe that there would be no crop without the magic. He does not, however, substitute a vital function in raising a crop, say putting the seed into the ground, with magic. The magic (to repeat) is a separate activity, varies from culture to culture, and is culturally determined. I quote Hook for more, I believe, than moral support. Speaking of the science of primitive people, he says,

> Malinowski points out that the realms of the profane or secular, and the realms of the religious or supernatural are not confused even when their respective activities are conjoined. The native plants his sweet potato with the most exacting care for the conditions of soil, moisture, and other elements which affect its growth: but in addition, he goes through some religious ritual, supported by a myth, before he believes he has a right to expect a successful crop. . . .

What all modern anthropologists seem to agree on, as I interpret them, is that the religious or mystical elements in primitive experience, with their myths and religious rites, arise not in competition with the secular knowledge of technology or as a substitute for such knowledge but as a "complement" in situations in which all the available technical means and know-how are not adequate to a desired end, or where events do not clearly or always prosper when the proper instrumentalities are employed. In a world full of dangers and surprises, in a world of time, pain and contingencies, it is not hard to understand the psychological place of religion. It is a safe generalization to say that the depth of the religious sense is inversely proportionate to the degree of reliable control man exercises over his environment and culture.[TQFB, 179, 180]

Not only is there a division of labor in the mind, but our science and metaphysics[t] are parallel activities as a rule. We are of two minds, to speak figuratively. One is the mind, the other is the heart, which has a mind of it's own. One is the physical realist the other is the guardian of the emotions. While I am speaking figuratively, I will carry it to extreme and call the one mind Nat, for passive naturalism, and the other one Emot, for active emotion and anxiety. Nat is mostly passive in using his (naturalistic) philosophy. Emot is not offended by that except as he is aware that it threatens his turf, namely those beliefs he holds to salve his emotions and allay his anxieties, in which cases, he is active, and sometimes aggressive and even vicious, in defending it. Those beliefs involve cause and effect in the metaphysical[t], and Emot feels that he uses the metaphysical[t] to affect his fortune or "luck," for the better, often with conative and kinetic urging to borrow a term from Thorstein Veblen (1857-1929) whose treatment of the "belief in luck" is quoted below, modified with words in brackets to fit my purpose. To Emot

> all the obtrusive and obviously consequential objects and facts in his environment have a quasi-personal individuality. They are conceived to be possessed of . . . propensities, which enter into the complex of causes and effect events in an inscrutable manner. . . . [Emot's] sense of luck and chance, or of fortuitous necessity, is an inarticulate or inchoate animism. It applies to objects and situations, often in a very vague way; but it is usually so far defined as to imply the possibility of propitiating, or of deceiving and cajoling, or otherwise disturbing the unfolding of propensities resident in the objects which constitute [Emot's world].[TLC, 184] The animistic congruity of things must decide for . . . a victorious outcome for the side in whose behalf the propensity inherent in events has been propitiated and fortified by so much of conative and kinetic urging.[TLC, 183]

Nat believes what he has to, and what makes life possible. Emot believes what he wants to, and what he has an emotional need to, which sometimes makes life more livable. Man does not live by truth alone. What may be intellectual rubbish on the one hand may be therapeutic on the other. For all their differences, Nat and Emot have something in common. The behavior of both is self serving and entirely natural.

Emot's forte is inventiveness; what mother nature does not supply for the needs of the emotions, Emot invents. What is not in reality is put into rhetoric which passes for wisdom. Facetiously, we might call this the conventional wisdom. In any given generation, most of the inventing has been done by previous generations, therefore, Emot's principal activity is purveying the conventional wisdom, resorting to invention only as changed conditions and pressures require new virtues. The collected inventions of Emots over the centuries make the most cherished literature of any society. These metaphysical[t] ideas have effects in society ranging from benefits to war. Nothing is too absurd for Emot to believe if it serves self interest in terms of great emotional needs. Take the case of death. Nat comes up with the cold clear fact of death. Emot invents ways around it, a happy hunting ground, perhaps, and rituals to aid him in getting there. But if Nat comes up with "apples are food," or even "an apple a day keeps the doctor away," Emot is not offended, is passive, and is content. He likes apple pie too.

I think this allegory helps elucidate a point. However, as presented, it needs to be modified to cover the "fact" that Emot has emotional needs to guard in cases of naturalistic against naturalistic theories and metaphysical[t] against metaphysical[t] theories. Also, if we put learning one's native language in Nat's domain, it is a variable in him. I now leave this and return to my theory of the physical composition of the mind and further explanation of the parallel activities of the naturalistic and metaphysical[t] "minds."

The basic assumptions of science, "built in" the mind, are some disposition of physical entities, as is the "knowledge" which arises with experience. Kant's categories, or whatever is valid in them, are part of this "native" or "constant" part of the mind, but I reject the Kantian characterization of them as "a priori", that is to say, as prior knowledge. They are prior only in the sense that a word processor is prior to the information put in it. This native or constant part of the mind (I say part because every new remembered idea or concept becomes part of the mind) is a capability or faculty that renders concepts (certainty[1], not certainty[2]) on experience. For examples I choose the concepts of space and time, which are exceptions to the rule that most new terms are learned by having them defined in familiar ones (page 128).

Any baby who has had to wait an inordinate time for his bottle experiences time, and the concept is immediate and ineffable. He will learn the term "time" to go with the concept by association as he grows and hears the term used, but "definitions" of time do not teach it to him. Any definition of time has the concept imbedded in it. The concept comes to him/her, shall we say, in "brute" experience, or to use Locke's term, he/she learns it "ostensively." He/she has the native capacity or faculty to acquire the concept of time, but acquires it only by experience. The same is true of space, say, if the bottle the baby waits for is just out of reach.

The parallel activities of naturalistic and metaphysical[t] concepts exist where the person has no conception of their incompatibility. He has no conception of incompatibility for some cause: either he is not aware of or conscious of the incompatibility, or cannot understand it, has rationalized compatibility, or for some other cause. A particular naturalistic concept such as those that are held by the primitive farmer in our example above are in fact some disposition of physical entities, partly acquired by experience, partly by accepting what he has heard, there being no impeding physical entities to the concept. His concepts of magic are likewise some disposition of physical entities, all acquired, but give an illusion of being confirmed by experience as the production of food followed the magic. The "constant" part of the mind (naturalistic assumptions) are subconscious in this case, and therefore are not an impediment to the belief in magic.

Should the primitive farmer hear it said that his magic has no effect, it is another matter. His receiving the remark is some disposition of physical entities but his previously held concept (some disposition of physical entities) is an impediment--*a physical impediment*--to the negative remark about magic and is rejected.

The mind (or minds) usually handles its naturalistic and metaphysical[t] concepts with some finesse. It does not, in most cases, let one interfere with the other. Here is an example of a metaphysical[t] theory interfering with a naturalistic one: in the manufacture of vaccine, magic was substituted for a vital step in producing it, say sterilizing the equipment. Here is an example of a metaphysical[t] theory not interfering with a naturalistic one: after a vaccine was produced by using a proven method, magic was performed to insure its efficiency. We have already seen our "primitive farmer" as an example, but examples are everywhere. To mention two eminent scientists, Priestley's "religious philosophy was his first interest and his major preoccupation,"[CTSOC, 51] and Newton left theological writings greater in bulk than all his scientific works, but he "never, despite his profound religiosity, mingled theology with the questions of science."[AOI, 255] Both men practiced their science and religion as parallel activities.

Rejection of incompatible metaphysical[t] conceptions can, and often does, occur. When a person holds one such conception strongly, say it is reinforced by being very emotionally satisfying, and hears of another which he conceives as different and opposing it, he rejects it. Those physical entities that are the conception inhibit in a physical way the new conception.

Exceptions to the rejection of an opposing concept occur when the new one is very compelling or rewarding and in cases where one realizes that two equally rewarding concepts he has held for some time conflict. In such cases, rationalizing comes into play and saves the day and provides for keeping both. An example is the belief that God is good and omnipotent on the one hand and the obvious fact that there are people in horrendous misery on the other. The rationalization is "God has a mysterious way his wonders to perform." This saves both concepts and saves God some embarrassment. The church settling on the Trinity after nearly four centuries of controversy is another example of resolving conflicting concepts without discarding any of them.

Problems of my theory to be dealt with are the "difference" between a conception held and the conception rejected, and the difference between opinion and "knowledge." Hume struggled with the former as he considered the difference between just having an idea and believing the idea:

> The idea of an object is an essential part of the belief of it, but not the whole. We conceive of many things which we do not believe. . . . There is a great difference betwixt the simple conception of the existence of an object and the belief of it.[TOHN, 94]

After some discussion, he concludes with what

> seems to me very evident, that an opinion or belief is nothing but an idea, that is different from a fiction, not in the nature, or the order of its parts, but in the *manner* of its being conceived. . . . An idea assented to *feels* different from a fictitious idea, that the fancy alone presents to us. And this different feeling I endeavor to explain by calling it a superior force, or *vivacity*, or *solidity*, or *firmness*, or *steadiness*. . . I confess that it is impossible to explain perfectly this feeling or manner of conception. [TOHN, 628, 629]

In my theory, both are some disposition of physical entities, and there is some difference in them. As I have no theory as to the details of the disposition, I have none of the difference, but I believe that we do not know anything that would justify a claim that science will not discover them if civilization lasts, say, a few more millennia.

There is not a difference in the disposition of physical entities that constitutes certainty[1] that would indicate certainty[2], no mark or telltale sign. The mind does not produce a certification from heaven for certainty[2] *Experience produces only conviction.* A concept held is certainty[1], and the learning process in whatever form, produces only conviction.

In making a physical theory of the mind, I have abandoned epistemology for psychology. Psychology, in learning or demonstrating the genesis of concepts, does not answer the epistemological question, "Is it true?" But if (in the millennia I give it) science establishes that experience, or whatever learning process, produces only conviction (certainty[1], not certainty[2]), epistemology as a pursuit of certainty[2] will be at an end.

But, in using certainty[1], all is not lost. Certainty[1] has natural selection to insure its usefulness. Man has had to be certain[1] correctly (certainty[2] if there were only a certificate with it) a sufficient percentage of the time to insure survival. Natural selection has selected for a capacity to make certainty[1] the *practical* equivalent of certainty[2] significantly often.

DETERMINISM AND CHOICE

The reader is perhaps asking, "You present a completely deterministic theory of the mind, the mind functioning completely by the laws of physics, but don't we make choices?" How can you deny that we make decisions? Indeed, we do make decisions, and for those who are satisfied with these terms, I have a solution.

My solution to this age-old problem cannot, given my definition of naturalism, include "free will" meaning "free from the laws of nature (indeterminism);" and it must include "decision" and "choice" the reality of which are held on good empirical grounds. We obviously make decisions. We choose between alternatives on almost a daily basis. How are these facts to be squared with a completely deterministic psychology? How do we do what is implicit in Bacon's aphorism, "we can only command nature by obeying it," namely interfere in nature naturally (the gods do it by overruling nature). No one has explained it better than John Stewart Mill:

> Though we cannot emancipate ourselves from the laws of nature as a whole, we can escape from any particular law of nature, if we are able to withdraw ourselves from the circumstances in which it acts. Though we can do nothing except through laws of nature, we can use one law to counteract another. According to Bacon's maxim, we can obey nature in such a manner as to command it. Every alteration of circumstances alters more or less the laws of nature under which we act; and by every choice which we make either of ends or of means, we place ourselves to a greater or less extent under one set of laws of nature instead of another.[ON, 13]

Thus, for example, if A is sitting on a railroad track when a train is coming, the laws of nature result in his death if he does not move. If he moves, he removes himself from the results of those laws of nature and puts himself under other laws of nature that insure he does not die in that instance. The laws of nature under which he chose to leave the tracks were such that he had knowledge and fear of what would happen if he did not, which determined his choice.

But the reader may not be convinced. He/she may insist that choice is "free will." The complete solution to this is in the identity of the self, but first it is necessary to dispose of a misconception about determinism. Mark Twain will do as an example. He said, "Whatever a man is, is due to his *make*, and to the *influences* brought to bear upon it by his heredities, his habitat, his associations. He is moved, directed, *commanded*, by *exterior* influences--solely."[HC, 521] Twain's mistake is in the last sentence. To explain it, let us use Hume's example of a billiard ball moving and striking a second one causing the second one to move. The first ball does not, as in Twain's analysis, hold all causation in itself. The second ball, although moved, has input. Its mass and material of construction are determining factors in the resulting movement; therefore, all of the determinants are not exterior to the second ball. Part of the causation is what the ball is made of, *the ball's self,* if you will. For the want of a better term, I will call Twain's rendition "one-directional determinism."

There were philosophers who made the same mistake. Herbert Spencer and followers in their theories of social evolution and William James in opposing it, are good examples. Charles Darwin did the science for the theory of evolution and Spencer did the philosophy, or at least, some philosophy.

> The famous slogan "survival of the fittest" is not Darwin's but Herbert Spencer's. Darwin himself was careful to disavow any supposed ethical implications of his theories, and the widespread view of the so-called "Social Darwinists" that those who are best adapted to survive aught to survive is no part of what Darwin himself sought to prove. Darwin was also very careful to observe the limits of his hypothesis. He did not profess to explain the origins of life itself; nor did he claim to know the precise causes of those variations which determine different organic species in the first place. And he rejected the implications which some sought to draw from his theory, namely, that the "higher" species are more perfectly adapted to their environment than the "lower" ones. It remained for his contemporary, Herbert Spencer, to draw out the major philosophical implications of the evolutionary theory. In his hands, it is transformed into a grand synthesis of human knowledge, complete with a cosmology, an ethics, and a politics. [AOI, 162]

Spencer's *System of Synthetic Philosophy*, 1862 to 1892, "is perhaps the greatest effort on the part of a nineteenth-century philosopher to organize and extend the scientific knowledge of his day into a grand speculative synthesis which seeks to provide general description of the entire natural world."[AOI, 163] All this was naturalism, of course, but much of it was naturalism run amuck.

In ethics Spencer was concerned with mental evolution. He accepted the Lamarckian theory of the inheritance of acquired characteristics. This was, he thought, a means by which species can originate, for if mental characteristics could be inherited the intellectual powers of man would increase over time and eventually producing the ideal or perfect man. This was not just possible but inevitable. He saw the environment and circumstances as completely controlling, and man as helpless to stop or effect the course of events. Therefore, he saw biological and cultural causes making man what he was and making his decisions, leaving no room for intelligent action to effect events, or so he is interpreted. It was what I have called one-directional determinism.

On the positive side, Spencer wrote *The Study of Sociology* (1873) which had a notable influence on the rise of sociology in the United States. The book defended sociology from the criticism of theologians and indeterminists, and was intended to show the desirability of a naturalistic social science. The purpose of sociology, however, is not to control the process of evolution, but rather to show that man's control is an absolute impossibility, and that the only thing and the best thing that can be done is to teach men to submit more readily to determinism, forgetting or ignoring, it seems, that according to his theory, man could do nothing but submit. This admission that a socialized society was possible was a contradiction of his position on cultural one-directional determinism.

"He predicted, prophetically, that in a socialized society, the bureaucracy would give rise to a new form of aristocracy, more powerful than any that had gone before."[AOI, 168]

William James, attracted to Spencer's first writings, soon was repelled by his complete determinism. James wanted and proposed a philosophy that acknowledged active human effort in effecting life for the better. James was quite right, in my view, but the limitations are more than James believed they were. Free will was his explanation for the obvious fact that we make choices and this was necessary because determinism was for him one directional.

Incidentally, there were reformers who opposed Spencer's determinism which in economics was unfettered free enterprise or laissez faire and no governmental aid to the unfortunate. The reformers were of several stripes with the most extreme being the socialists and communists. Recent events have proven that human intervention into economics in the form of communism did not work, so Spencer was partly right. But, the reformers have scored one also; today we mix social legislation with a market economy. We have the anti-trust laws and subsidies and regulations, and conservatives and liberals fight over how much of what is best.

The big three (my term) of pragmatism were Peirce, James, and Dewey. They believed in the possibility of novelties and that ideas had effects. Spencer proclaimed determinism and the control of man by the environment. The pragmatists took the opposite view and were for freedom and control of the environment by man. Dewey, however, did not accept James's assertion of freedom of the will. Nevertheless, they all thought they had found a chink in the armor of determinism. For James, as we have seen, it was free will. For Peirce it was "tychism," a word he used for chance events.[DOP, 339] Dewey believed in the potentialities of intelligence and that it operates within a series of objectively indeterminate situations. Still, he insisted that knowledge is a part of nature and that thinking is not a series of transcendent states or acts interjected into a natural scene. This makes it hard for me to understand why he used the term "indeterminate."

Dewey called his philosophy instrumentalism and it was to some degree in opposition to Spencer's, all-is-determined, man-is-helpless-to-interfere stance. If he meant by instrumentalism that ideas and man's action on them had effects without being part of the chain of physical (which in my terms includes mental) cause and effects, and I am not certain[1] that he did, then he held a view in common with Spencer who used "lubricant" to describe the effects of his theories. Spencer, as we saw above, wrote one book to promote the science of sociology, and he claimed that his evolutionary philosophy determined certain ethical conceptions (discussed below). Surely he expected these to have effects. In an effort to make his theory sound he described the function of a true theory of society as a lubricant for progress not a motive power. It would seem that the term instrumental would apply to Spencer in this case. I have, at last, come to my solution.

My solution to the free-will/determinism problem, given my theory of the mind, rests on the identity of the self (which explains why this subject follows rather than precedes my theory of the mind). As in the case of the second ball in the example used above, all of the causes for actions are not external to us. In my theory of the mind (self), ideas and/or concepts, among other things, *are* the mind (page 194); therefore, when one chooses, the concept (some disposition of physical entities), which is the choice, *is* (a component of) the person. Within the context of this theory, when we say "I choose," we state a fact, and to include the modifier, free, would be unnecessary and inaccurate. The terms "will, decision, and choice" communicate the facts without "free." The identity of the self and the concept (as part of the self, and the pertinent part in this instance) removes any mystery as to the self at once making a choice and it being determined. It is not a contradiction to say that determinism is true and that we make choices, because the determined choice is, among other things, the person. The person therefore chooses. The person is both the determinee, to coin a term, and determiner. I would like to say as Russell said of his theory of descriptions that this "clears up two millennia of muddle-headedness about" free will, but I will just say that I am certain[1] about it; besides free will has been a problem for more than two millennia.

I have pointed out that we use induction (assume universal natural law) in every step we take in applying means to ends. Some are tacit or instinctive and some are cognitive. I can now say, with expectations of not being misunderstood, that in many cognitive steps we take, we are choosing between two or more alternatives in a determined universe.

ETHICS AND ESTHETICS

The subject of ethics, as I present it, is allied to, or is an adjunct to, my theory of the mind; however, because of its deterministic nature, it best follows my position on free will and determinism.

There is no philosophy that engenders more disagreement than ethics. It is another area that for many is a stumbling block for naturalism. Before discussing the subject of ethics I want to show that the ethics of Spencer, the claim that what is natural is right, is not, as some might suppose, part of naturalism as a philosophy.

> As a man with all the moral severity of the mid-Victorian, Spencer was especially sensitive to the problem of finding a new and natural ethic to replace the oral code which had been associated with the traditional faith. "The supposed supernatural sanctions of right conduct do not, if rejected, leave a blank. There exist natural sanctions no less pre-emptory, and covering a much wider field."
>
> The new morality must be built upon biology. "Acceptance of the doctrine of organic evolution determines certain ethical conceptions." . . . Spencer felt that a moral code which could not meet the test of natural selection and the struggle for existence, was from the beginning doomed to lip service and futility. Conduct, like anything else, should be called good or bad as it is well adapted, or maladapted, to the ends of life: "the highest conduct is that which conduces to the greatest length, breadth, and completeness of life."[SOP, 289, 290]

Thus Spencer made an ethic of evolution. In nature the "survival of the fittest" he said was bettering the human race, therefore it was *right* that the fittest survive and that the less fit perish. He opposed state interference with the natural function and growth of society. He opposed state aid to the poor. They were unfit and should be eliminated. The over all function of nature, as he saw it, is to clear the world of them, and make room for the fit.

He was forced to defend himself from accusations of brutality, however, by repeatedly insisting that he did not opposed voluntary private charity to the unfit. Altruism resulting from private charity would be part of evolution. This, of course, contradicted his main theme that evolution came only from competition.

James was incensed by all of this and his answer was an attack on determinism. He called it a "monistic superstition" among other things.

This seems an odd position, for he had a scientific education, having been trained at Harvard's Lawrence Scientific School.

With a philosopher of James's stature insisting on indetermininsm in human behavior, it is well to consider what this would mean. I let a professional explain.

> If human behavior, both individual and social, does not exhibit cause-effect sequences, then the scientific method is essentially irrelevant to the elucidation of the nature of man and scientific psychology and the social sciences are permanently barred from achieving the status of sciences. . . . To deny the existence of uniformities in human behavior, both individual and social, is to assert that significant lessons cannot be drawn from the past and the man's future is capricious and elusive. . . . The distinction between wisdom and foolishness in practical affairs first becomes meaningful through the existence of cause-effect relationships in human behavior and by reference to the predictions which the existence of these relationships makes possible. [CRGP, 329]

It is not a point well taken to cite the poor showing of psychology in comparison to the physical sciences.

> We have learned to reject physical theories which fail to pass the test of observable fact, no matter how ingenious the theory or how dear it may be to our hearts when first propounded. For this reason the history of physical science is in a sense the history of discarded theories. What an advance toward sanity it would be, if it were equally generally accepted that theories of human nature, like physical theories, need careful, disciplined checking through observation. [CRGP, 130]

James had an acute moral and aesthetic sensitivity and an emotional attachment to religion. To use my allegory (page 198) the Emot in him dominated the Nat in him. He identified choice with free will and declared that there can be no morality where there is no free will and chance. James's position had an appeal to the public and to many philosophers, but it was John Stewart Mill who exposed Spencer's ethic as ridiculous. This is ironic, for Mill at one time offered to finance some of Spencer's work that was financed by advanced subscriptions.

> After the publication of [Spencer's] the *First Principles* in 1862, many subscribers withdrew their names because the famous "Part One," which, attempting to reconcile science and religion, offended bishops and pundits alike. . . . Spencer's subscribers fell away with every instalment, and many defaulted

on payments due for installments received.[SOP, 273]

When funds ran out and Spencer announced that he could no longer continue the work, Mill wrote him in 1866 and offered to guarantee the publisher against loss. Spencer refused but later accepted help from another source and continued. This was long before Spencer wrote his ethics.

In an essay "Nature" published after his death, Mill shows the absurdity of the "what is natural is right" ethic. Among the ambiguities of the word nature, Mill cites the two principal uses.

> In one sense, it means all the powers existing in either the outer or the inner world and everything which takes place by means of those powers. In another sense it means, not everything which happens, but only what takes place without the agency, or without the voluntary and intentional agency, of man.[ON, 9]

He then proceeds "to inquire into the truth of the doctrines which make Nature a test of right and wrong. . . ." When it is asserted that Nature or the laws of Nature, should be conformed to, . . in the first sense of the term, meaning all which is--the powers and properties of all things,[ON, 11,12]

> there is no need of recommendation to act according to nature, since it is what nobody can possibly help doing, and equally whether he acts well or ill. There is no mode of acting which is not conformable to Nature in this sense of the term, and all modes of acting are so in exactly the same degree. Every action is the exertion of some natural power, and its effects of all sorts are so many phenomena of nature, produced by the powers and properties of some of the objects of nature, in exact obedience to some law or laws of nature. . . . To bid people conform to the laws of nature when they have no power but what the laws of nature give them--when it is a physical impossibility for them to do the smallest thing otherwise than through some law of nature, is an absurdity.[ON, 12]

Mill then considers "whether we can attach any meaning to the supposed practical maxim of following Nature, in the second sense of the word, in which Nature stands for that which takes place without human intervention."[ON, 13]

> In nature as thus understood, is the spontaneous course of things when left to themselves, the rule to be followed in endeavoring to adapt things to our use? But it is evident at once that the maxim, taken in this sense, is not merely, as it is in the other sense, superfluous and unmeaning, but palpably absurd and self-contradictory. For while human action cannot help conforming to Nature in the

one meaning of the term, the very aim and object of action is to alter and improve Nature in the other meaning. If the natural course of things were perfectly right and satisfactory, to act at all would be a gratuitous meddling, which, as it could not make things better, must make them worse. Or if action at all could be justified, it would only be when in direct obedience to instincts, since these might perhaps be accounted part of the spontaneous order of Nature: but to do anything with forethought and purpose, would be a violation of that perfect order. If the artificial is not better than the natural, to what end are all the arts of life? To dig, to plough, to build, to wear clothes, are direct infringements of the injunction to follow nature.[ON, 13, 14]

Mill wrote of the ambiguities of the word nature. I suggest there is no ambiguity but rather they are different words spelled the same, the two Mill so precisely defined and others. If we recognize the fact that they are different words there is no confusion such as the word ambiguity denotes.

I recall vividly when I had a second awakening from my dogmatic slumbers, this time regarding ethics. It was about 20 years after the first one, and I can recall where I was when it occurred. Suddenly, I "realized" (as I experienced it) that there are no such things as right and wrong and justice. The term central to my thinking was "absolute;" there are no absolutes in ethics. I had been reading some comments by Justice Oliver Wendel Holmes. One was in a review of a book, which, as I recall, was of the letters of Holmes and Harold Laski. In it, Holmes said something to the effect that as to "rights," he did not believe in anything that the crowd would not fight for. The other was a conversation between Holmes and a young lawyer, Learned Hand, I think it was, who spoke of Holmes's job of "doing justice." Holmes replied that his job was not justice but rather was to administer the law. "Justice," I then saw, was rhetoric; "administering the law" was the reality. The first comment was in *Time* magazine, but I cannot recall where I saw the second.

There are many theories of ethics with nothing like a consensus on the subject by philosophers. To cover what has been found inadequate in them would be tedious and worthless to this discussion. I will mention only one more theory, that of G. E. Moore. I have mentioned Moore elsewhere regarding common sense and analysis. Before going into analysis, Moore made a case for common sense that appealed to me. He deflated some ethical theories by calling them a "naturalistic fallacy," a handy way of disposing of an opponent. One of Moore's theses was "that philosophers who have identified good with pleasure, or progress in evolution, or any other natural property, have committed "the naturalistic fallacy." Good, he claimed, "is a simple unanalysable non-natural quality,"[PTC, 41, 42] and intuition tells us what is right and wrong. I have just made the case against deriving ethics from evolution, so I have some agreement with Moore. I believe that the terms good and bad are, as such, unanalysable and indefinable, but what a non-natural quality could be, I do not have a clue. Moore made some analysis of definitions in support of his position (which I have not attempted to understand), which has been called a "mare's nest."[PTC, 44]

Up to a point Moore's common-sense philosophy was, as I see it, the best kind of naturalism, believing, as he did, that "external" things have the properties they are normally experienced to have. This has been discussed on page 176.

But Moore evidently retained the validity of moral terms as part of his "common-sense" philosophy. Here we part. For me, as most often used, common sense *is* naturalism; and moral terms, as undefinable, with no empirical content (it is behavior that can be empirically investigated), and without criteria for settling just what is "right and wrong," etc., are metaphysics[t]. Moore, in insisting that good is an intrinsic property or quality, held roughly the position that I had abandoned with my second awakening.

People do have (to continue my view) the *concepts* of right, wrong, justice, and obligation, the latter two being subsumed under the former two. The concepts, as such, are real; there is some disposition of physical entities, something happening in the brain cells, when they have these concepts. They have effects, that is, (at least) most people, part of the time, are motivated to behave according to the "morals" they espouse. But these traits are not alone in producing "civilized" behavior. People learn that it is often in their self interest to be good neighbors.

Our parish priest of Etrepigny in Champagne in the 18th century (page 134) gave some natural motives for "morality" (acceptable behavior) (page 138) but he had more to say on the subject. Of the motives man has for "morality" without supernatural sanctions he wrote:

> He can have the motive of pleasing himself and his fellow-creatures; of living
> happily and tranquilly; of making himself loved and respected by men. . . . He
> can fear men, their contempt, their disrespect, and the punishments which the

> laws inflict; and finally, *he can fear himself*; he can be afraid of the remorse that all those experience whose conscience reproaches them for having deserved the hatred of their fellow-beings. Conscience is the inward testimony which we render to ourselves for having acted in such a manner as to deserve the esteem or the censure of those with whom we associate.[SIAA, 242, 243]

Having put ethics in metaphysics[t] and believing that metaphysics[t] avails us nothing, I find the only area of investigation left to us is the natural history of "morals"--the cause of the terms, right, wrong, justice, and whatever else comes under that head.

But, what is the origin, the natural history, of society's "morals"? I theorize that principal among the factors causing the belief in, or the use of, moral terms is (1) they are acquired by association in the process of living and learning by hearing them used as absolutes (best word I can think of), and (2) they serve the wants and interests of the very self-interested human animal. The acquired concepts are reinforced by the experience of hearing them used in regard to acts which (a) in the case of "wrong", are disapproved, undesired, abhorred, etc. and (b) in the case of "right", are approved, desired, etc. Concerning obligation, people do in fact feel obligated, and in some cases feel rewarded (virtue is it's own reward) when fulfilling an obligation (part of the people all of the time and all of the people part of the time, possibly). The feeling reinforces what is heard. The concept of justice satisfies desires for recompense to self, and satisfies wrath and hatred in the case of penalties inflicted on others. In short, and to speak figuratively, moral terms are wants made holy. We find wants, our self interest, enshrined as the criteria of goodness in no less a precept than the Golden Rule. I quote Hobbes for moral support. For him *good* and *bad* are subjective terms (repeating from page 62):

> The object of any appetite or desire . . . a man calleth the *good*; the object of his hate or aversion, *evil*; for these words . . . are ever used with relation to the person that useth them, there being nothing simply and absolutely so, nor any common rule of good and evil to be taken from the nature of the objects themselves.

Spinoza has been quoted (page 68) to the effect that we do not desire anything because it is good. We call it good because we desire it.

> "In no case do we strive for, wish for, long for, or desire anything, because

we deem it to be good, but on the other hand we deem a thing to be good, because we strive for it, wish for it, long for it, or desire it." And again: "By good I mean that which we certainly know to be useful to us."

And I can quote Hume to my advantage here. Having laid down his skeptical pen and picked up his scientific one (observation), (to repeat from page 120) he observed that

> in every system of morality which I have hitherto met with . . . the author proceeds for some time in the ordinary way of reasoning . . . when of a sudden I am surprised to find that, instead of the usual copulation of propositions *is* and *is not*, I meet with no proposition that is not connected with an *ought* or *ought not*. This change is imperceptible; but is, however, of the last consequence. For this *ought* or *ought not* expresses some new relation or affirmation, it is necessary that it should be observed and explained.

Hume found no logical explanation for *ought* to be derived from *is*. To the contrary, he declared, in what is sometimes known as Hume's Law, that *ought* cannot be deducted from *is*, and he gives us a naturalistic theory of the origin of the moral sense (interpreted):

> Our moral sense comes not from Heaven but from sympathy--fellow feeling with our fellow men; and this feeling is part of the social instinct by which, fearing isolation, we seek association with others. "Man's very first state and situation may justly be esteemed social"; a "state of nature" in which men lived without social organization "is to be regarded a mere fiction", society is as old as man. Being members of a group, men soon learned to commend actions advantageous--and to condemn actions injurious--to the community. Furthermore, the principle of sympathy inclined them to receive or imitate the opinions that they heard around them; in this way they acquired their standards and habits of praise and blame, and consciously or not they applied these judgements to their own conduct; this and not the voice of God. . . is the origin of conscience. This law of sympathy, of communal attraction, is, says Hume, as universal and illuminating in the moral world as the law of gravitation in the material cosmos.[AOV, 146]

Hume further held that reason is a slave to the passions.

When an individual comes into this world (to continue my theory), he finds an "ethic" ready made for him/her, a cultural hand-me-down. It is accepted, by and large, quite mechanically on hearing it, except as it conflicts with his/her self interest. A community's moral code is not clearly defined in all respects, sometimes leaving us in a quandary, in which cases our self-interest takes over or we consult a trusted authority, trusting authority being part of the inherited moral code, and, if the trust is complete, mechanically (immediately) accept it.

The unwritten moral code our culture gives to us has largely evolved from, or grown out of, self-interest. Other "forces" such as a sense of duty and fairness, conscience, guilt feelings, sympathy, and a little love for fellow man, play a minor role. There is enough coincidence of self interest that a large body of "ethics" evolves which is more or less a constant held by the majority of the community. The moral code of the community can never have any other authority than the majority opinion. We can only go to common usage to learn what it is. Within this nucleus, there is slow change due to the pressures of self interest. Thus we find that in one age lending money for interest was usury ("sin") and in another quite respectable. In Holland in the 17th century, religious intolerance, a cardinal virtue of the time, gave way to tolerance under economic needs. As a great commercial center, good business in Holland required tolerance of the religion of sailors from many parts of the world. When money talks, ethics listens. Also, within the majority nucleus, various interest groups bend the rules toward their interest; thus there is always some "legitimate" debate as to what is "right" and "wrong." However, there is considerable getting around the code which does not change it. Having made our "ethics" of our wants-- what we want others to do and not do--we sometimes find ourselves with strong wants in opposition to the "ethical" code. In pursuing this want (or need) it is no small problem to find a self-interested answer with a clear conscience and dress it in a legitimizing rhetoric, but we often manage. As I write this, I think of what Russell said about Gladstone, (*Unpopular Essays*, which is, "He had all the skill of a clever politician, but was sincerely convinced that every one of his maneuvers was inspired by the most noble purposes. . . . Invariably he earnestly consulted his conscience, and invariably his conscience earnestly gave him the convenient answer."[UE, 169]

Outside of the majority nucleus, there are usually subcultures with their own moral codes, based on varying interest; and, in most societies there are some who have no conscience and disregard their people's moral code.

I would describe moral terms as akin to universals, not a close "family resemblance" to borrow a term from Wittgenstein, but something like a non-kissing cousin. It is an attempt to generalize, but there the resemblance ends. Moral terms, although used as such, are not based on empirically identifiable entities as universals are. Therefore, I would describe them as phony generalizations. Right and wrong and their synonyms are ostensive generalizations, but they do not generalize. Moral terms do refer to empirically identifiable acts, but nothing in philosophy is in worse disarray than the attempt to define the terms.

Having pronounced ethical terms phony (pseudo generalization), I suggest that we can get along without them. I suggest that in the third paragraph above, "moral code" can be replaced by "behavioral code" without any loss of meaning. We can use behavioral terms, approval, disapproval, codes, rules, etc., to express whatever makes sense regarding ethics, so-called. It is behavior that is the object of the teaching, preaching, persuasions, exhortations, condemnations, and threats to effect "morals," so why call it anything else? If an "ethics" committee in the US Congress sets down, under the title of ethics, a behavioral code for members of Congress, it is just that, a behavioral code. Behavior is what it is concerned with, empirically identifiable behavior, and it can be dealt with in those terms without any loss in communicating about what is being done.

If moral terms are not valid as such, then there are no categorical imperatives, Kant notwithstanding. There is no "must" or "ought" without an "if." All imperatives are hypothetical. This theory could stand some refinements, but none of them would pose problems for naturalism. There can be no philosophy of "ethics," however, moralists by their exhortations exhibit behavior. This behavior and the genesis of "ethical" beliefs can be investigated by science. If one genetic theory is found wanting, it is corrected by more science.

Much the same can be said about esthetics. Science cannot provide knowledge of what is beautiful and ugly. It is limited to showing *what* people hold to be such. In humans, the only animal that articulates these terms, it is the average that is "seen" to be beautiful (beauty is in the eye of the beholder). A scientific confirmation of this has been made in recent years by work with composite pictures. Composite picture were made of several faces with varying features. People were then asked to pick from these pictures the face, including the composite, they thought the most beautiful. The composite, which is the average, won. I would add to my theory that beauty is the bull's-eye of recognition. Every species recognizes its own kind, and humans see the average of theirs on a scale of facial features--ears, nose, etc.--from the smallest to the largest, as beautiful. The bull's-eye is, say, the 45th to 55th percentile. Science, having shown the genesis of the concept of beauty cannot then answer the esthetics question, "What is beauty?" on that basis. To do so would be to commit the genetic fallacy (see page 188). People are attracted to and emotionally moved by art and beauty whether in nature or "naturally" man made, but the only "knowledge" we can have, other than this fact, is the genesis and the expression of these feelings. This is not to say that the one experiencing these feelings does not have "knowledge" of their occurrence. To the contrary, he/she does in the same sense that one has "knowledge" of a sensation.

FINALLY

I cannot close without making one more criticism of philosophy and philosophers.

Given my position or prejudice--let us say prejudice--in philosophy, I see most philosophers in two camps: (1) philosophers of science, those who believe knowledge is scientific knowledge, and (2) metaphysicians[t], those who believe there are other kinds of knowledge. Science does not need the former and gets along, at least in modern times, quite well in spite of the latter. The latter type, who have more work to do, far out number the former. Principal among these are idealists, theologians, and those who claim to have knowledge of "being," as well as some who deal with esthetics and ethics. They produce a large volume of contradictory philosophy, but agree on a deprecatory attitude toward science. Their position, generally, is that science is all right, *but*. Science gets along quite well in spite of this opposition. As to the philosophers of science, those who attempt to make philosophy a support for or a proof of science and who also contradict each other, science doesn't need them (except as they contribute to science itself) and that includes what I have written here. Witness that Galileo was not led to his great discoveries by Francis Bacon's postulations on scientific method, nor did Bacon's understanding of that method help him understand some of Galileo's discoveries.

Of those philosophers who attempted to bolster science and failed, I will give two examples, John Stuart Mill and Ernst Mach (1838-1916). The following account of Mill's attempt to prove the validity of induction is taken from his *System of Logic* Book III.

His position was that the entire inductive process depends on the validity of its underlying assumption, the law of causation. He bases his method on direct observation. An a priori principle or reason does not obtain. For him

> the belief we entertain in the university, throughout nature, of the law of cause and effect, is itself an instance of induction. . . We arrive at this universal law by generalization from many laws of inferior generality. We should never have had the notion of causation (in the philosophical meaning of the term) as a condition of all phenomena, unless many cases of causation, or, in other words, many partial uniformities of sequence, had previously become familiar. The more obvious of the particular

uniformities suggest, and give evidence of, the general uniformity, once established, enables us to prove the remainder of the particular uniformities of which it is made up.[SOL]

These inductions do not belong to the rigorous inductions that conform to the cannons of scientific induction but is a "loose and uncertain mode of induction" which he calls induction by simple enumeration, or "generalization of an observed fact from the mere absence of any known instance to the contrary." He admits this a fallible process which must precede the less fallible forms of the inductive process, and states that "the precariousness of the method of simple enumeration is in an inverse ratio to the largeness of the generalization."[SOL]

As the sphere widens, this unscientific methods becomes less and less liable to mislead; and the most universal class of truths, the law of causation, for instance, and the principles of number and geometry, are duly and satisfactorily proved by that method alone, nor are they susceptible of any other proof.[SOL]

This brief account may not do justice to Mill's argument, but it is useless to pursue it further. What he believes he is showing is that the warrant for the thesis that the course of nature as a whole is uniform is proven by the individual instances in which natural law is experienced. It is one thing to be convinced of universal natural law by experienced instances of natural law and another to have proof. It is the problem of induction which we have discussed at length. Mill's method, which is capable only of rendering the result of a particular case of causation probable, assumes the validity of induction. Probability assumes the validity of induction. Mill's argument is simply circular. Natural law is incapable of, because antecedent to, demonstration.

Mach's project is much more ambitious. Mach looked back fondly to the enlightenment when, in his words, "humanistic, philosophical, historical, and physical science here met and gave each other mutual encouragement."[AOI, 253] This was no longer the case and confusion was destroying the tranquility.

Toward the end of the nineteenth century philosophical interest in science revived after being largely dormant for a century, coming not from the professional philosophers, but from the scientist themselves. Nonempirical concepts were creeping into physics. This posed a problem for the empiricist theories of knowledge that had long held that the scientific method was the only vehicle of rational belief. This view was under fire from philosophical idealists, theologians and those in allied fields who had much to gain and nothing to lose from the confusion among scientists. If the empirical integrity of science could not be maintained, how could it claim superiority as knowledge to empirically indefinable notions such as God, immorality, and freedom.

Some solution to this problem, it was felt, had to be found if science of physics was still to be upheld as the paradigm of human knowledge. To this problem Mach applied himself holding to the thesis of empiricism which we first met in Berkeley, (page 95): Any statement purporting to be about physical objects in the external world must be reducible to or analyzable into statements about the contents of immediate sense experience. Mach, however, included the "interior" world in his radical empiricism and believed that there are no methodological differences between physical science and the sciences of the mind. Sensations, for Mach are to be both physical and mental (as is my theory) and there is no reason that any sensation should not be perceivable by more than one person (about which I am doubtful). Intersubjective (available to all observers; public) methods are to be used. Subjective (available to only one observer; private) are ruled out. "For once it is admitted, on principle, that access to the facts of emotion, feeling, and memory can be gained only through certain private modes of observation, then the whole ideal of the unity of science is doomed from the outset. And in that case at least one basic contention of the idealists would have to be sustained, namely, that there is an ineradicable difference in kind between the sciences of nature and of behavior and those disciplines which have to do primarily with the inner life."[AOI, 250, 251]

Mach did recognize auxiliary concepts that are necessary for the purpose of organizing hypotheses into a coherent system. What are these concepts? Just those that science cannot do without such as cause and number and "thing words." These concepts are calculating devices, not terms of reference and, according to Mach, do not designate. These may be used to make possible a sound scientific theory.

It is not worth our time to follow Mach's endeavor--dream, we might say-- further. His goal was not reached. Indeed, as he proceeded he got deeper into a subjective world with such statements as "there is no cause nor effect in nature" and "properly speaking the world is not composed of 'things', but of individual sensations," pushing his ideas to the brink of idealism which he professed to oppose.

Mach's position that intersubjective methods of verification alone are to be used seems on the surface to be correct. If someone claims to have observed something by some occult method not accessible to others, we just don't call it science, but to say that subjective data are impossible calls for a little investigation. Consider medical science, for example, which is pretty close to home, so to speak, for everyone. A subjective element is constantly involved. It is obvious that we must separate naturalistic subjective evidence from the metaphysical[t]. Mach's criteria were too narrow. We call it medical science when a doctor asks a patient for his/her symptoms. When the patient has a pain it is obviously a subjective sensation and admissible in the science at hand. When he/she reports it to his/her doctor and the doctor uses it in the diagnosis, it is indispensable to the doctor's science. The doctor's experience teaches that the patient's report is correct more often than not, thus bringing its use under the domain of probability, which is good scientific practice. The doctor may be able to confirm the probability that the patient was telling the truth, with an x-ray of the back on report of back pain, for example, but the sensation of pain itself is not made intersubjective--and Mach hangs his project entirely on verification by sensation.

It is enough to say that the mind and physical objects are the same kinds of stuff, namely that kind of stuff that obeys the laws of nature. Method must be left to science. The position for those who hold that all knowledge is scientific knowledge is naturalism.

The philosophers of science fail because they attempt to appropriate to reason what we have by instinct. They are reaching for certainty[2], that certification, if I may use my figure again, from heaven, and it is out of reach.

Science forges its own way and is it's own justification as knowledge. Science in its broadest meaning is simply being honest and careful with the information that comes from both experience and that acquired from others about the natural universe. The useful analysis of that process is made within science, not for it.

SOURCES OF QUOTATIONS

The sources of quotations are indicated at the end of each quotation by superscripted notations. The notations consist of the codes listed below, followed by the number of the page on which the quotation appears, except for electronic copies which have no page numbers.

CODE   SOURCE

AECH   David Hume. *An Enquiry Concerning Human Understanding*, Harvard Classics vol. 37, 1910. P.F. Collier & Son http://www.knuten.liu.se/~bjoch509/works/hume/human_underst.txt

AOA   Morton White. *The Age of Analysis: Twentieth Century Philosophers*. The Great Ages of Western Philosophy, vol. 6. New York: George Braziller, 1957. Reprinted with the permission of Morton White.

AOAv   Giorgio de Santillana. *The Age of Adventure: The Renaissance Philosophers*. The Great Ages of Western Philosophy, vol. 2. New York: George Braziller, 1957. Every reasonable effort has been made to find the copyright holder.

AOB   Ann Fremantle. *The Age of Belief: The Medieval Philosophers*. The Great Ages of Western Philosophy, vol. 1. New York: George Braziller, 1957. Every reasonable effort has been made to find the copyright holder.

AOE   Isaiah Berlin. *The Age of Enlightenment: The Eighteenth Century Philosophers*. The Great Ages of Western Philosophy, vol. 4. New York: George Braziller, 1957. Every reasonable effort has been made to find the copyright holder.

AOI   Henry D. Aiken. *The Age of Ideology: The Nineteenth Century Philosophers*. The Great Ages of Western Philosophy, vol. 5. New York: George Braziller, 1957. Every reasonable effort has been made to find the copyright holder.

AOR   Stuart Hampshire. *The Age of Reason: The Seventeenth Century Philosophers*. The Great Ages of Western Philosophy, vol. 3. New York: George Braziller, 1957. Every reasonable effort has been made to find the copyright holder.

AORB   Will and Ariel Durant. *The Age of Reason Begins*. The Story of Civilization, part 7. Reprinted with the permission of Simon & Schuster from *The Age of Reason Begins* by Will and Ariel Durant. Copyright ©1961 by Will and Ariel Durant.

AOV   Will and Ariel Durant. *The Age of Voltaire*. The Story of Civilization, part 9. Reprinted with the permission of Simon and Schuster from *The Age of Voltaire* by Will and Ariel Durant. Copyright ©1965 by Will and Ariel Durant.

C   Baruch Spinoza. *Correspondence*, (1677) translated to English by R.H.M. Elwes. Numbers in accordance with Gebhardt. No. 67 (73) Sept 3, 1675 and No. 76 (74), end of 1675. http://bdsweb.tripod.com/en/let/leti.htm

COM   Gilbert Ryle. *The Concept of Mind*. New York: Barnes and Noble Books, 1949.

CPR   Immanuel Kant. *Critique of Pure Reason*. Rev. ed. 1787. Translated by J. M. D. Meiklejohn. New York: Willey Book Company, n.d.

CRGP   *American Scientist*, October, 1952. Reprinted by permission from American Scientist Magazine of Sigma Xi, The Scientific Research Society, *American Scientist* 40 (4) 665-676, October 1952.
        Also, this article appears in Robert D. Daniel, ed. *Contemporary Readings in General Psychology*. Boston: Houghton Mifflin, 1959. The page numbers given with the quotations are from this publication.

CTSOC   Bernard Jaffe. *Crucibles: The Story of Chemistry from Ancient Alchemy to Nuclear Fission*. 4th ed. New York: Dover Publications, 1976. Reprinted by permission of Dover Publications.

DH   A. P. Cavendish. *David Hume*. 1958. New York: Dover Publications, 1968. Reprinted by permission of Dover Publications.

DOP   Dagobert D. Runes, ed. *Dictionary of Philosophy*. Revised. Savage, MD: Rowman and Littlefield, 1983. Reprinted by permission of Rowman and Littlefield.

E   Baruch Spinoza. *Ethics*, 1677. Translated from the latin by R.H.M. Elwes (1883). MTSU Philosolphy WebWorks. Hypertext Edition (©) 1997. http://www.mtsu.edu/ ~ rbombard/RB/Spinoza/ethica-front.html

ECB   Basil Willey. *The Eighteenth-Century Background*, London 1949.

ECHU   John Locke. *An Essay Concerning the Human Understanding*, 1690. http://humanum.arts.cuhk.edu.hk/Philosophy/Locke/echu/

EGP   Milton C. Nahm. *Selections from Early Greek Philosophy*. 4th ed. New

York: Appleton-Century-Crofts, 1964.

EIEL   John Dewey. *Essays in Experimental Logic.* 1916. New York: Dover
Publications, n.d. Reprinted by permission of Dover Publications.

FD   Plato. *Five Dialogues: Euthyphro, Apology, Crito, Meno, Phaedo.*
Translated by G. M. A. Grube. Indianapolis: Hackett Publishing, 1981.
Reprinted by permission of Hackett Publishing Company, Inc.

FDTW   Roger Scruton. *From Descartes to Wittgenstein.* New York: Harper
Torchbooks, 1985. London; Routledge & Kegan Paul. Reprinted by
permission of Taylor & Francis Books, London.

GTP   C. E. M. Joad. *Guide to Philosophy.* New York: Dover Publications,
1936. Reprinted by permission of Dover Publications.

HC   John Hospers. *Human Conduct: An Introduction to the Problems of Ethics.*
New York: Harcourt Brace and World, 1961. Reprinted by permission of
Harcourt Brace & Company.

HP   Gordon H. Clark. *Selections from Hellenistic Philosophy.* New York:
Appleton-Century-Crofts, 1940.

HWP   Bertrand Russell. *A history of Western Philosophy*, Simon and Schuster,
New York, and George Allen & Unwin, Ltd., London, copyright © 1945
by Bertrand Russell.

L   Thomas Hobbes. *Leviathan*, 1651
http://www.ets.uidaho.edu/mickelsen/ToC/Hobbes%20-%20Leviathan%20
ToC.htm

LTL   Alfred Jules Ayer. *Language, Truth and Logic.* 1946. New York: Dover
Publications, n.d. Reprinted by permission of Dover Publications.

NO   Francis Bacon. *Novum Organum*, 1620
http://www.constitution.org/bacon/bacon.htm

OKEW   Bertrand Russell. *Our Knowledge of the External World.* New York: The
New American Library of World Literature, Inc. Copyright © 1956,
Bertrand Russell.

ON   John Stewart Mill. *On Nature.* 1874. Electronic copy taken from *Nature,
The Utility of Religion and Theism*, 1904, Watts & Co.
http://www.lancs.ac.uk/users/philosophy/texts/mill_on.htm

PALA   Maxwell John Charlesworth. *Philosophy and Linguistic Analysis.*
Duquesne Studies Philosophical Series, No. 9. Pittsburgh: Duquesne

University Press, 1959. Reprinted by permission of Duquesne University Press.

PP   Moore G. E. *Philosophical Papers. Collier*, New York, 1962. See "A Defence of Common Sense."

PTC   A. J. Ayer. *Philosophy in the Twentieth Century*. New York: Vintage Books, 1982.

SAAF   George Santayana. *Skepticism and Animal Faith: Introduction to a System of Philosophy*. 1923. New York: Dover Publications, 1955. Reprinted by permission of Dover Publications.

SE   Bertrand Russell. *Skeptical Essays*. 1928. New York: Barnes and Noble Books, 1961. Reprinted by permission of Routledge/TIPS, England.

SIAA   Jean Meslier. *Superstition in All Ages*. Translated by Anna Knoop. 1889. New York: Truth Seeker Company, 1950.

SOL   John Stewart Mill. *System of Logic, Book III*, 1843.
        The Internet Encyclopedia of Philosophy
        http://www.utm.edu/research/iep/m/milljs.htm

SOP   Will Durant. *The Story of Philosophy: The Lives and Opinions of the Great Philosophers*. 2d ed. New York: Simon and Schuster, 1953. Reprinted with the permission of Simon and Schuster from *The Story of Philosophy* by Will Durant, Copyright © 1962 by Will Durant.

TC   Augustine. *The Confessions*. http://www.knuten.liu.se/~bjoch509/works/ augustine/confessions/confessions.html

TCOG   Giorgio De Santillana. *The Crime of Galileo*. Chicago: University of Chicago Press, Copyright 1955. Reprinted with the permission of The University of Chicago Press.

TCPH   George Berkeley. *Treatise Concerning the Principles of Human Knowledge*, 1710. E-text originally from the Virginia Tech Eris project. http://www.knuten.liu.se/~bjoch509/works/berkeley/princ_knowl.html

TFWT   Marjorie Strachey. *The Fathers Without Theology*. New York: George Braziller, 1958.

TE   Francis Bacon. *The Essays* (an undated reprint). The Peter Pauper Press, NY.

TLC   Thorsten Veblin. *The Theory of the Leisure Class: An Economic Study of*

Institutions. 1899. New York: New American Library. Copyright 1899, 1912 by The Macmillian Company.

TOHN   David Hume. *A Treatise of Human Nature* © Oxford University Press Copyright 1978. Reprinted from David Hume: *A Treatise of Human Nature* edited by L. A. Selby-Bigge, revised by P. H. Nidditch (2nd edition, 1978) by permission of Oxford University Press.

TP   Ludwig Wittgenstein. *Tractatus Philosophicus*, 1921 http://www.kfs.org/ ~ jonathan/witt/ten.html

TPA   Vernon J. Bourke, ed. *The Pocket Aquinas*. Reprinted with the permission of Pocket Books, a Division of Simon & Schuster from *The Pocket Aquinas*, translated by Vernon J. Booke. Copyright © 1960 by Washington Square Press. Copyright renued © 1988 by Simon and Schuster.

TQFB   Sidney Hook. *The Quest for Being: And Other Studies in Naturalism and Humanism*. New York: Dell Publishing, 1963. Copyright © 1991 by Sidney Hook. From: *The Quest for Being* by Sidney Hook. Reprinted by permission of St. Martin's Press, LLC.

TR   Plato. *The Republic*. Baltimore: Penguin Books, Translated by H. D. P. Lee (Penguin Classics 1955, third revised edition 1987) copyright (©) H. D. P. Lee, 1953, 1974, 1987. Reprinted with the permission of Penguin, London.

UE   Bertrand Russell. *Unpopular Essays*, Simon and Schuster, copyright © by Bertrand Russelll, 1950.

INDEX